WILLIAM FULBRIGHT AND THE VIETNAM WAR

WILLIAM FULBRIGHT AND THE VIETNAM WAR

THE DISSENT OF A POLITICAL REALIST

William C. Berman

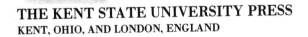

THE KENT STATE UNIVERSITY PRESS
KENT, OHIO, AND LONDON, ENGLAND

© 1988 by The Kent State University Press, Kent, Ohio 44242
All rights reserved
Library of Congress Catalog Card Number 87–2260
ISBN 0–87338–351–6
Manufactured in the United States of America

The paper in this book meets the guidelines for permanence and durability of the
Committee on Production Guidelines for Book Longevity of the Council on
Library Resources

Library of Congress Cataloging-in-Publication Data

Berman, William C., 1932–
  William Fulbright and the Vietnam War.

  Bibliography: p.
  Includes index.
  1. Fulbright, J. William (James William), 1905–
Views on foreign relations.   2. Vietnamese Conflict,
1961–1975—United States.   3. United States—Foreign
relations—1961–1963.   4. United States—Foreign
relations—1963–1969.   I. Title.
E840.8.F8B47   1988   973.9′092′4   87–22600
ISBN 0–87338–351–6 (alk. paper)

British Library Cataloguing in Publication data are available.

TO RACHEL AND DANIEL

CONTENTS

ACKNOWLEDGMENTS

This study could not have been completed without the cooperation of former Senator William Fulbright of Arkansas. His grant of copyright and his willingness to discuss at length, and on the record, his recollections of the Vietnam years allowed me to proceed with my work. I am grateful to him for his generous sharing of time and information.

Others also aided me, including the many people I interviewed, some more than once. Samuel A. Sizer, former curator of special collections at the University of Arkansas Library, organized the Fulbright papers so well that his work can serve as a model for similar collections everywhere else. He and his wife, Betty, and his fine staff at the University of Arkansas Library made my trips to Fayetteville a special treat. David Humphrey and his coworkers at the LBJ Library in Austin, Texas, were helpful, providing me with what materials they had in such a nicely professional way. Merill Distad of the John Robarts Library of the University of Toronto and Vivian Monty of the York University Administrative Library offered valuable assistance too. The University of Toronto's Office of Research Administration generously funded my many research trips; its help was always appreciated.

William Callahan, my former chairman at the University of Toronto, always listened with interest to my latest discovery. John Cairns, William Gibbons, John Hubbell, Stanley Kutler, Walter LaFeber, Herbert Parmet, Stephen Randall, and Paul Rutherford offered timely advice and/or letters of support. Robert Accinelli and Richard Sandbrook, my colleagues at the University of Toronto, read the manuscript with professional rigor, and improved it in so many ways, as did Florence Cunningham and Hilah Selleck of the Kent State University Press. I alone am responsible for its final form, structure, and content. My wife, Debbie, and my children, Rachel and Daniel, were always encouraging and supportive; they sustained me from start to finish. Finally, Sally, our family cat, provided me with companionship during the many long days and evenings of composition and labor necessary to produce a book that, I hope, will be of interest to students of recent American history.

INTRODUCTION

Historians continue to disagree about why the United States intervened in Vietnam. Was that intervention a "most selfless" act, as Ernest May would have us believe? Was it the result of "ignorance, improvisation and mindlessness," as Arthur Schlesinger, Jr., argued some years ago? Or was it a counterrevolutionary undertaking designed to make credible American power in a global context, as Gabriel Kolko contends?[1] Faced with such a division of opinion, a new generation of scholars, working with fresh materials, is seeking again to reconstruct the history of that tragic episode in American and world history.

A topic of current interest among historians is the antiwar opposition in Congress. Of those opponents, no one was more important or prominent than William Fulbright, the chairman of the Senate Foreign Relations Committee. With the opening of those papers that he deposited at the University of Arkansas Library, it is now possible to trace in far greater detail than before his relationship to that war.

Fulbright initially supported Lyndon Johnson's effort to hold the line in Southeast Asia, but in early 1966 he broke with the prevailing consensus and emerged as the best-known congressional critic of that intervention. Once Fulbright publicly rejected the official explanation for those events in Vietnam, he also began to rethink his position on a number of other foreign policy issues, including the role of the presidency in the conduct of foreign policy. Consequently, he functioned not only as a major opponent of the war, but also as a thoughtful critic of the world view which gave rise to that intervention. His own vision of what constituted a proper foreign policy for the United States in the nuclear age thus grew directly out of his long and painful experience with the Indo-Chinese war.

Interestingly, Fulbright's dissent embodied an outlook and perspective that went back to the foreign policy of America's Founding Fathers. As Norman Graebner reminds us, that policy was rooted in their realistic awareness of the limits of power, in their primary commitment to the safety and security of the people at home, in their disdain for ideological crusades, and in their recognition that diplomacy was a valuable tool for resolving international conflicts.[2]

As an heir to that tradition of "unsentimental realism," Fulbright sought to relate it to the events of his day via speeches, lectures, and a variety of publications. His hope was that others would be sufficiently educated to see the need to impose limits and constraints on American global power, if for no other reason than "to bring back into balance our economic and political system."[3]

Earlier in his career, Fulbright found himself in agreement with another part of the realist tradition which came of age after World War II. Thanks to the writings of Hans Morgenthau, among others, a national-interest school emerged to dominate the debate and discussion about the future course of American foreign policy. Stressing the primary importance of power in defining the options available to policymakers, that school provided a conceptual framework and analytic justification for the politics and practice of containment in a global context.[4] Years later, as a result of Vietnam, Fulbright and others, including Morgenthau, launched an attack on globalism from within the realist tradition itself.

This study is not a biography. Its object, rather, is to explore the impact of the Vietnam war on Fulbright's foreign policy views and opinions, as well as his political behavior. Throughout, an effort will be made to relate those views to a broader discussion of the war and its relationship to the making and shaping of American foreign policy.

1 | *H*OLDING THE LINE IN ASIA

William Fulbright was born in Sumner, Missouri, in April 1905, but he soon moved to Fayetteville, Arkansas, the home of the University of Arkansas. Subsequent to his graduation from that school, Fulbright attended Oxford University's Pembroke College as a Rhodes scholar. While there, he broadened his academic horizon and developed a strong attachment to and admiration for the British parliamentary system. Most important for Fulbright's future political and intellectual growth was the orientation he received from his history tutor, R. B. McCallum, who taught him to think in internationalist terms, and to view history and politics from that perspective.[1]

After returning to the United States, Fulbright earned a law degree from George Washington University, and, in 1934, went to work in the Department of Justice's Antitrust Division. Two years later, he moved back to Fayetteville and soon became a part-time law professor at the University of Arkansas. In 1939, Fulbright was appointed president of the University of Arkansas. While president, he came to realize, ahead of many, that Hitler's Germany was a profound threat to the values and security of the entire Atlantic community. Believing that America's "vital interest" was now directly connected to the survival of Britain, Fulbright, in 1940, became an ardent military interventionist and a strong supporter of William Allen White's Committee to Defend America by Aiding the Allies.[2]

In June 1941, Fulbright's career took an unexpected turn. He was fired from his position at the university by Governor Homer Adkins, who took this step because Fulbright's mother, the publisher of a local newspaper in Fayetteville, had opposed his bid for governor in 1940. (In 1944, Fulbright had the last word; he defeated Adkins—a conservative Democrat—in a Democratic primary runoff to win the party's senatorial nomination.)[3]

Turning next to politics, Fulbright was elected to the House of Representatives in 1942, where he soon established himself as a spokesman for an enlightened American internationalism. In 1943, he sponsored a resolution calling on the United States to participate in a postwar international organization. In 1946, two years after winning a seat in the Senate, he developed the legislation which established the means by which American academics and their counterparts from elsewhere could visit each other's countries in a teaching capacity. As an experiment in international education, this program expressed well Fulbright's hope that the promotion of mutual understanding and cultural awareness among peoples might just contribute to the easing of tension and the lessening of conflict inside the international system.[4]

Fulbright took these steps because he was searching for a creative alternative to war. As a longtime student of Tocqueville, he was aware of the great Frenchman's argument that war enhanced the power of the executive to the detriment of the legislature, a body which served as the chief protector and safeguard of the people's liberties.[5] On a different and more profound level, he saw that, with the coming of the atomic age, war in the twentieth century had become so lethal that it could lay waste to the social life and cultural endowments of the human race.

Facing that reality, Fulbright sought, in 1945, to find the means by which to head off an atomic arms race. What he knew for certain was that any international organization predicated on the principle of national sovereignty would lack the institutional power and authority to do the job. For that reason, he found the United Nations Charter deficient because it guaranteed the power of the veto inside the Security Council. He was equally critical of an American policy of going it alone on the central issue of how to control the future use of atomic energy. The fact that the United States, in the fall of 1945, had "already fallen to quarreling with Russia like two dogs chewing on a bone" distressed him greatly.[6]

Suffice it to say that Harry Truman had no use for such criticism coming from either Henry Wallace or William Fulbright. Unlike Wallace, however, Fulbright rejoined the team in 1946 after the Russians rejected in the United Nations the American-sponsored Baruch Plan, which he mistakenly thought was consistent with the recommendations of the earlier Acheson-Lilienthal Report to internationalize controls over atomic energy. (The Baruch Plan allowed the United States to retain its monopoly over atomic materials for an indefinite period.) Also making it easier for Fulbright to move back into the mainstream was his genuine disgust with Russian behavior in eastern Europe and Iran. A fact not to be discounted, too, was his awareness that Truman was very popular with the voters in Arkansas.[7]

For these reasons, then, Fulbright generally went along with the Truman administration's European initiatives. He reluctantly supported the Truman Doctrine, while responding positively to the Marshall Plan and the creation of NATO. During this period, he also became a champion of a politically and economically federated Western Europe, seeing in this arrangement the best possible defense against the threat from the East.[8]

As a staunch Europeanist, Fulbright was happy to back those administration policies, but during the first few months of the Korean War, he said next to nothing about the American involvement. Soon after the Chinese entered the fray, it appeared to him that the Truman administration was committed to fighting communism on all fronts. Alarmed by this development, Fulbright recommended on 18 January 1951 a withdrawal from Korea rather than risk a wider war with China, especially because he believed that the Soviet Union—not China, a Soviet "satellite" in his view—was the real enemy.[9] But once the Chinese threat receded, he backed away from this position.

Fulbright did not back away from the controversy created by President Truman's April 1951 firing of General Douglas MacArthur for insubordination. He quickly came to Truman's defense, arguing that the president's authority in this matter was not only final but in keeping with the spirit and the letter of the American constitutional system.[10] Later, Fulbright, a member of the Senate Foreign Relations Committee (to which he had been appointed in 1949), engaged MacArthur himself over the key question of how to fight the Korean War: it was a revealing debate on both sides of the issue.

MacArthur saw a permanent threat to American interests emanating from communist ideology. Consequently, he insisted that the United States had no choice but to seek total victory over communism, which perforce required the expansion of the Korean War into a larger and more compelling struggle against Mao's China itself.[11] Fulbright countered MacArthur by informing him that "I had not myself thought of our enemy as being communism, I thought of it as primarily being imperialist Russia."[12]

Fulbright's comment captured well the vital difference which separated him, a political realist, from those on his right. He preferred to see international crises and conflicts in the broad context of power relationships. Such a perspective, he believed, could help to make American foreign policy more flexible with respect to means and less absolutist and rigid with respect to ends. The MacArthurites, with their ideological fanaticism and calls for military crusades against communism, frightened him because he feared that their policy recommendations would most likely trigger a world war.[13] In other words, containment, not liberation, was the policy Fulbright preferred to pursue in the atomic age.

Interestingly, Fulbright's definition of containment sometimes varied from what one would hear during the Truman years inside either the White House or the State Department. In 1952, Fulbright, worried about inflation and the growing influence of the military on policy-making, wondered whether the rapid and very substantial military buildup undertaken by the administration was necessary. He argued that since the Soviet Union was not about to provoke a full-scale, hot war, it would be far better to spend more funds on the political and ideological struggle and less on military preparations for a war that was unlikely to occur.[14]

Such a fugitive sentiment constituted a radical heresy in the world Dean Acheson had struggled to create. By questioning the rationale for military containment, Fulbright had briefly stepped outside the consensus which existed in Washington to justify a massive spending program for arms—a corollary of the Truman administration's globalizing of foreign policy on behalf of the international status quo.

Also of great concern to Fulbright in the last years of the Truman era and the first years of the Eisenhower administration were the various rampages of Joseph R. McCarthy, whose political demagoguery and bullying style he detested. Fulbright saw McCarthy as a powerful spokesman for the radical right and feared that unless the Wisconsin senator's power was either curbed or checked, the country's domestic institutions and international standing would fall victim to a "swinish blight of anti-intellectualism."[15]

After the Army-McCarthy hearings in the spring of 1954, Fulbright recruited Republican Senator Ralph Flanders of Vermont to introduce a censure resolution that ultimately led to the downfall of this talented desperado. Thanks to Fulbright and others, McCarthy was defeated. Still, McCarthyism lived on as a powerful new force inside the American political system. In the years to come, as Fulbright well knew, leading Democratic politicians, including John Kennedy and Lyndon Johnson, could not allow themselves to be labeled as "soft on communism" for fear that they would suffer an irreversible decline at home.[16]

Such was not a serious problem for Fulbright in Arkansas. He easily won reelection in 1950 and 1956 by working hard on behalf of powerful oil and

gas interests, as well as poultry producers, and by showing his white constituents that he fully shared their commitment to racial segregation.[17]

From 1952 to 1957, Fulbright was identified as a strong political supporter and close friend of Adlai Stevenson, whose urbane style and cold-
war perspective appealed to him. Like Stevenson, he was critical of the
Eisenhower administration's excessive moralism and its rhetoric, while
supporting the continuing military and political buildup of NATO in the
name of collective security. In other words, Fulbright did not take issue
with the substance of the administration's policies; his occasional disagreements with the White House were mostly over methods and means,
not ends or goals.[18]

After Stevenson's defeat in 1956 and his own reelection the same year,
Fulbright emerged as a more outspoken critic of administration policy,
especially with regard to the Middle East. Angered by the administration's
inability to respond positively to the new currents of Arab nationalism as
represented by Gamal Nasser, and worried that its militarized approach
was playing into the hands of Moscow, Fulbright took his case to the Senate floor on 11 February 1957. There, he registered his opposition to an
administration-backed proposal designed to give the White House advance
authority to operate in the Middle East as it saw fit. Contending that this
resolution, if passed, would violate the spirit of consultation between the
Congress and the White House, and would be tantamount to giving the
president a blank check, Fulbright called on his colleagues not to abdicate
their constitutional powers. Only nineteen senators later opposed this resolution; Fulbright, absent on the day of the vote, was paired against it.[19]

In 1958, Fulbright addressed the current state of American foreign policy, finding it "inadequate, outmoded, and misdirected." He was critical of
the argument that the Soviet Union was "the sole source" of America's
troubles. Some of the blame belonged closer to home, and that included, in
his view, the parochialism of Congress and inadequate presidential leadership. Congress, according to Fulbright, was prone to see global problems in
military, not economic and cultural, terms, and the administration was
"impetuous and arbitrary" when it was not "weak and desultory."[20] Without a strong and effective president to educate public opinion, little could
be done to overcome the deepening crisis in American foreign policy.

In more specific terms, that crisis, argued Fulbright, resulted from the
failure of policy elites to understand and to appreciate the new forces of
nationalism now at work in the Third World. By overemphasizing strategic
deterrence and military containment, the administration was losing pre-

cious opportunities to win friends and influence people, as was reflected earlier in the case of Nasser. Fulbright believed that the creation of a more complex global political environment meant that if American foreign policy was to be effective, it had to focus sympathetic attention on political and economic developments in the Third World. Here was a realistic way, he thought, of avoiding the charge that the United States "was the defender of the status quo throughout the world."[21] More would be heard from Fulbright on this point once he moved into opposition to Lyndon Johnson's foreign policy in 1965.

As the Eisenhower era was ending, a new mood of political activism began to sweep the country, a mood that was palpably tied to the presidential candidacy of Senator John F. Kennedy.

During his primary campaign, the young man from Massachusetts had made the point that, if elected, he would seek to mobilize all the necessary resources to get the United States moving again. Fulbright did not then back Kennedy, but he agreed with him that the country needed fresh leadership. Eisenhower, thought Fulbright, "is hesitant and indecisive on the most important issues . . . and he is reluctant to ask of the country anything that looks like it might entail hardship or sacrifice. Peace and prosperity is the current slogan which lulls the country into a rather dull state of complacency and smugness." To counter that "complacency," Fulbright had earlier endorsed Lyndon Johnson for the nomination, because he knew that the case for Adlai Stevenson in 1960 was hopeless, and because he thought Johnson was "probably the best qualified man—by experience and temperament—to make a forceful president."[22] Knowing Johnson well, Fulbright respected his legislative skills and talent, which Johnson had employed to help him obtain the chairmanship of the Foreign Relations Committee in 1959. (That is, Johnson managed to persuade the aged chairman, Theodore Francis Green, to step down, thereby allowing Fulbright to succeed him.)

Although Fulbright thought that Kennedy was too young and inexperienced for the responsibility of the presidency, he endorsed the ticket that came out of the Los Angeles convention. And subsequent to the election, Fulbright's name figured prominently in the deliberations of the president-elect who was busily involved in selecting members of his cabinet. Kennedy, it seems, had initially favored appointing Fulbright secretary of state, a choice which had been strongly recommended to him by Vice President-elect Lyndon Johnson and Walter Lippmann, a close friend of Fulbright. Despite Kennedy's feeling that Fulbright was probably the best man for the job, he turned to Dean Rusk, president of the Rockefeller Foundation, after encountering growing opposition to Fulbright from pro−civil rights advocates and friends of Israel inside the Democratic party.[23]

While Kennedy awaited his inauguration, Fulbright mused about the state of the nation and the world. He was afraid that

> the Democrats are inheriting some extremely difficult problems in the domestic as well as the foreign field. Our economy shows signs of a serious recession, our national payments continue to show a large deficit, and of course trouble has broken out in Africa, South Asia, and Latin America. I do not believe that the problems inherited by Roosevelt in 1933 were anything like as ominous and difficult as the ones now confronting Kennedy.

Noting that Kennedy had filled many top positions in his administration with talent drawn from Harvard and several other universities, Fulbright thought that their performances would be better than the businessmen who largely dominated the Eisenhower administration—but, he added cautiously, "how much better remains to be seen."[24]

After the debacle of the Bay of Pigs, Fulbright may have seen enough to wonder if "better" was not worse. He had advised Kennedy to abort that CIA-sponsored mission, but the new president went ahead with it—only to suffer acute political embarrassment after the undertaking ended in disaster. That failure, along with Kennedy's difficult meeting with Nikita Khrushchev in Vienna, led, in Fulbright's opinion, to the hardening of the American resolve in Southeast Asia and elsewhere.[25]

Of the greatest concern to Kennedy, besides Cuba, was the crisis in Laos. That breakdown in the Laotian equilibrium, for which the United States bore considerable responsibility, soon led to discussion in Washington in the spring of 1961 about the need to intervene in Laos to save the situation. Like others in Congress, Fulbright opposed such a move, believing that the terrain and political conditions were not "proper for sending in our troops."[26] Fortunately, Kennedy opted for a negotiated settlement for Laos, culminating in an agreement with Moscow that saw both sides accepting the restoration of a neutralist regime in Vientiane.

Fulbright opposed the use of American troops in Laos, but in 1961 he publicly supported their possible introduction in South Vietnam because he agreed with the view that South Vietnam was strategically important to the defense and security of the United States, and because he knew that the

Kennedy administration had discussed such a move.[27] Furthermore, since the people and government of South Vietnam appeared to him to be interested in their own defense, he believed that it was only proper to assist them with whatever means both they and Washington deemed necessary and appropriate.

Fulbright's support of the regime in the spring of 1961 was consistent with the stand he had taken in the mid and late fifties. For example, in the spring of 1954, Fulbright recommended that American military force be used to prevent a communist victory in Indochina.[28] In 1955, he voted for the creation of the Southeast Asian Treaty Organization. And in the late fifties, he went along with the Eisenhower administration's commitment to aid the Diem regime as the best way to construct a bulwark against possible communist expansion from the North.

Yet Fulbright and his colleagues Hubert Humphrey, John Kennedy, and Mike Mansfield were not altogether happy with the thrust of administration policy in Vietnam. Hence, in September 1958, they asked President Eisenhower to give more economic aid and less military assistance to Diem in order to stimulate economic development and to encourage social stability. On the other hand, when Albert Colegrove, a journalist, exposed in 1959 the pervasive waste and corruption in that regime which was tied to foreign aid, Fulbright, like Mike Mansfield, felt that his reportage did "a great deal of damage . . . to our efforts in Vietnam."[29] Fulbright's concern, oddly enough, reflected the prevailing American consensus that South Vietnam was already an important geopolitical asset for the United States in Southeast Asia.

Unfortunately, that consensus was based in part on a colossal ignorance of the history and the politics of the region. Fulbright, like most people in Washington, knew virtually nothing about the background and evolution of the conflict that began in 1946. Senator Mike Mansfield was the Senate's resident expert on the subject and only he, in private, and Wayne Morse, Ernest Gruening, and George McGovern, in public, dared to raise questions about John Kennedy's growing commitment to Saigon after 1961.

During the early Kennedy years, Fulbright focused on other issues, most notably Soviet-American relations. On that subject, his views were conventional; he was a strong proponent of the containment doctrine. But as a result of the Cuban Missile Crisis and the Limited Nuclear Test Ban Treaty, he was converted to the cause of détente with the Soviet Union. As Fulbright now understood, more clearly than ever before, the transcendent issue of the age was the need to prevent a nuclear war; and if that ultimate catastrophe was to be avoided, he felt that attitudes had to be changed inside the United States.[30]

The attitudes which most worried Fulbright were those he associated with Senator Barry Goldwater, an articulate spokesman for the Republican right wing, who was something of a throwback to Douglas MacArthur in his call for "total victory" over international communism. How that victory was to be achieved Goldwater did not say, but Fulbright, having heard that cry before, was concerned that if Goldwater's crusade was unleashed it could produce a nuclear war. And in the event the United States won such a victory, Fulbright wanted to know if the next step would require an American occupation of the Sino-Soviet land mass.[31]

As a cold-war realist, not a right wing utopian, Fulbright made it clear, in a Senate speech of 24 July 1961, that he supported the current alliance system and favored all efforts to assist "many more nations toward the fulfillment of their legitimate political, economic and social aspirations." Although he opposed indiscriminate military interventions and rejected policies that would overextend the United States, especially when such policies found "little or no support elsewhere in the non-communist world," Fulbright was not backing down in the face of the communist challenge. As he said: "the program which I support is one of long range intervention in depth, one which employs all the instrumentalities of foreign policy, the political and economic as well as military. Its object is the realization of our national interests and not merely the piecemeal frustration of Communist ambitions."[32] Having committed himself, in John F. Kennedy's words, "to the long twilight struggle ahead," Fulbright came down on the side of a rationally managed, interventionist-oriented global foreign policy.

Such was Fulbright's perspective in the summer of 1961, as he sought to educate his colleagues to recognize the current complexities of that global environment. It was a frustrating experience, as he admitted. When writing a faculty member at the University of Arkansas, Fulbright remarked that "I have been trying to persuade my committee and the administration to re-evaluate our policy in all of these areas [Russia and China], and I encounter a most stubborn resistance in every instance."[33] That "resistance" to any such reappraisal was rooted, he believed, in the legacy of McCarthyism, which was enough to chill discussion and curtail debate almost before it began. The problem, according to Fulbright, was a dominant public opinion, which he feared was nothing more than an expression of prevailing ignorance and ideological rigidity about the cold war. Fulbright agreed, then, with the analysis of George Kennan and Walter Lippmann that mass opinion had a deleterious effect on the foreign policy process, particularly with respect to Congress. Reiterating the view he held since at least the late fifties, Fulbright expressed little or no confidence in the ability of Congress to grasp either the subtleties or complexities of policy-making, or to work beyond the reach of various pressure groups for whom local concerns were far more important than an abstract general good or a national-interest approach to foreign policy.

Thus Fulbright, out of necessity and choice, turned to the presidency as the best way of avoiding the parochialism of the Congress. The presidency, he argued, was the one institution that "constitutes a forum for education and political leadership on a national scale." Accordingly, he believed that it was necessary to enhance even further the authority of the presidency in foreign affairs. In the period from 1961 to 1964, Fulbright repeatedly emphasized this point.[34] His perspective, of course, was one which many liberal Democrats of the day shared—and it contributed to the ideological buildup of the office which under Kennedy became the driving force behind the further growth of the new imperial state and the strengthening of its warmaking potential.

If Fulbright was attracted to the presidential system for institutional reasons, he also found it useful as a personal vehicle for political education. It provided him with the opportunity to exert some influence on the inside either through a well-argued memorandum or a quiet discussion with officials from the White House or the State Department. As befitted his style and way of doing business, Fulbright felt comfortable in that kind of setting; it allowed him to make his point and at the same time to avoid the glare of publicity, which he did not want or seek.

Because of the Buddhist protests in Hue and Saigon, Kennedy's Vietnam policy was beginning to receive media attention in the summer of 1963. The fact that Vietnam had suddenly become newsworthy was not welcomed by the administration, as it was in a quandary as to how best to confront this new crisis. Some officials in Washington favored dumping Diem as soon as possible in favor of a more reformist-oriented regime; others wanted to pressure him into promoting change from above. Kennedy hoped that the latter course would work, and he sent his good friend Congressman Torbet McDonald to Saigon on several private missions to see Diem.[35]

The administration made other moves to force Diem to act on its demands. Assistant Secretary of State Roger Hilsman asked Senator Frank Church to introduce a resolution calling on Diem to make changes or face the prospect of the withdrawal of American aid and personnel.[36] Although

Kennedy quickly disavowed any American intention of leaving Vietnam, it is clear that Church's move was simply another device used by the administration to pressure Saigon into making the necessary reforms in order to better cope with the Viet Cong insurgency.

When the Church resolution was presented to the Senate, it was cosponsored by twenty-three senators, but Fulbright was not among them. His own views concerning the Church resolution and the general situation in South Vietnam were spelled out during a 15 September appearance on the CBS program "Face the Nation." He believed "Vietnam is the most serious crisis at the moment, obviously it is; and what we do there is very, very important." And although he endorsed the spirit of the Church resolution, Fulbright made it clear that he opposed the withdrawal of the American forces "at this time." Yet he declared that unless the Saigon government was willing to accommodate demands for internal reform, the government was destined to fall no matter how much American aid it received.[37]

Indeed, questions regarding the viability of Diem's regime had been on Fulbright's mind for several years. In February 1962 he wanted to know whether an alternative to Diem could be found. Later, like others, he indicated that he would not oppose efforts to bring about a change at the top. Nor would President Kennedy, who in October 1963 allowed events to unfold in Saigon, leading, in the first days of November, to a coup d'état against Diem which the United States had encouraged.[38] Subsequently, matters in Saigon were now even more confused and uncertain.

On 22 November, John Kennedy was assassinated in Dallas. Fulbright felt Kennedy's loss sharply, because he thought the young president had proven himself to be educable. Whatever private doubts he had earlier about Kennedy's capacity to lead and grow were dispelled by the events which followed upon the Cuban Missile Crisis. With his American University speech of 11 June 1963 and his efforts to reach a test ban agreement, Kennedy had shown Fulbright that he had the imagination and political skill to reach out in the direction of détente, and to begin the process of seeking an accommodation with the Soviet Union.[39] And that for Fulbright was the acid test, the sine qua non of any constructive foreign policy.

Yet, despite this new beginning in relations between Washington and Moscow, the problem of Vietnam had continued to vex Kennedy. By putting in many more troops and by talking about war in the manner he did, Kennedy had deepened and intensified the American commitment in Vietnam far beyond the point where Dwight Eisenhower had left it. Even in the last weeks of his life, the president referred to Vietnam as "this critically important contest with the communists." Admitting years later that it was nothing more than "pure speculation or a hunch," Fulbright thought that Kennedy, had he lived, could have changed his mind about Vietnam. His attempt to improve relations with Moscow had shown Fulbright that he "was not so set in his ways or so ideologically bound up" that he was incapable of "taking a different turn."[40]

Yet, at the time, Fulbright also supported Kennedy's approach to Vietnam, in the belief that a proper mix of economic aid and military support for Saigon would suffice to prevent a communist victory. A supporter of the center, Fulbright fully accepted the need to contain communist expansionism in South Vietnam, which he and others thought was undertaken by Hanoi but inspired and directed by Peking.

After the tragedy in Dallas, Lyndon Johnson assumed the responsibility for making the key decisions, promising to continue Kennedy's work. With Johnson in the White House, Fulbright had every reason to assume that the new president would continue to consult with him and to seek his advice on crucial foreign policy matters.

2 | *F*ULBRIGHT GOES ALONG

Shortly after Lyndon Johnson returned to Washington from Dallas in the late afternoon of 22 November 1963, he met with William Fulbright, along with several other old friends and associates. That Johnson would speak with Fulbright at such a time was evidence of their solid friendship, which had been nurtured by years of service together in the Senate. Now that Johnson was president, he would surely continue to seek the advice of that senator he was wont to call "my Secretary of State" during the years when he was majority leader of the United States Senate.[1]

For his part, Fulbright had high regard for Johnson's political skills, recognizing that he brought to his new office "talents which may well prove to be of great importance under the circumstances that exist in the nation, and especially in the Congress, at this time." Also encouraging to Fulbright was Johnson's apparent inclination to "follow President Kennedy's views quite closely, at least for some time," precluding then "any radical departure in matters of foreign policy within the near future."[2]

If continuity in politics was LBJ's chief objective, then there was no doubting his intention to hold to the Kennedy course in Vietnam, a point he made in a telephone conversation with Fulbright on 2 March 1964. Because Fulbright was in total agreement with that position, he responded by saying, "I think that's right . . . that's exactly what I'd arrive at under these circumstances at least for the foreseeable future."[3]

There was nothing exceptional about Fulbright's support; like almost everyone of prominence and importance in Washington, he shared the general outlook of a generation which believed in the necessity of applying the containment doctrine to Asia. Consequently, those few individuals, such as Senators Mike Mansfield, Wayne Morse, and Ernest Gruening and columnist Walter Lippmann, who in early 1964 urged a qualitatively different approach to Vietnam, had no impact on policy-making. Nor could they, since Lyndon Johnson, holding to a centrist position, summarily rejected all advice which to him smacked of capitulation. For precisely the opposite reason, he rejected Senator Barry Goldwater's demand for considerably greater escalation, seeing in that approach a likely threat to world peace.[4]

More to Johnson's liking were the views on Vietnam he found in a speech Senator Fulbright delivered to the Senate on 25 March 1964, only three days after the senator had shared dinner and discussion about Vietnam at the White House in the company of Johnson, Secretary of Defense Robert McNamara and Walter Lippmann. Yet Vietnam was not really the major issue on which Fulbright focused his speech "Old Myths and New Realities." The primary reason he had spoken out was to provoke a fresh discussion of other substantive foreign policy issues and concerns, including American relations with the Soviet Union, China, Cuba, and Panama. Before any serious discussion of these issues could begin, it was necessary to dispel certain myths which he felt were responsible for the wide divergence between so many existing policies and "current realities."[5]

Hoping then to "cut loose from established myths and to start 'thinking some unacceptable thoughts,' " Fulbright offered the following: that the communist world was pluralistic, not monolithic, in character, and that some communist regimes—like China—posed a threat to the United States while others did not; that as a result of the Cuban Missile Crisis and the Test Ban Agreement, the Russians were now behaving less aggressively than in the past; that Mao's China was the only China worth considering; that Castro's Cuba was not on the verge of collapse or a "great threat" to the United States; and that Panama's wish to revise the terms of the 1903 treaty governing the American control of the Canal was in the interest of the United States to pursue. By challenging the conventional wisdom of the day with each of these statements, Fulbright produced spasms of outrage and indignation from conservatives on all sides of Capitol Hill, as well as a show of irritation from the Oval Office.[6]

Still, what most commentators or critics generally overlooked or ignored were Fulbright's very important remarks about Vietnam, which seemed out of character with the rest of the speech. Carefully recapitulating the then *official* American position on Vietnam, Fulbright spelled out what he thought were

> the three options opened to us in Vietnam: first, the continuation of the anti-guerilla war within South Vietnam, along with renewed American efforts to increase the military effectiveness of the South Vietnamese Army and the political

effectiveness of the South Vietnamese Government; second, an attempt to end the war through negotiations for the neutralization of South Vietnam or of both North and South Vietnam; and finally, the expansion of the scale of the war, either by the direct commitment of American forces or by equipping the South Vietnamese armed forces to attack North Vietnamese territory, possibly by means of commando-type operations from the sea or air.[7]

Rejecting any call for negotiations until the American bargaining position had been strengthened sufficiently to secure "the independence of a non-Communist South Vietnam," and repudiating any French mediating role on behalf of neutralization, Fulbright made it clear that the United States could either expand "the conflict one way or another," or "bolster the capacity of the South Vietnamese to prosecute the war successfully on its present scale." Either position, he argued, would call for "continuing examination by responsible officials in the executive branch of our government." Whatever the means or the method, the object remained the same. Declared Fulbright: "the United States will continue to defend its vital interests with respect to Vietnam."[8]

After Fulbright finished his speech, he was challenged on the Senate floor by Wayne Morse, a sharp and persistent critic of American policy in South Vietnam. Unhappy with Fulbright's defense of the administration's position, Morse wanted to know why the matter could not be taken to the United Nations. Fulbright responded by saying that he did not "see any feasible way to apply any rules of law." And he added that "rightly or wrongly, we are deeply involved . . . we are committed to the point where it would be quite disastrous for this country to withdraw."[9]

Interestingly, Fulbright's views were remarkably similar to those expressed by Secretary of Defense Robert McNamara in a speech he delivered in Washington on 26 March. This textual correspondence suggests that Fulbright and Seth Tillman, his chief speechwriter, had a copy of that speech and simply incorporated the views contained therein into the speech Fulbright gave the day before on the Senate floor. Apart from that likelihood, the question remains: why did Fulbright so identify himself in such a public way with Johnson's slowly evolving policy? The most important reason is that Johnson asked him to make those remarks, probably to offset Senator Ernest Gruening's recent speech calling for an American withdrawal from Vietnam. Given Fulbright's special relationship with Johnson and his awe of the presidency, it would have been out of character for him not to include those remarks if LBJ had so requested. In addition, he could speak with a good conscience because he thought that Johnson and his advisers were responsible and had a firm grasp of the situation.[10]

In the meantime, the administration discovered in the late spring of 1964 that the situation in both Laos and South Vietnam was beginning to deteriorate, as insurgent forces continued to make headway against those American-backed regimes. Yet the Johnson administration continued to operate within the guidelines spelled out in a presidential directive of 17 March 1964, which provided a solid administration commitment to protect the independence of South Vietnam; in short, it was not yet prepared to go beyond its current program to assist Saigon, a program which included CIA-directed commando raids up the North Vietnamese coast, known as OPLAN 34-A, and the beginnings of an electronic surveillance program designated DE SOTO.[11]

At this stage, Fulbright remained generally conversant with the administration's approach and thinking, as evidenced by Johnson's invitation to him to join Secretary of State Dean Rusk and Secretary of Defense Robert McNamara for lunch at the White House on 15 May, the day after McNamara returned to Washington to brief the president about his latest trip to Saigon.[12] By including Fulbright, Johnson was being both gracious and shrewd, for Fulbright was not only a good friend of long standing and a Johnson confidant, he was also a key member of the Senate Democratic leadership. Furthermore, he earlier had displayed his trustworthiness on the issue by including at Johnson's request those remarks on Vietnam in his speech of 25 March.

With that speech, Fulbright put himself on record in opposition to any effort to neutralize South Vietnam, a position Walter Lippmann was advocating in late May 1964. On the other hand, Fulbright was not certain there was a need for major escalation. Appearing with former Vice President Richard Nixon on the 27 May edition of the "Town Meeting of the World," Fulbright replied guardedly to Nixon's demand for attacks on the "so-called privileged sanctuaries in North Vietnam and Cambodia" as the most direct way of producing victory:

> I would say that this Vietnamese question is, of course, a most critical one. It is currently under discussion and consideration by the President. I have great confidence in the President and his ability to understand these matters. He consults with his Leadership in the Senate, in the House, and in the Executive. I have

hesitated to go into detail and say that I wish that we should do this or that for fear of making his problem more difficult than it is.

Agreeing then with Nixon that the goal was to win the war, Fulbright added: "We differ as to the means . . . so what we are really arguing about is what is the wisest way to proceed or to achieve our common objectives."[13]

Fulbright was certainly aware that the situation facing the United States in Vietnam was "vicious and difficult." In early June he believed the administration was seeking to contain the problem. Writing to an Arkansas constituent, he stated "that many people, in addition to McNamara, are studying how best to solve this problem without a general war. I know that the President is giving his closest attention to this matter, and I am sure he will not do anything rash that would cause many thousands of deaths."[14]

The administration was indeed hard at work trying to devise an appropriate strategy to cope with the interlocking problem of Laos and South Vietnam. In the first days of June, a high-level policy review was held in Honolulu. Among those present were Robert McNamara; Dean Rusk; General Maxwell Taylor, chairman of the Joint Chiefs of Staff; Henry Cabot Lodge, American ambassador to Saigon; John McCone, director of the CIA; and George Ball, under secretary of state. High on their agenda for discussion was a proposal for a congressional resolution "in support of U.S. resistance to communist aggression in Southeast Asia." A consensus for such a resolution was quickly forged thanks to the arguments advanced by McNamara and Rusk. McNamara felt it was needed to prepare for the possibility of a strong Chinese and North Vietnamese response to contemplated American military action against Hanoi. Rusk saw in the resolution the means of affirming support for the president "at a time when public opinion on our Southeast Asia policy was badly divided in the United States."[15]

While the Honolulu meeting was in progress, President Johnson met with the congressional leadership on 2 June to review American policy aims in Southeast Asia. Restating them later that day at a press conference, LBJ insisted that "like a number of other nations, we are bound by solemn commitments against Communist encroachment. We will keep this commitment . . . a commitment to help these people help themselves."[16]

Given that objective, the administration moved quickly to line up support for a proposed congressional resolution providing Johnson with the authority he desired to deal with the changing situation in Southeast Asia. Hence a series of closed-door meetings was held at the White House and the State Department in June and July, as first the president, and then Secretary of State Dean Rusk and Under Secretary of State George Ball, met with select members of the Senate Democratic leadership, including Mike Mansfield, Fulbright, Hubert Humphrey, Richard Russell, and John Stennis, as well as Republican Minority Leader Everett Dirksen. At those meetings, Johnson, Rusk, and Ball gave these senators assurances that the administration did not contemplate or desire a wider war, and, furthermore, that it only sought this resolution as a means of showing Hanoi that the country, even during an election year, was united in pursuit of limited goals, namely, the need to prevent Hanoi from taking over South Vietnam and/or Laos.[17]

It was a particularly masterful stroke on Johnson's part to have assigned Ball the responsibility of shepherding the resolution through Congress, a task Ball certainly did not relish because he had avoided contact with the Vietnam problem for many months both out of disgust with and despair over the growing American intervention. A next-door neighbor and a longtime friend of Walter Lippmann, Ball shared Lippmann's belief that Vietnam was not a strategically important issue for the United States.[18] Thus when Ball spoke on behalf of the resolution to the somewhat skeptically minded Fulbright, who, after all, helped to bring Ball back into government in 1961, Fulbright's doubts about the need for such a resolution could be suppressed or overcome because of Ball's reputation for honesty and his own known opposition to a wider war.

Ball was not the only one who did Johnson's bidding. Frank Valeo, the secretary of the Senate, helped to bridge the differences between Fulbright, Mansfield, and the White House. Years later Fulbright confirmed that Ball and Valeo had each played a role, and he mentioned that Pat Holt, the acting staff director of the Foreign Relations Committee, had been involved.[19] The net result of all this pressure was that Fulbright, who had opposed the 1957 Middle Eastern Resolution, was persuaded to go along with the Southeast Asian Resolution in order to accommodate the White House.

What also seems clear is that Mike Mansfield, a dove and a longtime critic of American policy in Southeast Asia, was largely responsible for involving the Senate in the process of participation, most likely at Johnson's instigation. Whatever steps he took could not have been taken without Fulbright's knowledge and support. Both men could have opposed the proposed resolution, but they felt there was no choice but to go along with it. For having been told by Johnson himself that he needed help in restraining the hard-liners in the administration, they thought it was necessary to have some role in heading off what they feared was a mounting campaign by high-ranking brass to escalate the American response to recent tensions in Laos and South Vietnam with a possible attack on North Vietnam or even China. A Senate debate, they thought (or may have been told) was one way "to slow down the escalation." Consequently, Fulbright and Mansfield acceded to Johnson's request: as loyal Senate Democrats seeking to protect their institutional base, they believed, in the words of George Ball, that "the president has got to take ultimate responsibility for this. If he needs ultimate authority from us, we'll give it to him. He is much closer to it; he sees the problem."[20]

Johnson had thus succeeded in winning the support of the Senate leadership by convincing Mansfield, Fulbright, Russell, and Stennis that he did not want a land war in Asia. In addition, he promised Fulbright that he would return to Congress to seek fresh authority if, for any reason, the American mission changed in character, and he also discussed with Fulbright in late July a diplomatic initiative to coincide with United Nations' Secretary General U Thant's forthcoming visit to the White House. So, given the goodwill manifested on all sides, an unspoken bargain was struck before 1 August 1964, one that seemed to serve the political and personal needs of all the participants: Johnson, facing an election battle, could buy time before having to make some hard decisions; Fulbright could hope for a negotiated settlement; Russell, fearful of repeating the bruising American experience in Korea, could see a way of avoiding the pitfall of another land war in Asia. And according to George Ball, Mansfield could involve the Senate in the process so as to obviate a possible jurisdictional challenge to its authority by a president he knew was intent on doing something.[21]

At the same time, in mid-July, the Republicans nominated their leading hawk, Senator Barry Goldwater, as the party's presidential candidate. In his acceptance speech, he attacked Johnson's "no-win" policy in Vietnam and demanded action to roll back the communist advance.[22] Hearing this tirade coming from the Cow Palace in San Francisco probably unnerved Johnson, since he was blessed with an acute political memory and remembered well what had befallen Adlai Stevenson in 1952 as a result of the deadlocked Korean War. And Johnson knew that the situation in Saigon was not good and could unravel at any time.

Like everyone else, Fulbright was aware in late July 1964 that Barry

Goldwater would contest Johnson for the presidency. The prospects of a Goldwater presidency frightened him, because—going back to his earlier battles with Douglas MacArthur and Joseph McCarthy—he associated it with all those forces in American society which, if unleashed, could push the country in the direction of nuclear war with the Soviet Union. Given his strong feelings about Goldwater, the issues he stood for, and the ideas he represented, Fulbright, like Walter Lippmann, was grateful that Lyndon Johnson "was a man for this season."[23]

On 26 July, Fulbright had dinner with Johnson at the White House at which the two men discussed the political situation at home and abroad. Fulbright sensed that Johnson—now under pressure from Goldwater—was looking for some way to strike at the communists in Indochina. Consequently, he knew that something was going to happen. Of importance to Fulbright was Johnson's indication that he would try to open a negotiating track with Hanoi via U Thant who was planning to visit the White House on 6 August. (Because Fulbright was eager for such an initiative, Johnson may have offered it to him for that reason.) Influenced by that gesture, Fulbright was also willing to help Johnson, both out of his own fear of Goldwater, and out of his awareness, too, that the Khanh regime in Saigon was in serious trouble. Hence Fulbright was disposed to go along with Johnson's argument that "united action" at home could probably save the day in Indochina by forcing Hanoi to come to terms, thereby bringing the war to a close.[24]

The Khanh regime, in the summer of 1964, was beset with many difficulties. Internal conflict, lack of administrative cohesion, and poor morale had further weakened this already shaky American satrapy. Nevertheless, General Khanh, on 19 July, publicly threatened an invasion of North Vietnam as the best way of ensuring freedom of his own regime in the south. Yet, according to American Ambassador Maxwell Taylor, Khanh's real objective was not to march north but to get the "United States committed to a program of reprisal bombing . . . a first step in further escalation against Hanoi."[25]

When Fulbright, on 30 July, appeared on NBC's "Today" to discuss the publication of his new book, *Old Myths and New Realities*, he briefly alluded to Vietnam, saying that unless the South Vietnamese government faced imminent collapse, he did not want to see the war expanded to North Vietnam. In short, he preferred a diplomatic settlement rather than an "all out victory route." He also remarked that small steps were being taken to establish better relations with the Soviet Union. For him that goal was of the highest importance, and he fully endorsed all moves to ease tensions between the two superpowers.[26]

Johnson, too, was committed to improving relations with the Soviet Union, which had to be another reason why Fulbright trusted him. Like other Democrats, then, he looked forward to Johnson's nomination at the Atlantic City convention; in his eyes, Johnson was a candidate who stood for restraint in foreign affairs and progress at home.

Fulbright was also supporting a candidate who was looking for the proper moment to attack North Vietnam and, perhaps, to ram home the Southeast Asian Resolution: a resolution which had been revised to give him greater authority for action than was contemplated in an earlier draft prepared by the State Department. But when the recently resumed 34-A and DE SOTO missions provoked an incident in the Gulf of Tonkin on 2 August 1964, Johnson failed to take advantage of an opportunity to do what he had planned to do all along. Then, according to Fulbright, who spoke years after the event, Johnson realized that this was the incident he had been looking for; so his administration "created" a fresh one in the Gulf of Tonkin on 4 August to provide him with an "excuse" to attack North Vietnam militarily and, later, to play upon the "chauvinism" of the Congress.[27]

It seems clear from the evidence that Fulbright did not know in advance about DE SOTO. Nor, for that matter, was he fully informed about the administration's intensive planning for escalation, which had commenced in late May. According to Fred Dutton, a former State Department official in both the Kennedy and Johnson administrations, Fulbright, unlike others, received from June to early October only a partial briefing about what was being considered in the inner councils of the Johnson administration.[28] Why was he, a longtime confidant and friend of Johnson, denied the full story? One can only surmise that Johnson possibly feared Fulbright's likely resistance to an incident of this nature. By not giving him the details, Johnson may have thought that it would be easier to obtain his cooperation in pushing the resolution through the Senate.

Although Johnson's handling of the Gulf of Tonkin affair later was to be fraught with controversy, there was very little dispute in Washington in the first week of August 1964. When Secretaries Rusk and McNamara and the chairman of the Joint Chiefs, General Earle Wheeler, appeared on 3 August before a combined meeting of the Foreign Relations Committee and the Armed Services Committee to discuss in secret session what had happened the day before in the Gulf of Tonkin, they faced few doubters or critics. What those administration spokesmen said that day has never been publicly revealed. But when Senator Wayne Morse, a member of the Foreign Relations Committee, described in a letter to Norman Thomas what he heard on 3 August, he was also indicating what Fulbright, Russell, Mansfield, Humphrey, Stennis, and Dirksen were told as well: "It was a briefing on not only the Maddox affair but on developments in both North and South Vietnam. When it was over, I said to myself, 'We don't need a sinking of the Maine maneuvered by the United States military this time, because we are already at war in North Vietnam and have been for some time.' " Little did Morse know then what additional maneuverings were yet to take place the next day, both in the Gulf of Tonkin and the White House, before Johnson could go to the country with his call for "united action."[29]

On the morning of 4 August, Secretary McNamara informed the president that the USS *Maddox* had been attacked in international waters in the Gulf of Tonkin. Even though this incident was never fully authenticated, then or later, Johnson decided to cash in those chips he had been accumulating since the early summer. He first met with the congressional leadership, among whom only Mansfield and George Aiken challenged his proposed course of action. Afterward, Johnson went on national television to announce that limited retaliatory raids were commencing at that hour and that he was also asking Congress for a resolution of support to show Hanoi, and by inference Peking, that the country was united "in support of freedom and in defence of peace in southeast Asia."[30]

By raising the flag, Johnson lowered the sights of his potential critics, including John Sherman Cooper and Allen Ellender, and he all but muffled the historic dissent of Senators Wayne Morse and Ernest Gruening. Most members of Congress did not know how and why events unfolded as they did in the Gulf of Tonkin. Three and a half years later, though, Fulbright and his colleagues on the Foreign Relations Committee had produced enough evidence to allow I. F. Stone to charge that the administration had "lied" to Congress when it presented its case for the resolution in August 1964. By 1968, of course, no one on the committee needed to be told that, in the words of George Ball, "if it wasn't Tonkin Gulf, it would have been something else." Nor would they have been surprised to learn "that even though DE SOTO patrols were not sent initially to serve as decoy ducks for the other side, this is not to say that once having gotten started they didn't see the utility of provoking some excuses. But not initially."[31]

Long before Fulbright was fully alert to that possibility, he had to perform as floor manager of the resolution, a responsibility Johnson wanted him to accept. Consequently, he went to the White House on 5 August to prepare for the debate to come, needing the best arguments and information administration officials could give him to counter the attacks Morse and Gruening, and perhaps others, were likely to make. At that time, he was told by William Bundy that there was no operational connection between the 34-A mission and the presence of the American destroyers in the Gulf of Tonkin. Believing Bundy, Fulbright would subsequently argue—contrary to the truth—on the Senate floor that the two missions were unrelated and that the United States had not provoked those attacks. Even more important, he was not informed about the communiqué from Captain John Herrick of the USS *Maddox* suggesting that the North Vietnam attack which had been reported earlier may not have occurred.[32]

Fulbright would later admit that he should have been more critical and more skeptical about what he had been told. But at the time, he was convinced that Johnson was acting prudently and that he was seeking to end the conflict, not to expand it.[33] So he went along with the president in the belief that it was necessary to send a message of firmness and resolve to Hanoi, render symbolic aid to a beleaguered Saigon, quiet congressional dissent, and contain Goldwater at home. In short, if he had not been apprised of the details surrounding the events in the Gulf of Tonkin, he surely knew enough to appreciate the multiple purposes which the administration intended the resolution to serve.

Years later Wayne Morse argued that Fulbright "had played the game when he should have known, and in fact, did know better." There is no denying that Fulbright played the game. By his own later admission, he knew that something was going to happen. Yet he could not bring himself to criticize the policy. Why not? The fear of Goldwater and a desire to contain Peking and Hanoi were part of it. Also important was his personal relationship with Johnson. Fulbright was eager to remain on the inside, and Johnson, no doubt sensing Fulbright's vulnerability, flattered him into believing that he was a wise and trusted counselor. Furthermore, because Fulbright trusted Johnson not to deceive him, he accepted his friend's assurances that the resolution, in the words of George Reedy, "was not going to be used for anything other than the Tonkin Gulf incident itself." Is it also possible that LBJ had encouraged Fulbright to think that Fulbright might replace Dean Rusk as secretary of state? Such an appointment—which he had not actively sought—had eluded him in 1961. By playing the game, was he hoping that Johnson—his earlier sponsor—would move him into the cabinet now that Rusk had informed Johnson of his desire to retire at the end of 1964? (Years later LBJ remarked that Fulbright had "never found" a president to appoint him secretary of state; Fulbright later denied ever having had any such ambition.)[34]

Whatever were the personal and private reasons leading Fulbright to support Johnson, he had to deal publicly with the crisis in the Gulf of Tonkin. Characteristic of Fulbright's approach to it was his Senate speech of 6 August. He declared that the United States had every right to protect itself against the aggressive and unprovoked attack from North Vietnam. Yet what struck him as being so "notable" about the American action "was its great restraint . . . in response to the provocation of a small power." But at the same time, he insisted that the goal of American policy was "to uphold and strengthen the Geneva agreements of 1954 and 1962—that is to say, to establish viable, independent states in Indochina and elsewhere which will be free of and secure from the combination of Communist China and Communist North Vietnam."[35] He hoped that this could be accomplished by diplomatic means or, if necessary, through a very discriminating use of military power.

According to Fred Dutton, then serving as executive director of the Democratic National Committee, Fulbright's remarks were quickly distributed in Washington and in the country. Fulbright could not have been more pleased, for he viewed his speech, in Dutton's words, as a way "of containing, to some extent, the military expansionist tendencies in the Johnson Administration."[36] Furthermore, because he believed he was getting "a considerable commitment" from Johnson for a diplomatic demarche via U Thant, Fulbright, according to Dutton, really thought he was "pinning things down" on behalf of a nonmilitary approach to the problem.

Fulbright's belief that Johnson would keep his word about negotiations influenced his behavior toward his Senate colleagues during the brief period of debate which preceded the roll call on 7 August. Although he never directly engaged either Morse or Gruening in debate about the resolution, Fulbright did face a small group of skeptically minded senators, including Daniel Brewster, John Sherman Cooper, Allen Ellender, Jacob Javits, George McGovern, and, above all, Gaylord Nelson, who pressed him for more details about the events themselves while seeking assurance that the Senate was not about to give Johnson a blank check to pursue a land war in Southeast Asia.[37] Fulbright, with the occasional assistance of Richard Russell, sought to allay the fears of his colleagues. After forcefully denying the possibility of any American provocation, he argued that the objective of the resolution was to put Congress on record in support of Johnson's limited and measured response to Hanoi's blatant attack. The two together—Johnson's action and the joint resolution—he hoped would be enough to persuade Hanoi and Peking to end their aggression.

What bothered the skeptics in the Senate was that the resolution was sufficiently open-ended to authorize Johnson to send troops in large numbers to Vietnam. Fulbright made it clear that he, too, opposed such a move, but he admitted that the language of the resolution "would authorize whatever the Commander in Chief feels is necessary." For precisely that reason, Gaylord Nelson wanted to offer an amendment specifying that the limited nature of the American commitment did not contemplate the use of troops. Fulbright talked him out of it on the grounds that the resolution was "harmless," while emphasizing, also, that if there was such an amendment, the resolution would have to go to conference, thereby frustrating Johnson's effort, in Fulbright's words, "to pull the rug out from under Goldwater."[38]

Fulbright also talked Allen Ellender out of an amendment he wanted to offer, ensuring that the resolution would apply only to American military activity on the sea, not land. What worried Ellender was that the newly revised language of the resolution—which he had seen earlier in its original form—now gave Johnson more authority than he, Ellender, thought the president needed to protect American forces in international waters. More specifically, what had caught Ellender's eye was Section 2, which declared that "the United States is, therefore, prepared, as the President determines, to take all necessary steps, including the use of armed force, to assist any member of protocol state of the Southeast Asia Collective Defense Treaty requesting assistance in defense of its freedom." Rightly worried by this section, Ellender, nevertheless, dropped his amendment after Fulbright assured him that Johnson had no intention of waging a land war, and that Section 2 "was simply designed to back him up in his efforts to get some settlement of the issues involved."[39]

On 7 August 1964, the Senate, by a vote of eighty-eight to two, joined the House in approving the Southeast Asian Resolution (also known as the Gulf of Tonkin Resolution). There is no doubt that Fulbright played a decisive role in attracting votes and quelling doubts, exactly the reason why Johnson had wanted him to serve as floor leader. From June to August, Fulbright had worried about the direction the war could take, so he went along with the resolution as a gesture for peace and because he was loyal to Lyndon Johnson. Fulbright knew that in order to get along with Johnson he had to go along with him. Making it easier for him to go along was the specter of Goldwater and his own belief—encouraged by Johnson—that he was very much a trusted and influential figure inside the Oval Office. In addition, he was committed to the principle of executive supremacy in the area of foreign policy. Having given Johnson his support, Fulbright was hopeful that Johnson's military retaliation would dovetail with a negotiating effort that together would bear fruit, leading to the independence and freedom of South Vietnam.

It didn't work out that way: Hanoi was not intimidated by Johnson's actions and simply ignored the tough American stand as expressed in the resolution, probably to the surprise of the White House, which had expected a positive response to its policy.[40] As far as negotiations were concerned, there was little likelihood that Hanoi would be interested in anything that Washington had to offer short of an American withdrawal. On the other hand, thanks to this action of Congress, the president had been given an awesome grant of power, to be used at his discretion and at his convenience. The passage of that resolution was simply one more step, a very important step, that made possible the ultimate Americanization of the war.

Looking back at the Senate's actions of 7 August 1964, Mike Mansfield, speaking six years later, tried to put the episode in perspective:

> Why did we do it? Why did the Senate adopt the Tonkin Gulf resolution in short order and with only two dissenting votes: Were we fearful of exercising an independent judgment? Was it because we accepted assurances that we were strengthening the hand of the president in protecting American forces already in Vietnam? Were we persuaded that a show of unity here would secure freedom in South Vietnam? Were we convinced that what was tantamount to a postdated declaration of war would so frighten the North Vietnamese as to forestall the further spread of the war and, hence, our deepening involvement?
>
> Such were the reasons for the Tonkin Gulf resolution that were propounded at the time. Such were the judgments of the executive branch. That was almost 6 years ago. The Senate passed the Tonkin Gulf Resolution. The Senate acted, we thought, to protect American servicemen already in Vietnam. The Senate gave the green light to go further into Vietnam in order the more quickly, we thought, to withdraw from Vietnam.
>
> The rest is history.[41]

This was a reasonable explanation of how Mansfield and Fulbright, too, viewed their respective roles and responsibilities in the summer of 1964.

The green light had indeed been flashed for additional military action of some sort. But because Johnson had at this time no desire or plans to use American troops, Fulbright had to be reassured. Even more reassuring was his belief that Johnson would do everything in his power to avoid a Soviet-American confrontation. After dining with Johnson at Clark Clifford's home on 15 August, Fulbright wrote a correspondent that the "whole purpose of my activities, and, I believe, of the President's, is to avoid a nuclear war, without in any way infringing upon the security and freedom of the United States and our allies."[42]

Seeking to help LBJ, Fulbright worked hard for him in the campaign of 1964. He delivered a number of pointed speeches directed at Goldwater which the speech division of the Democratic National Committee had prepared for him. He also traveled to Florida, Texas, and even Arizona to speak on behalf of the candidate whose nomination he had seconded at the Atlantic City convention on 26 August with the following words: "His approach has always been a positive one. In recent months, for example, he made positive and clear-cut decisions in the Bay of Tonkin and at the same time exercised the restraint which lessens rather than enhances the possibility of a major war in that area. . . . His problem is to find a solution to a dangerous situation which he inherited—I believe he will."[43]

While Johnson was busy campaigning, Vietnam was put on hold: LBJ had no desire to take more active measures now that he had Goldwater on the run. However, he was intent on keeping the pressure on Hanoi. On 9 September, the White House authorized further 34-A and DE SOTO missions. The next day, a few members of the Foreign Relations Committee, including Fulbright, heard General Maxwell Taylor, the American ambassador to Saigon, say that there would be no bombing of North Vietnam until or unless a stable government could first be established in Saigon.[44] Or to turn it around, the bombing of North Vietnam could begin once a stable government had been established in Saigon.

Earlier in the summer, as Fulbright knew, the president's chief advisers had favored an escalation of the war, but Johnson held back because of his own uncertainty about what to do next and because of election pressures. In late September, he was telling the electorate that he was not going to send American boys to fight Asian boys. But at the same time, McGeorge Bundy was busy in the White House preparing the case for the escalation to come. He sent the president a memo on 1 October, suggesting that "it will be better than an even chance that we will be undertaking some air and land action in the Laotian corridor or even in North Vietnam within the next two months."[45]

Because of such views, George Ball was convinced that the administration was moving ineluctably towards a bombing decision, once the election had passed. Consequently, Ball tackled the problem of escalation in a lengthy memorandum which he prepared for his colleagues in October 1964. He offered for their consideration a variety of options, including the Americanization of the war or the bombing of North Vietnam for the purpose of either forcing Hanoi to drop the insurgency or negotiating a settlement acceptable to the United States.[46] What Ball clearly preferred was a political settlement that could be negotiated in advance of any military escalation.

Fulbright learned of this mounting support for the bombing from Ball himself, though Ball is not certain whether he told Fulbright before or after the election. Suffice it to say that Ball remembers Fulbright—with whom he was in close contact—sharing his concern and perspective about developments, but he is vague about the specific details of Fulbright's position, other than to confirm that Fulbright went along with the administration's incremental escalation in the hope that enough pressure could be applied at each stage by the United States to contain the problem, with the objective of either forcing Hanoi to negotiate or making the insurgency fade away.[47]

Just after the election, Fulbright left for a three-week trip to Europe, which included a stop in Belgrade, where he had a useful discussion with Marshal Tito about the current conflict in Zaire. Fulbright was impressed with Tito's point that outside parties should stay out of the affair and let those engaged in a civil war settle the matter by themselves. When he returned to Washington in late November, Fulbright apparently learned from Ball that the matter of sending more advisers to Vietnam had been raised at a 24 November meeting of senior administration officials. Hence, Fulbright, surely aware of the clear drift of policy, expressed his increasing anxiety about that drift in a letter he sent on 27 November to his old Oxford mentor R. B. McCallum, the Master of Pembroke College:

The President is still in Texas, and I have not seen him since I returned. We were all so worried about Goldwater that very little attention has been given to what the President's program may be. . . . As I have told you before, he is essentially an "activist" rather than a "thinker." And how he performs, particularly in foreign relations, will depend to a great extent upon the sources of his information and advice; and I need not tell you that good advice is a rare commodity, especially in Washington.[48]

FULBRIGHT GOES ALONG

As Fulbright's letter indicated, he was out of touch with Johnson, having had no contact with him since 19 October, the day he attended a White House briefing following the political demise of Nikita Khrushchev and the explosion of a Chinese nuclear device. Nevertheless, Fulbright, who looked critically at administration plans to intensify the conflict, tried to reach Johnson by other means. On 8 December, he told a press conference in Dallas that he agreed with General Douglas MacArthur in opposing another land war in Asia, calling it "a senseless effort."[49] Yet once more, he repeated his long-standing opposition to any unilateral American withdrawal from Vietnam.

The day after Fulbright's press conference in Dallas, McGeorge Bundy sent a memo to the president, informing him that he had heard from Carl Marcy, staff director of the Foreign Relations Committee, that Fulbright was out of sorts because he feared the prospects of war in Vietnam: "Marcy told me this extremely personally, and I relate it not to add to your troubles, but simply to mark it down as an objective report in case you happen to want to give Fulbright a coat of butter."[50]

It is not likely that Bundy would have taken such a liberty at Fulbright's expense without Johnson's encouragement. When asked years later what LBJ said to him about Fulbright, Bundy answered that his memory was too dim, and that he would have to consult his records to find out. Needless to say, Bundy's remark captured well Fulbright's current standing at the White House. Now that preparations for escalation were proceeding, Johnson no longer needed his advice, wanting only his loyalty and public cooperation. How did Fulbright reach such a state with a former colleague who had helped to make him chairman of the Foreign Relations Committee and who had supported him for secretary of state in late 1960? All the available evidence suggests that Fulbright was particularly vulnerable to Johnson's wiles because of his fear of Goldwater, his belief that Johnson would not escalate the conflict, and because of his strong desire to remain close to him. Having thus misread Johnson, Fulbright had, by his own later admission, deceived himself in 1964 into believing that his old friend was reliable and well intentioned. When Fulbright finally realized, months later, that a Johnson "coat of butter" had helped to keep him under the president's thumb, at a time when LBJ needed his cooperation and support in the Senate, he was embarrassed.[51]

By the time Fulbright discovered that he had been used, Johnson had long since initiated the bombing of North Vietnam and set the stage for the landing in South Vietnam of tens of thousands of American troops. In that altered context, Fulbright still lagged far behind Senators Frank Church and George McGovern in his public criticism. He was not yet psychologically or intellectually ready to challenge in the open the very presidential authority and official wisdom which had made the Vietnam intervention possible in the first place.

3 | *T*HE BREAK WITH JOHNSON

Once Lyndon Johnson won the election, he was in a secure position to make fresh moves in Vietnam. Mike Mansfield, aware of what was on the agenda in that postelection period, warned President Johnson on 9 December 1964 of the consequences that would surely follow the Americanization of that war. He wrote the president that "we will find ourselves saddled in South Vietnam, no matter what we will, with a situation that is a cross between the present South Korean quasi-dependence and the preindependence Philippine colony and at the 1964 level of cost in lives and resources." LBJ responded that "given the size of the stake, it seems to me that we are only doing what we have to do."[1]

Other voices were soon heard. On 3 January 1965, Senator Frank Church called for a full-fledged debate on Vietnam. In a survey of eighty-three senators the Associated Press reported that only seven favored the dispatching of troops or the bombing of North Vietnam, while a substantial number supported negotiations either then or whenever the military balance would permit.[2]

Fulbright was himself caught on the horns of a dilemma, not wanting a major escalation but unwilling to countenance an American pullout. Given what would come later, it's ironic that Fulbright's views were close to those then held by Secretary Dean Rusk. In January 1965, Rusk supported fully the American commitment, but he, like Fulbright, opposed a land war in Vietnam, and in January 1965, he looked skeptically at a proposed bombing campaign in the north. During his appearance before the Foreign Relations Committee on 8 January, he ably defended the administration's position without revealing his concern about the future. When Fulbright asked him on that occasion if he, Fulbright, would be consulted by the administration in advance of any decision to escalate the conflict, Rusk offered only to bring the matter to the president's attention.[3]

On 22 January, Fulbright went to the White House with other senators and saw Johnson for the first time since 19 October. While there, he expressed the hope that the war could be administered more effectively, and he raised questions about the quality of the American team in Saigon. Fulbright's participation in the evening's discussion came only a few days after he publicly revealed his intention not to serve as floor manager for the administration's foreign aid bill unless the military and economic requests were divorced from each other and offered as separate proposals. He argued that "military aid should be in the Military Budget," and that economic aid should be funneled through multilateral lending institutions such as the World Bank or United Nations development agencies. Fulbright took this stand because he now felt that the traditional bilateral approach to foreign aid had helped to foster the initial and growing American involvement in Vietnam after 1954.[4]

Greater involvement in Vietnam was what the president had in store for the American people. By initiating the bombing of North Vietnam, LBJ quickly upped the ante in what was fast becoming a high-stakes poker game. He ordered an attack on North Vietnam following a Viet Cong raid on an American military base at Pleiku; and he subsequently authorized the implementation of Operation Rolling Thunder. Long in the works, Rolling Thunder was designed by the administration to pressure Hanoi in the north to end the insurgency in the south.[5]

At first the opposition to Johnson's bombing was restrained. Senators Church and McGovern, moving to a more critical position, were among the very few who dared to question current American policy and call for negotiations with Hanoi. Once the bombing campaign began in earnest, protests soon mounted on college campuses in the form of teach-ins, and in mid-April 20,000 people assembled at the Washington Monument to denounce American policy, marking the emergence of a nascent antiwar movement.[6]

Unlike Church and McGovern, Fulbright did not speak out, but he was concerned. On 8 February, he spoke to the president about the bombing of North Vietnam just as Aleksei Kosygin, the Soviet premier, was visiting Hanoi. On 9 and 10 of February, Fulbright, in the company of other senators, returned to the White House to receive briefings from Johnson and senior administration officials, who discussed the bombing and informed those in attendance that the administration was thinking of sending troops to Vietnam. Upon hearing such news, Allen Ellender challenged the president's use of the Gulf of Tonkin Resolution to justify his action, only to be severely rebuked by him in front of all those present. Neither then nor in the next several months, recalls McGeorge Bundy, did Fulbright oppose at various White House meetings the incremental steps that led in time to the full-scale Americanization of the war.[7]

After having talked with Johnson on 8 February and 14 February, Fulbright evidently believed that the bombing was necessary to force Hanoi to negotiate a settlement. As he put it on 22 February,

> We face several bad alternatives. The thing is to find one resulting in the least evil. The raids in North Vietnam are intended to create conditions that will make the Communists want to negotiate. As of now, there is no one to negotiate with and nothing to negotiate about, so we have to build up pressure for negotiation. We obviously could hit the North harder but the targets have been very carefully chosen to show our teeth, but not to escalate matters much further. The President has resisted pressures from the hawks to hit a wide range of targets.[8]

Admitting in early March that Vietnam "is a hard-nut to crack," Fulbright remained publicly loyal to Johnson's policy. When he appeared on the 14 March edition of "Meet the Press," Fulbright reiterated his support of the air attacks, seeing them as a means by which Hanoi could be brought to the conference table for the purpose of reaffirming the independence of South Vietnam. Although Fulbright expressed his concern about the current situation, he did not think that "present conditions are so critical in Vietnam that a public debate either by my Committee or the Congress would serve any good purpose." On the other hand, he was worried that the conflict there could lead to a superpower confrontation. To prevent such an outcome, Fulbright recommended continuing the policy of cooperation with the Soviet Union "as being the most practical way to create conditions which can lead, I hope, to a further détente."[9]

For Fulbright, the central issue of the age was the prevention of war between the United States and the Soviet Union. His fear that the Vietnam war could damage the prospects for détente led him to seek to influence policy on the inside. Consequently, in late March, he tried to enlist his good friend Richard Russell, whose views carried weight with Johnson, for the purpose of making a joint proposal for a negotiated settlement, this at a time when the administration was preparing to send more troops to Vietnam. But Russell refused Fulbright's entreaty, even though he firmly believed that South Vietnam had no strategic value for the United States. It was his staunch belief, according to Fulbright, that once the flag had been committed, the country had no choice but to conclude the affair with honor.[10]

Russell's rebuff left Fulbright feeling frustrated. That feeling was captured in a letter he sent on 31 March to R. B. McCallum, his old Oxford mentor: "I need not tell you that the Vietnamese war is causing all of us great concern, and I am very afraid it may get out of hand. I am not at all sympathetic to our policy there, but so far have been unable to influence the Administration, and I am frustrated about what to do about it."[11]

Moving on his own, Fulbright had Seth Tillman, his chief speechwriter, prepare a memorandum for LBJ that was given to the president in early April. Much of what Fulbright recommended to Johnson indicated that he was beginning to rethink his position. His main suggestion was that the United States accept the legitimacy of an independent, nationalist, and united Vietnam. The object of such an approach would be to encourage the development of a Titoist-like entity in Southeast Asia that could serve as a buffer to China while strengthening ties with a détente-oriented Soviet Union.[12]

Fulbright had taken this tack because he was convinced that the Saigon regime could only survive if the war was expanded. There were three reasons why Fulbright did not think it was worth expanding:

First, because the existence of an independent Communist regime in a united Vietnam may be compatible with American interests; second, because the commitment of a large American land army would involve us in a bloody and interminable conflict in which the advantage would lie with the enemy; third, because a full-scale air war against North Vietnam would not defeat the Viet Cong in the South and could lead directly to the intervention of the North Vietnamese Army and quite possibly the Chinese Army as well.

Turning his attention to the home front, Fulbright also reminded Johnson "why a major war in Asia would be disastrous for American interests." He wrote that

like the Korean war and the various crises we have experienced over Cuba, it would strengthen irresponsible political groups and encourage highly emotional public attitudes in our own country. A major war in Asia, especially if it lasts a long time, could be expected to poison the political life of the United States, undoing the beneficial results of the election of 1964 and reviving the influence of irresponsible and extremist political movements.[13]

THE BREAK WITH JOHNSON

Fulbright's memorandum is revealing for several reasons. For one, it shows that his genuine fear of an expansionist China still colored his views about Vietnam. Whatever Fulbright told Johnson about Vietnam, the fact that they were still in agreement about the need to contain the greater menace probably convinced the president that the rest of the memorandum either made no sense or was not to be taken seriously. For another, the memorandum points out that Fulbright no longer viewed a communist-dominated Vietnam as representing a serious threat to the vital interests of the United States. (This argument would be at the heart of his challenge to the administration in the months to come.) Finally, it underscores Fulbright's fear that any escalation of the war would play into the hands of the radical right.

Johnson's experience with American politics took him in a different direction; he feared that if Vietnam fell to communism, it would precipitate a resurgence of McCarthyism, which had already made life so difficult for the Democrats in the 1950s. He also shared the view of his advisers such as McNamara and Bundy that the war had to be fought to protect and to maintain America's global credibility. For these reasons, then, Johnson, who had already decided to send more troops to Vietnam, completely disregarded the advice he received from Fulbright, among others, not to escalate the conflict. On the other hand, he was constrained to deal somehow with that token opposition on his left, including not just Morse and Gruening, but Church and McGovern, who also feared a wider war. Moreover, he still hoped to deflect the growing criticism of Walter Lippmann and, perhaps, to co-opt Fulbright and Mansfield, as he did so successfully in 1964. In addition, he could not altogether ignore growing international demands from seventeen unaligned or neutral nations for some kind of diplomatic gesture that could end the conflict.[14]

Given this domestic and international context, Johnson sought to sweep the table clear of his critics by offering to start unconditional discussions (note: not negotiations) and to underwrite a billion-dollar multinational economic development program for the immediate area affected by the hostilities. Those views were contained in a politically adroit speech—written by Richard Goodwin—that he delivered at Johns Hopkins University on 7 April.[15]

Just prior to making that speech, Johnson managed to persuade Eugene Black, a former president of the World Bank and a friend of Fulbright, to head that program. Johnson's last-minute acquisition of Black, whose name had been presented to him by Fulbright the very afternoon of this speech, suggested to the Arkansan that the White House was serious about its willingness to push for large-scale economic reform as well as possible negotiations. It was that approach which Fulbright saw at the time as the only realistic alternative to a military solution in Vietnam. Consequently, he was pleased with Johnson's speech, since it appeared to him to be not only a positive response to one of his key recommendations, but a strong indication that Johnson was earnestly listening to what he and Mike Mansfield were saying on the inside about the need to avoid escalation.[16]

Not long afterwards, Fulbright publicly suggested that the White House consider both a temporary bombing halt and a temporary ceasefire so that both sides could reflect on their respective positions, thereby helping to ease tensions sufficiently to get some kind of discussion underway.[17] Dean Rusk quickly rejected his proposals. Since Johnson's call for unconditional discussions had already been denounced by Hanoi as a fraud, the less the president heard about bombing halts from friends on the home front, the better. Ironically, of course, he later ordered a brief respite from the bombing, no doubt to coincide with the national teach-ins occurring in late April and early May.

In late April the sudden crisis in the Dominican Republic temporarily diverted attention away from Vietnam. Contesting factions, including one that sought to return Juan Bosch, the liberal constitutionalist to power, were engaged in armed struggle for the control of the country. Once the American ambassador on the scene reported to Johnson that Castro-like Communists were ostensibly behind and gaining control of the uprising, he dispatched more than 20,000 Marines there to restore order. What was so extraordinary about Johnson's behavior was not just his overreaction to the crisis, but the hyperbole and distortion he employed to justify this latest expression of big-stick diplomacy in the Caribbean.[18] At first Fulbright, like the rest of his colleagues, went along with the White House; later, though, he would see the matter in an entirely different light, and when he spoke out, his remarks would rupture a friendship the two men had enjoyed for many years.

On 30 April, Dean Rusk appeared before the Foreign Relations Committee to discuss the Dominican situation, but Vietnam was not ignored. In the course of that hearing, Fulbright made it clear that he was distinctly unhappy with the developments in Vietnam, suggesting that administration policy was not making it easier to get a settlement. He also reminded Rusk that when the Tonkin Gulf Resolution was presented to the Congress, there was no mention of troops. Now that American forces in South

THE BREAK WITH JOHNSON

Vietnam were growing in number, Fulbright wondered if it would not be advisable for the administration to obtain a fresh mandate from Congress:

> This operation in Vietnam has obviously become quite controversial. A lot of us have been quiet. We do not want to embarrass the administration. We have not discussed it in public. Some have, some have not. I am quite sure some would like to have, but they did not wish to embarrass the administration, because we realize this is a very difficult situation.
>
> However, I would think it would be wise if the administration could make up its mind to present the matter to this Committee and at least to the Congress, as to how much and how far they are contemplating going.

In response, Rusk said only, "Well, Mr. Chairman, it is very hard to look into the future."[19]

As Fulbright grew more apprehensive about the war, he largely refrained from entering the public debate. Having been encouraged by Johnson to believe that his advice was still welcome, Fulbright felt he had no choice if he wanted to retain his effectiveness at the White House. He sought to explain his public reticence in a letter to a correspondent who had asked why he had not spoken out about Vietnam or the Dominican intervention:

> I am sure I need not tell you that there have been numerous executive meetings and conversations on these matters, but I have not believed it appropriate to take issue in public with the Government's policy at this time. . . . Personally, I have not believed that my making public statements about it would result in any beneficial change. I have always made the distinction between an immediate critical situation and long-term policy in indulging in public discussions.[20]

The "immediate critical situation" facing Fulbright in June was the intensification of the bombing of North Vietnam. Like Mansfield, he was afraid that if a major attack was directed at Hanoi and other sensitive targets, as some proponents of a harder policy wanted, both Russia and China might enter the war. Because Johnson seemed to be exercising restraint in his bombing policy, Fulbright was encouraged. His general agreement with stated administration policies and objectives was also making it difficult for him to speak out. He opposed any American withdrawal from Indochina, and he thought that Johnson was seeking a military stalemate to open the way for a negotiated settlement that would protect the independence of South Vietnam.[21]

On another level, Fulbright's hands were tied by Johnson's enormously shrewd move to push ahead on a program for economic assistance employing the talents of Eugene Black. Fulbright had great respect for Black's talents, including his negotiating skills.[22] Thus whether it was to support Black's new mission, or to keep his lines of communication open with Johnson, or both, Fulbright finally agreed—after talking with Vice President Hubert Humphrey—to do what he had long opposed—assume the responsibility of floor manager for the administration's foreign aid bill.

Fulbright's willingness to go along was prompted in part by LBJ's request on 1 June for an $89 million appropriation measure to begin the social and economic reconstruction of South Vietnam. That proposal, offered as an amendment to the foreign aid bill, cleared the Foreign Relations Committee on 7 June and was immediately brought to the Senate for floor action that same day. Speaking on its behalf, Fulbright argued that support for the program was essential because "the stakes of political and economic development are as high as the stakes of war itself. Indeed, the meeting of human needs, so far as the Vietnamese people are concerned, is both the only meaningful objective of the war and the probable condition of success in the war." And he further contended that "the struggle in Vietnam is, after all, part of a general struggle in which the peoples of Asia, Latin America and Africa are engaged." And if the United States was to befriend "the new nationalism," he insisted that "it has to be wary indeed of the arrogance of great power" and remain alert to the fact that "the sense of capacity and dignity in the emerging countries is a delicate thing indeed."[23]

That amendment to the foreign aid bill cleared the Senate on 7 June by a vote of forty-two to twenty-six, but there was no chance that this measure by itself could arrest the military escalation and direct attention to the root causes of the conflict. As if to underscore the point, a number of senators, including John Sherman Cooper and Wayne Morse, noted how essentially futile and ill-conceived the program was.[24] Upon reflection, Fulbright may have agreed with them. Perhaps it was time for a more forceful presentation of his views.

Because Fulbright still believed that Johnson was the major advocate of restraint in an administration full of hard-liners, he tried his best to cooperate with him and to encourage him to avoid rash action. After talking with LBJ on 14 June, Fulbright agreed, at Johnson's suggestion, to include in a forthcoming speech praise for past administration efforts to reach a settlement with Hanoi. The next day, he delivered a speech on the Senate floor in which he cited those diplomatic initiatives undertaken by the administration to bring peace. Having done this much, Fulbright then pleaded for an end to the escalation, fearing that it could lead in time to a large-scale land war, more bombing, Chinese intervention, and, finally, nuclear war.[25]

Central to Fulbright's appeal for restraint was his call for "a negotiated settlement involving major concessions by both sides." In order to facilitate such settlement, it was necessary, he believed, to use only that degree of military force which would promote a deadlock or a stalemate—leading, he hoped, to a concerted effort by both sides to find an appropriate formula for ending the conflict. As a basis for such a negotiation, Fulbright suggested that "there may be much to be said for a return to the Geneva accords of 1954, not just in their essentials but in all their specifications."[26]

The following morning Fulbright appeared on "Today," where he was interviewed about his speech by NBC correspondent Sandor Vanocur. It was a particularly significant interview because Fulbright both extended and refined the remarks he made the day before on the Senate floor. When asked by Vanocur whether the administration was prepared to concede the point of recognizing the Viet Cong at the conference table, Fulbright replied: "Well, I can't speak for the Administration, but I certainly would and I would suggest that they do. I think that they should recognize the parties involved whether or not they are legitimate in the sense of traditional legitimacy, but they are the major force there."[27] Fulbright further noted that since the administration had no objections to Hanoi's bringing the Viet Cong to the conference table, it seemed reasonable to assume that the administration would be willing to accept the Viet Cong in any future negotiations.

When questioned about the ongoing troop buildup, Fulbright was equally candid and revealing:

VANOCUR: Sir, when you spoke out now, as you did after what some believe was a long silence, did you feel we were in some danger of getting into a major land war if the troops increased all the time?
FULBRIGHT: Well, really the danger that bothered me most was the possibility of escalation in the north, and bringing in confrontation with the Chinese and ultimately the Russians. I'm more apprehensive about that aspect of it than I am of more manpower in South Vietnam, which as I interpret it, is intended to stabilize and establish the independence of South Vietnam. I think that this is less likely to escalate the war than the extended bombings.[28]

Although Fulbright approved the troop buildup then underway, this is not to say that he necessarily favored sending 300,000 troops to Vietnam, a number that some in the Pentagon were promoting. Simply put, he was prepared to support those moves which prevented a Viet Cong victory and enhanced the possibility of a stalemate—the necessary precondition, thought Fulbright, for a negotiated settlement.

Fulbright's insistence on such a settlement reflected two other concerns which he discussed that morning. The first was his now stated belief that, in the context of American security needs, Vietnam, unlike Europe, was not a "vital interest" requiring an all-out American effort, and the second was his consuming fear that the war might get out of hand and thereby produce a global disaster. For this reason he sharply attacked the "crusading spirit" which Secretaries Rusk and McNamara had employed in support of the American intervention. He feared that their efforts at ideological mobilization could lead in time—depending on the battlefield situation—to a general weakening of those restraints which so far, at least, had made a general war unthinkable.[29]

Fulbright's remarks indicated that he was now beginning to join the public debate about American policy in South Vietnam. Like George Ball and Mike Mansfield, he recognized the imperative need to contain the military escalation. Furthermore, he understood the necessity of including the Viet Cong in talks designed to end the conflict. And most important, he now argued that Vietnam was not a "vital interest" of the United States. Yet he still talked about the need to stabilize and establish the independence of South Vietnam. Ironically, then, if he was beginning to question the president's approach, his goal—an independent South Vietnam—was the same as Johnson's.

During this period, Fulbright still trusted Johnson and thought the president was doing everything possible to avoid a general war, while pursuing a reasonable compromise in Vietnam. At the same time, however, Fulbright's television interview revealed that he was starting to move away from the ideological embrace of the White House, even though he still tried to position himself well within reach of the Oval Office. In other words, by sending Johnson a signal, albeit a friendly signal, it can be argued that he was moving to a new stage in his now ambivalent relationship with the president.

Although Fulbright believed he was helping Johnson with his remarks, Johnson clearly thought otherwise. Only minutes after the conclusion of Fulbright's interview on 16 June, Johnson called him, presumably to say that his views on the Viet Cong did not, and would not, represent those of the administration. The next day LBJ made this point at a press conference, where he denounced any attempt to legitimize the Viet Cong. Having turned down that piece of advice which he had received publicly from Fulbright and Senator Joseph Clark, Fulbright's colleague on the Foreign Relations Committee, Johnson also made it clear to everyone that in August 1964 Congress had given him sufficient authority to do what he was currently doing in Vietnam.[30]

Johnson's quick rejection of the Fulbright and Clark proposal was probably due in part to a desire to placate House Republicans, whose spokesman, Melvin Laird, had made it plain on 14 June that continued Republican support for the war would evaporate if the White House sought a "negotiated settlement which would include Communist elements in a coalition government." That statement highlighted Johnson's dilemma which Fulbright captured well when he remarked: "As the Republicans see it, the President is damned if he does and damned if he doesn't. If there are a lot of American casualties, they'll talk about the 'Johnson war' the way they talked about 'Truman's war' in Korea. If the war is settled by negotiation, they'll claim we 'lost' Vietnam the way we 'lost' China." Despite that Republican threat, Johnson's standing in the country during the summer of 1965 was extremely high; a solid majority endorsed both his Great Society programs as well as his handling of the war.[31] With that kind of popularity and approval he was, for the time being, safely beyond the reach of his critics from either the right or left.

As Johnson prepared his next moves in Vietnam in July 1965, Fulbright and his colleagues on the Foreign Relations Committee were themselves investigating the circumstances which had led to the American intervention in the Dominican Republic. After several weeks of closed-door testimony and hard work by the committee staff, Fulbright and some other committee members concluded that Johnson had received bad advice from American officials on the scene, advice which sparked the intervention. (It was precisely that same point which Fulbright communicated to Johnson many weeks before he delivered his Dominican speech to the Senate on 15 September.)[32] Fulbright's committee was too split between administration supporters and critics to permit the publication of any report disclosing the committee's findings. But its investigation revealed to Fulbright just how blatant were the discrepancies between what Johnson said to justify the intervention and what the realities really were at the time.

Ever astute about such matters, Johnson realized in July that Fulbright was now becoming more restless and less dependable. Boat rides on the Potomac, a government-sponsored "business trip" to Brazil, and approval of Fulbright's candidate, Professor Charles Frankel, for assistant secretary of state for educational and cultural affairs were some of the devices Johnson employed in the late summer of 1965 to keep him a contented passenger on the LBJ ship of state.[33]

Yet that ship was sailing on rough seas. Johnson knew that by late July he had to take additional steps to prevent a Viet Cong victory. Not only did he give General William Westmoreland more troops to continue the battle, he was prepared to take major offensive action to prevent a Viet Cong victory in the field. This momentous decision was made in the face of George Ball's warning of 1 July 1965 that it could lead to "a protracted war involving an open-ended commitment of U.S. forces, mounting U.S. casualties, no assurance to a satisfactory solution, and a serious danger of escalating at end of the road."[34] Clark Clifford had argued similarly; and Mike Mansfield had repeatedly warned Johnson about the dangers inherent in the approach he was following.

Fulbright had initially accepted Johnson's rationale for the bombing. But when he saw that the bombing risked conflict with China or even the Soviet Union, he publicly endorsed the policy of sending more troops because it seemed to him to be the best way of promoting a military stalemate and limiting the escalation. This same point Fulbright made as late as 19 July, when he wrote to R. B. McCallum that he was more unhappy about how the United States got into its current predicament than with the state of the current policy. However, that policy had been under review and was now subject to change or alteration or both. Until then, Fulbright trusted Johnson, hoping and believing that he would opt for a compromise settlement.[35]

In late July 1965, Fulbright suddenly realized that Johnson had used and manipulated him. His awareness of how things really stood between himself and Johnson probably resulted from his conversation with the president on 28 July, the day Johnson informed a group of senators that the war could last six or seven more years. Adding to his dismay, Fulbright admitted years later, were the Foreign Relations Committee's secret hearings on the Dominican intervention, which revealed the full extent of Johnson's disregard for the truth.[36] The knowledge that he had been misled and that the war in Vietnam was going to get worse, not better, combined to shake Fulbright's confidence in the president's judgment and leadership.

Subsequently, on 17 August, Fulbright received a memorandum from Carl Marcy, staff director of the Foreign Relations Committee. According to Marcy, the American position in the world had deteriorated since the death of President Kennedy. Given that situation, Marcy suggested that a public review of the current state of affairs might well be in order. But Marcy warned Fulbright that if he gave such a speech, it "would break you with the Administration and make Borah and Hiram Johnson and Cabot Lodge, look like pikers. But it is a line of action that you should perhaps consider. I don't know whether I would do this if I were you!"[37]

In late August, Seth Tillman prepared a speech for Fulbright, though it was not the one Marcy had in mind. His speech was based on the findings of the staff, including Pat Holt's careful study of the cable traffic that flowed between Washington and Santo Domingo in late April, and it offered a devastating indictment of the Johnson administration's handling of the affair, with Johnson himself being held responsible for what happened. As Fulbright did not wish to personalize the issue, he removed from the text those particular references to Johnson, hoping in this way to make his point.[38]

By the time Fulbright delivered his speech on 15 September, the situation in Vietnam had changed for the worse. LBJ again had intensified the bombing of North Vietnam, thereby scuttling any chance at that time for a diplomatic settlement. In short, he ignored those pleas from Fulbright and others for patience and restraint. Johnson made it clear—at least to Ho Chi Minh—that he was not opting for any compromise settlement. So when Fulbright arose to speak that day to a virtually empty Senate, he had Vietnam very much on his mind.[39]

Fulbright's speech was well crafted and to the point. It was his view that "U.S. policy in the Dominican crisis was characterized initially by over-timidity and subsequently by over-reaction. Throughout the whole affair, it has also been characterized by a lack of candor." After recapitulating the story of the American intervention, he pointed out that because of administration actions "we have lent credence to the idea that the United States is an enemy of social revolution in Latin America and that the only choice Latin Americans have is between communism and reaction." Refining that point, Fulbright noted that "if there is no democratic left as a third option, then there is no doubt of the choice that honest and patriotic Latin Americans will make: they will choose communism, not because they want it but because U.S. policy will have foreclosed all other avenues of social revolution and, indeed, all other possibilities except the perpetuation of rule by military juntas and economic oligarchies."[40]

This was a remarkable speech for that time and place, and, not surprisingly, it produced a strong reaction, both pro and con, in the Senate. Vietnam doves, such as George Aiken, Joe Clark, Mike Mansfield, George McGovern, Wayne Morse, and Steve Young, praised the speech. Vietnam hawks, including Everett Dirksen, Thomas Dodd, and George Smathers, denounced him, their talons having been sharpened at the White House for that purpose.[41]

Fulbright had earlier sought to mollify Johnson by sending him a copy of the speech and a covering letter explaining that his objective was simply to raise some questions about past American action. That gesture was wasted, as Johnson was not assuaged. He launched a fierce counterattack, against Fulbright, even enlisting Mike Mansfield in his defense. Secretary McNamara publicly denounced Fulbright's analysis as well. By pulling out all the stops, Johnson put everyone on notice that he had no patience for well-intentioned criticism coming from friends, not to speak of enemies. Why was Johnson so wrathful? As George McGovern pointed out years later, the Dominican Republic intervention, unlike Vietnam, was his decision and responsibility, not Eisenhower's or Kennedy's.[42]

A few days after he delivered that speech, Fulbright, in an interview with Gannett News Service, elaborated on what he thought the issues really were in this now swelling controversy. He had spoken out, he said, because "speeches are the only way I have of conveying my views to my colleagues in the Senate and policy makers in the Executive Branch. It is the only way I know to get across. If the press associations pick them up, if the newspapers carry stories and discuss them in editorials, then it will impress the Executive." And since he felt there was very little opportunity to influence foreign policy in the various briefings that took place from time to time at the White House, this attempt to reach out to a wider public through speech making was his way of trying "to influence the course of our foreign policy."[43]

Again, Fulbright was careful not to attack Johnson directly, insisting that what he said was not a criticism of the president, who was, in his judgment, "a political genius." Underlying the conflict, Fulbright observed, was the basic question of how to deal with the demands for social change in Latin America; for that reason, he felt that "it was my duty as a member of the Foreign Relations Committee and as its chairman to state my conclusions. . . . Things are not clearcut; it is always a matter of judgment."[44]

Before making his speech, Fulbright had been warned by members of his staff what he could expect from Johnson if it was delivered, but he never expected Johnson to react as he did. Johnson was outraged and unforgiving. So Fulbright sought to repair the damage wrought by his speech. He sent LBJ a friendly letter while Johnson was hospitalized for gallbladder surgery. But included in that letter was a sentence which had to catch Johnson's trained eye: "Subservience cannot, as I see it, help develop new policies or perfect old ones."[45] Johnson, who equated public criticism with personal disloyalty, never answered Fulbright's letter.

Because of Johnson's studied silence, Fulbright subsequently contacted Jack Valenti, a senior White House aide, to find where matters stood with his old colleague and friend. According to Valenti's 19 October memorandum to Johnson, Fulbright "grieved" over what had happened and hoped that he could see the president "to discuss this and other matters." Fulbright's effort was rebuffed. By October 1965, Johnson wanted nothing more to do with him. The outcome was fairly predictable: a major rift caused by Fulbright's Dominican speech would soon widen ever more, once the two men finally went their separate ways over the issue of Vietnam. Years later, Fulbright admitted that Johnson's harsh and hostile treatment in the fall of 1965 pushed him toward a more clearly defined and outspoken dove position on the war.[46]

Before Fulbright made that move, he first confronted those critics who told him that he was silly, foolish, or irresponsible for having given that speech on 15 September. Repairing to the high ground of general principle, Fulbright defended the right of dissent, saying:

Insofar as it represents a general reconciliation of differences, a consensus is a fine thing, insofar as it represents the concealment of differences, it is a miscarriage of domestic procedure. I think we Americans tend to put too high a value on unanimity—on bipartisanship in foreign policy, on politics stopping at the water's edge, on turning a single face to the world—as if there were something dangerous and illegitimate about honest differences of opinion honestly expressed by honest men.

And he added:

In the case of the Dominican crisis, I felt that, however reluctant I might be to criticize the administration—and I was very reluctant—it was nonetheless my responsibility to do so, for two principal reasons.

First, I believe that the Chairman of the Committee on Foreign Relations has a special obligation to offer the best advice he can in matters of foreign policy, it is an obligation, I believe, which is inherent in the chairmanship, which has nothing to do with whether the Chairman's views are solicited or desired by people in the executive branch.

Second, I thought it my responsibility to comment on United States policy in the Dominican Republic because the political opposition, whose function is to criticize, was simply not doing so. It did not because it obviously approved of United States intervention in the Dominican Republic and presumably, had it been in office, would have done the same thing. The result of this peculiar situation was that a highly controversial policy was being carried out without controversy—without debate, without review, without the necessary calling to account which is a vital part of the democratic process. Again and again, in the weeks following the Committee hearings, I noticed the absence of any challenge to statements appearing in the press and elsewhere which clearly contradicted evidence available to the Committee on Foreign Relations.[47]

Having defined a fresh role for himself as an outgrowth of the Dominican affair, Fulbright may have also opened the door for a public airing of the Vietnam issue as well. Retrospectively, then, this speech marked an important turning point in his career, indicating that he was moving in a new direction in order to address important national issues.

On 24 October, Fulbright appeared on "Meet the Press" to discuss not just his Dominican speech but Vietnam as well. Contending that the military balance was no longer so one-sidedly in favor of the Viet Cong, he suggested that the White House could enhance the peace prospects by stopping the bombing "for a more reasonable time" than, say, the brief period in the spring. Fulbright also observed that without such a halt the prospects for talks were dim. The president could help matters, he said, by risking such a move "at this time."[48]

Of interest, too, were Fulbright's remarks about the role played by the Department of Defense, particularly Secretary McNamara, in the making of Vietnam policy. Though Fulbright readily acknowledged LBJ's complete dominance of the administration, and freedom from anybody's control, he was plainly worried that McNamara had more influence than was necessary. Yet according to Fulbright, the problem went beyond McNamara; the Pentagon's influence in Vietnam and most other areas depended not just on McNamara's talent and powers of persuasion but on "its awesome and ever expanding budget."[49]

Fulbright's remarks captured his long-standing fear of the military's impact on policy-making. He knew that some high-ranking officers in the Air Force and the Navy, along with their allies in Congress, wanted to expand the air war beyond the limits imposed by the White House. Because they represented a potentially powerful force, the president and his advisers could not easily disregard or ignore them. If Johnson's policy of the center was to prevail at home and abroad, he would have to contain his critics on both the right and left.

In the meantime, LBJ responded to Fulbright's criticism by having Bill Moyers, his press secretary, defend McNamara while announcing, also, that the bombing would end whenever Hanoi was willing to negotiate. Moyers's remarks indicated to Fulbright that the Oval Office was in no mood to conciliate him. Thus having been cut off from Johnson and denigrated by colleagues who thought he was "silly" for speaking out, Fulbright felt that an "avalanche of vituperation had descended upon me in recent weeks." It was a heavy price to pay for a speech he characterized as a "very moderate statement." Granted, he had not expected Johnson's response, and he was surprised by the intensity of the administration's resentment. Dean Rusk, for example, not only heaped scorn on Fulbright's assistants who had researched his Dominican speech, he expressed a dislike for that educational undertaking.[50] Rusk—like Johnson—made it clear that Fulbright had become a pariah for having spoken out of turn.

Fulbright, nonetheless, continued to discuss the issues. On 8 December, in a speech to the Eleventh Commonwealth Parliamentary Conference in Wellington, New Zealand, he declared that nationalism was the major force promoting change in Asia, and that the best thing the United States could do was to allow that process to unfold as autonomously as possible. While speaking about Vietnam, Fulbright repeated his opposition to both an American withdrawal and the pursuit of military victory. Arguing against withdrawal, he said, in words Dean Rusk could have used, that it "would dishonor the American commitment to those South Vietnamese who have fought long and hard against the Viet Cong and would reduce the value of American commitments all over the world." He also rejected the goal of a military victory because it would greatly intensify the suffering of the Vietnamese people and increase the danger of a "general Asian and even world war." The only alternative to either course, Fulbright said, was a negotiated settlement tied to an "honorable compromise." If Hanoi still refused to bargain, the senator urged that "we must repeat offers already made, spell out at least the broad outlines of the kind of peace settlement we are prepared to accept, and take whatever new initiatives that seem promising." He then reminded his audience that it was Chinese imperialism, not communist ideology, which threatened Asia, and he also remarked that if

China possessed a revolutionary ideology, its current behavior seemed cautious and controlled.[51]

(Like Rusk, then, Fulbright believed that China was now acting in a restrained manner. But unlike Rusk, he would soon reject the argument that China was a potential aggressor, or that it was somehow responsible for major developments inside Vietnam. By viewing the China problem in terms less apocalyptic than the secretary of state, Fulbright would come to see that events in Indochina had their own internal logic and history.)

Fulbright's speech thus summed up his thinking as it had changed during the course of the year. His fear of escalation was now related to a search for some kind of formula to end the war. Moving from supporting an independent South Vietnam to a compromise with Viet Cong power, Fulbright had become far more critical of Johnson's intervention. And as the war intensified, his foreboding about the future also grew. Writing to a constituent in Arkansas, he said that "it appears likely that the Administration is going to step up the war effort in Vietnam and I anticipate that there will be a thorough airing of the Administration's policies in the Congress shortly after the first of the year. It is a difficult situation and I do not think there is any simple solution to it."[52] Faced with that "difficult situation," Fulbright was in need of a fresh approach that would give him the opportunity to question Johnson's policy. As the new year commenced, he was ready to move in a fresh direction and with means he never before desired or even contemplated. By initiating open hearings, he would seek to educate his colleagues and the country to the fact that the United States did not have a vital interest in a country already ravaged by a civil war and torn apart by the legacy of French colonialism.

4 | JOINING THE OPPOSITION

In the aftermath of his Dominican speech, William Fulbright made a concerted effort to learn as much as possible about the origins and history of the Vietnam War. Thanks to his conversations with the noted scholar Bernard Fall, a professor of International Relations at Washington's Howard University, he was able to see the conflict in Vietnam in a new and different light. (A French citizen, Fall was the author of several illuminating and analytically sophisticated works on the French involvement in Indochina since the end of World War II.) With Fall serving as a catalyst, Fulbright was led to a growing literature on the subject. The writings of Philippe Devillers and Jean Lacouture, *I. F. Stone's Weekly*, and *Viet Reports*, along with Fall's already distinguished work, provided him with a framework for understanding events in the region which was diametrically opposed to the one held by the administration. He now realized that the conflict there was both a civil war and an expression of revolutionary nationalism. By the time Fulbright was through educating himself about those realities, he was, according to Carl Marcy, far more aware of the historical context and the political dynamics of the region than was Dean Rusk, Lyndon Johnson's most trusted and indefatigable spokesman.[1]

While Fulbright was talking with Fall, Senators Mike Mansfield and George Aiken and several of their colleagues were preparing a report the president had requested about their recent world trip, which included a visit to Southeast Asia. That report was released on 6 January 1966, and it emphasized (far more concretely in the private version given to Johnson) that the conflict in Vietnam was teetering on the brink of disaster; that is, it was quickly becoming "open-ended" and had the potential for spilling over all of Southeast Asia, perhaps touching China as well.[2]

Even before Johnson received that report, he was fully engaged in a massive public relations effort to convince friends and foes alike that he wanted peace. He had stopped the bombing in December 1965 and made a worldwide diplomatic push to end the war. Others may have been fooled by Johnson's legerdemain but not Fulbright, who saw the problem as one which still required the sticking of an "olive branch in Uncle Sam's fist."[3] For months, he had tried to persuade Johnson to work for a compromise solution in Vietnam, but that was the last thing the president desired. And after the senator delivered his Dominican speech, Johnson wanted nothing more to do with him either, thus dooming efforts by Bill Moyers, White House press secretary, and Mike Mansfield to effect a reconciliation between the two men.

Their falling-out was intensified by Fulbright's opposition to the likely resumption of the bombing. At a closed-door meeting of the Foreign Relations Committee on 24 January, Fulbright urged Secretary Rusk to consider prior consultation with the committee before the administration made its final decision. He also repeated to Rusk his earlier recommendation that the Viet Cong be included as "a proper party" to any peace conference. Of greater significance than these two points was Fulbright's line of inquiry. Showing that he had learned a great deal from Fall, Fulbright argued that the conflict in Indochina was a product of civil war and a struggle for national independence. Taking strong exception, then, to Rusk's contention that the war was externally imposed rather than indigenously sparked and prolonged, Fulbright had grasped an essential historical truth that ran completely counter to the administration's various efforts to justify a now massive American intervention.[4]

That session with Rusk was not a pleasant encounter for either individual—marking a step on the road to a very prickly relationship between the two men. Later a reporter asked Fulbright: "Did you finish with him?" He answered that "I don't think we will ever be finished with him." The next day, 25 January, Fulbright voiced the fear that if the bombing was resumed, it "would mean that we have given up any hope of a negotiated settlement and it would proceed to a higher ever increasing escalation."[5] And he reiterated his point that the war was civil in character as most of the Viet Cong fighters in the South were from that region. Having taken the time to spell out his views to the press, Fulbright was beginning to reach out to the media in order to get his message across to political elites in Washington and elsewhere.

Both Fulbright and Mansfield declared their opposition to the resumption of the bombing at a White House meeting on 25 January. Mansfield contended that "the best chance of getting to the peace table is to minimize our military action." Fulbright agreed with Mansfield, adding that "we ought to negotiate a way out. . . . If we win, what do we do? Do we stay there forever?" But Richard Russell called on the president to resume the bombing on the grounds that the lull had not been militarily productive. He wanted Johnson to let the North Vietnamese "know they are in a war."[6]

While Johnson deliberated over his decision, fifteen Senate doves, including his old Senate protégé Vance Hartke, petitioned him to delay the bombing. An even more important development was taking place on Capitol Hill. On 28 January, the Foreign Relations Committee, contrary to administration desires, was meeting in open session with Secretary Rusk to discuss the administration's request for a $415 million supplement to the foreign aid bill. The barrage of questions and critical comments which were directed at Rusk that day, especially over the administration's interpretation and use of the Tonkin Gulf Resolution to justify escalation, spelled the end of the committee's public acquiescence in the administration's war policy.[7] For spilling now into the public arena were the fears and anxieties of committee members that could no longer be bottled up in executive sessions.

The committee's questions that day were consistent with its legislative function. By scrutinizing the administration's foreign aid request, it was in a position to raise questions about administration policy in Vietnam. But although some committee members were now willing to display their concern about that policy in a public setting, there was no consensus inside the committee as to what should be done in Vietnam. The committee, in fact, was split almost down the middle with respect to administration policy. Fulbright's public position was shared by Democrats Frank Church, Joseph Clark, Albert Gore, Eugene McCarthy, Wayne Morse, and to a lesser degree, Claiborne Pell. Mike Mansfield, the Senate's majority leader, had little to do with the committee's day-to-day business, but inside the Oval Office he was a dove. Other Democrats, including Thomas Dodd, Frank Lausche, Russell Long (soon to be replaced by Gale McGee), John Sparkman, and Stuart Symington, were hawks, as were Republicans Bourke Hickenlooper and Karl Mundt. Frank Carlson and Clifford Case either went along with the administration or said little that could be construed as unfriendly or antagonistic to the White House. Among Republican members, then, only George Aiken favored de-escalation.

Despite the lack of consensus inside the committee, the power of the chairman in that uniquely Senate setting was of salient significance. His prerogatives, attitudes, work habits, and ways of transacting committee business all blended to gether to give him enormous authority to define the committee's agenda and operating methods. The chairman could, within limits, determine how to proceed on specific matters. Church, for example, had asked Fulbright in the summer of 1965 to open public hearings on the war, but he had refused to do so.[8] By January 1966, Fulbright's personal and political situation had changed, justifying in his view the need to move in a new direction.

Another area of importance which came under the chairman's authority was the makeup of the staff. Carl Marcy, whose association with the committee went back to the days of Tom Connally and Arthur Vandenberg, was Fulbright's staff director. He was assisted by Pat Holt, Norvill Jones, James Lowenstein, and Seth Tillman, among others. But it must be pointed out that if the staff advised and aided Fulbright in a variety of ways, he still made the key decisions, a point generally overlooked by the White House, which thought that he was a captive of Marcy, a committed dove.[9]

On 31 January, LBJ made public his decision to renew the bombing of North Vietnam. The committee, with Fulbright's endorsement, subsequently agreed to hold all future hearings on the supplemental authorization in public session. That move was to have unforeseen consequences, as it opened the door of the committee chamber to the eye of the television camera. Earlier, both Fred Dutton, a former assistant secretary of state, and Marcy had discussed the best way of publicizing the doves' opposition to the war, but they never anticipated the response the committee would elicit from the White House once these hearings commenced in full view of the country.[10]

There are several reasons why the committee moved into public session. They were spelled out in a conversation that White House aide H. H. Wilson had with Don Oberdorfer, a *Washington Star* reporter. In a memorandum to the president, which recapitulated the gist of that conversation, Wilson mentioned that Oberdorfer felt that "the present troubles go back to the Dominican thing, and to what Fulbright regards as the deep freeze of him by the Administration during the fall." The Mansfield Report also stirred up a lot of people who were even more incensed by the administration's failure to answer it. Moreover, according to Oberdorfer, a speech that Senator John Stennis had given to the Mississippi State Legislature on 27 January had a "tremendous impact." Stennis, the second-ranking member of the powerful Armed Services Committee, was considered by his colleagues to be extremely well informed; so when he suggested that there would ultimately be 680,000 men in Vietnam and that he favored the use of nuclear weapons in case China entered the war, his remarks "just scared the hell out of people." Committee members thus went into action, wrote Wilson to the president, because they felt that it was "the last chance to avert a major war."[11]

As the committee was busy lining up prospective witnesses to testify on the supplemental request, Fulbright appeared on a prime-time CBS television special on 1 February to discuss the war with Eric Severeid and Martin Agronsky. Taking advantage of this opportunity, he tried to engage the minds of the viewing audience. When discussing China, Fulbright rejected at once Secretary Rusk's argument that China was another version of Hitler's Germany on the march. He deftly noted the long history of western domination of China, going back to the Opium Wars, and he tried to explain current Chinese "hatred" of the West in that context. When discussing Vietnam, Fulbright expressed his strong desire for a settlement that would allow for an American withdrawal; it was his view that "the reconvening of the Geneva conference under the chairmanship of Great Britain and Russia would be the appropriate way to approach the matter."[12]

Most revealing was Fulbright's public apology for the role he played in pushing the Tonkin Gulf Resolution through the Senate. After mentioning that he was not proud of that role, Fulbright remarked

> that at the time of the Bay of Tonkin I should have had greater foresight in the consideration of that resolution. That would have been a good time to have precipitated a debate and a reexamination and reevaluation of the involvement. . . . It was during the presidential campaign. I was very much a partisan in that campaign for Johnson, for the administration. I disapproved of the statements of Mr. Goldwater and I went along with the urging. I may say, of the administration, I think it is a terrible situation we are in. I am hoping we can find an honorable way out of it.[13]

Although Fulbright had spoken the truth about his role in pushing the resolution through the Senate, he had not told the whole story. Left out was the fact that he had accepted the president's assurances that the resolution had no purpose beyond the incident itself. Left untold was that he went along with Johnson in order to remain close to him.

That Johnson-Fulbright relationship was altogether different on the morning of 4 February 1966, as the Foreign Relations Committee resumed its public hearings, focusing attention on David Bell, the administrator for the Agency for International Development. Bell was sharply questioned by committee members, though perhaps unfairly since he was no policymaker as were McNamara, Rusk, and McGeorge Bundy. Of importance that day was not what Bell said, but the fact that his testimony was carried on live television across the country. Once Lyndon Johnson saw those cameras, he decided on the spot to announce that he and a number of senior officials, including Robert McNamara and Maxwell Taylor, were going to Honolulu to meet with the leaders of the Saigon regime. Committee members never realized that the introduction of television into those hearings had produced sheer "turmoil" at the White House.[14]

On the afternoon of 4 February, Professor Bernard Fall appeared before the committee in an informal executive session. He saw the United States victimized by the same illusions of military power that had earlier defeated the French. After calling for a negotiated settlement that would leave neither side with a victory, Fall left the committee members to ponder his calculation that for every Viet Cong casualty, the "United States pays $311 in a country whose per capita is $102 a year."[15]

When the committee again met on 8 February, it heard testimony from General James Gavin, who presented a case for "the enclave strategy." He argued that the United States should make do "with what we have," while seeking to stabilize its position by securing easily defended installations along the coast that would deny the Viet Cong a military victory. His approach was soon endorsed by General Matthew Ridgway in a letter he sent to Fulbright, who later inserted it into the *Congressional Record*.[16]

On 10 February, George Kennan appeared before the committee. The father of the containment doctrine, former American Ambassador to Belgrade and Moscow, and distinguished scholar, Kennan was a model of decorum and precisely the eminent figure Fulbright needed to question Johnson's policy. During his testimony, Kennan agreed with Gavin that it was essential to avoid further escalation, and he urged also that the war be liquidated "as soon as this could be done without inordinate damage to our prestige or to the stability in the area."[17] Like Gavin, he also warned about a possible conflict with China in the event the United States pursued the goal of military victory.

When queried the next day about the Gavin and Kennan testimony, the president sought to minimize the import of their remarks, saying that he could not see "a great deal of difference" between their position and his own. That was not Maxwell Taylor's slant. A former ambassador to Saigon, chairman of the Joint Chiefs of Staff, and currently a special consultant to the president, Taylor had no qualms about emphasizing the basic incompatibility between his views and those of Gavin. This disagreement was highlighted in his testimony by his defense of air power and his rejection of the enclave strategy as "inglorious" and "disastrous."[18]

This bold inquiry into the administration's policy ended on 18 February, as Secretary Rusk and Fulbright sparred on whether or not the SEATO agreement justified and legitimized whatever steps the United States had taken to defend South Vietnam. Ultimately, though, the issue boiled down to what would be a good negotiating position for the United States to take to enhance the prospects of a settlement. Rusk rejected any de facto or de jure recognition of the National Liberation Front as the sole spokesman for the people of South Vietnam. Such a move would mean, he submitted, "our acceptance of the Communist position as to the indigenous nature of the conflict and thus our acceptance of a settlement of Hanoi's terms. . . ." Fulbright pointed out that the United States was receiving little help from its SEATO allies because, he thought, they did not believe Rusk's argument that "this is a clear case of international Communist aggression. I think they believe rather that it is more in the nature of a civil war in which outside parties have become involved." Because the United States refused to accept the reality of a civil war, it seemed to him that Johnson was demanding unconditional surrender from the other side. That was a "policy objective" which—he feared—could bring the Chinese or even the Russians into the conflict.[19]

Those hearings, which received considerable media attention, did not alter administration policy, but, speculated Fulbright, they may have moderated prospects for increased escalation. It is certain that they helped to make dissent somewhat more respectable and institutionally more significant. Years later, Church and McGovern both agreed that Fulbright's decision to open those hearings to the public was the single most important act of his career. He made it possible for Gavin and Kennan to give LBJ's critics a respectable character which Johnson found hard to challenge. In addition, he helped to revive the spirit of debate and discussion which had laid dormant inside the committee ever since the coming of the cold war.[20]

On 21 February, the United Press International released the transcript of a recent interview in which Fulbright remarked that the public responses to the hearings had been "encouraging."[21] Implicit in his comment was the hope that public pressure would force Johnson to change his policy. Those hearings thus marked the beginning of an extended public relations battle between a powerful administration and a few doves, led by Fulbright, to sway the voters one way or another.

Fulbright's attempt to educate the public was tied to his realization, in

1966, that public opinion, especially elite opinion, had to be mobilized against the war. For this reason, he would henceforth seek to influence that opinion through Senate speeches, television appearances and interviews, lectures and publications. Whether he could change many minds was an open question; but at least he was committed to a course of action that would have been unthinkable for him in the years when he was so disdainful of public opinion. Thanks to that shift, Fulbright had taken his "teach-in" directly into the nation's living rooms.

Johnson was very much aware of the impact the committee had made, and he also sensed the latent danger to him which resulted from Senator Robert Kennedy's prompt identification with the committee's work. Consequently, he sought to answer his critics—in a manner suggested to him via Richard Goodwin—with a "simple and clear" statement to dispel "the confusion" generated by the Foreign Relations Committee. On 23 February, the president provided a New York audience with a detailed rebuttal of the criticism which had emanated from the committee during the hearings; and he assured everyone there that the United States contemplated no "mindless escalation" of the war.[22] The fact that Johnson took the time to reply so specifically to his critics was an indication that he was concerned with the possible ramifications of their opposition within both the Democratic party and the country.

On 1 March, many prominent senators, including Russell, Fulbright, and Morse, debated the matter of funding the war. And in the course of that freewheeling, charged, and often tense discussion, Fulbright delivered a speech calling for neutralization of the entire region. He made this proposal in an attempt to advance the discussion beyond where Gavin and Kennan had left it and because he was searching for some kind of mechanism that would prevent the war from spilling over into Thailand. Thus an argument for neutralization appealed to him because it would involve an "accommodation" with China as one way of securing an end to the conflict in Vietnam, while at the same time promoting the stabilization of the entire region.[23]

Neutralization was, as Fulbright well knew, a thin reed on which to build a platform for peace. But it was all he could publicly offer at a time when he privately believed that the United States "ought to get out." But if he had proposed withdrawal, in line with the position taken earlier by Gruening, it would have left him politically vulnerable in a hawkish state like Arkansas, where its popular, vote-getting governor, Orval Faubus, was considered by many observers a likely challenger for Fulbright's Senate seat in 1968.[24]

As Hanoi and Washington were not interested in neutralization, Fulbright's proposal was at best a fugitive hope. And so was the 1 March vote on Wayne Morse's amendment to the Vietnam authorization bill to rescind the Southeast Asian Resolution, the legal basis and justification for Johnson's war. Although Fulbright disagreed with Morse's tactic (for fear that Johnson would rightly construe the results as further evidence of congressional support for his policy), he nevertheless supported Morse as a matter of conscience. By joining Morse, Gruening, Steve Young, and McCarthy in opposition to ninety-two other senators, Fulbright sought to atone for the role he had played in August 1964. Two days later, Morse wrote him, "I want to tell you how moved I was the afternoon when you cast your vote in support of my amendment to the Vietnam authorization bill. . . . I am receiving great strength and inspiration from your courage and leadership on the Foreign Relations Committee." To which Fulbright responded: "I appreciate more than I can say your thoughtful letter. . . . You should certainly be proud of the record you made."[25]

Fulbright, too, was beginning to make a record. He had scheduled hearings in early March on the long tabooed subject of China. For years—because of McCarthyism and the deadlock in Korea—it had been guaranteed to generate considerable controversy full of sound and fury. Fulbright's efforts to demystify the issue, especially at a time when people in Washington were talking about war between China and the United States, was a notable and exceptionally important undertaking. Fulbright himself was very concerned about that possibility of war. Like others, he had heard rumors that such figures as General Curtis Lemay wanted to bomb China's nuclear installations. And, like others, Fulbright had long believed that behind Hanoi stood Peking; in order to deal with the former, he thought, mistakenly, that it was necessary to reach the latter.[26] Fulbright's China hearings were, as he admitted, an extension of the recently concluded Vietnam hearings.

On 7 March, the day before the China hearings began (though, this time, without the benefit of television), Fulbright addressed the Senate on the subject of China. His speech, full of apt historical allusions and thoughtful commentary, stressed the point that if China and the United States were to avoid war, both countries had to be less fixated on matters of doctrine and ideology. Fulbright recognized that because each country had demonized the other for so long, it was a difficult situation to rectify. He could only hope that it was not too late to reach "the ultimate political objective: the prevention of war between China and America."[27]

During the next several weeks, a number of leading sinologists and specialists in international relations, including Doak Barnett, John K. Fairbank, and Donald Zagoria, presented testimony to the committee. Barnett, for one, advocated a policy of "containment but not isolation" of China. He also urged a de facto recognition of the regime in Peking as the only government of mainland China. Fairbank, like Fulbright earlier, sought to explain current Chinese behavior in historically oriented terms, and he recommended more contact with China "on every front." Zagoria argued that "our only hope to achieve a stable and tolerable relationship with Communist China is to do all we can to promote not a change of the system—which can be done only by war—but a change within the system."[28]

Fulbright was delighted with the response that the hearings had evoked. CBS even produced a television seminar on China and Vietnam, with him and Fairbank serving as discussants. That program suggested that the Foreign Relations Committee had helped to break new ground. And for Fulbright himself, the hearings had been a valuable learning experience, reinforcing his recent discovery that China was not the driven expansionist power he had so long believed.[29] Not all the testimony necessarily pleased him. Most of the experts saw the problem of Sino-American relations in conflict-oriented terms which largely exculpated the United States of any responsibility for the tensions between the two powers. Their discussion of recent Chinese political behavior and history was such that one could scarcely believe that John Foster Dulles had ever existed or that the Korean War had ever taken place.

Vietnam was not divorced from the general discussion. Barnett, in his prepared statement, warned of the danger inherent in Johnson's bombing campaign, fearing that it had the potential to precipitate a war with China. And Zagoria raised the matter of neutralizing Southeast Asia as a possible outcome of the ending of the Vietnam War. On the other hand, Fairbank disappointed Fulbright by defending so-called nation-building activities in South Vietnam.[30] Clearly Fulbright's general approach to both Vietnam and China, characterized by his recent Senate speeches and public remarks, was simply too unconventional to be shared publicly by some specialists in the field of Asian studies, let alone by the White House.

Fulbright and his fellow doves had tried to reach the general public, but as a Louis Harris poll revealed, only 37 percent of those queried had heard about the committee's recent hearings, and a majority of those who had were college-educated. Of people with opinions, 55 percent believed that the hearings had been helpful, while 45 percent believed otherwise. Most revealingly, 60 percent felt that Wayne Morse had been more harmful than helpful, while 45 percent of those polled classified him as a "radical."[31] Despite those hearings, the Harris poll showed that public confidence in both Secretaries Rusk and McNamara remained high, in fact higher than in President Johnson himself.

Meanwhile, Fulbright could only hope that future public hearings, speeches, and continued discussion would ultimately affect Johnson's standing in the polls, forcing him then to change his policy. He recognized how difficult it would be to change anything in the near future. Listening to Secretary Rusk "discuss with much fervor or glibness our purposes in Vietnam," he was "reminded of Torquemada." When he sent a letter to the president suggesting that a neutralization scheme might have possibilities for ending the conflict, Johnson replied that "until Hanoi and Peking are prepared to permit solutions other than force against South Vietnam and Laos, I see no prospect of achieving the result you have in mind. They won't even talk about what you have in mind."[32]

What Fulbright had in mind was the principle of "no clear victory for either side," which he saw as the "crux of the difference between the Secretary of State and myself." When Fulbright delivered the Brien McMahon lecture at the University of Connecticut on 22 March, he sought to clarify that difference and explain his own position. On that occasion, he argued that the war was undermining Johnson's Great Society programs, programs which he himself supported. As Fulbright put it, "the President simply cannot think about implementing the Great Society at home while he is supervising bombing missions over North Vietnam; nor is the Congress much inclined to debate—much less finance—expanded education programs when it is involved in debating and paying for—an expanded war." If that loss of direction and élan at home was a tragedy, so, in his view, was Vietnam, where a "revolution against social injustice and foreign rule has become a contest between Asian communism and the United States." Fulbright suggested that "American interests are better served by supporting nationalism than by opposing communism, and that when the two are encountered in the same country, it is in our interest to accept a Communist government rather than undertake the cruel and all but impossible task of suppressing a genuinely national movement."[33]

Fulbright also called for "a new relationship between the United States and China in the rimlands of Asia," which, he asserted, was the "issue on which everything else depends." If a reconciliation between the two powers could be arranged, it would contribute, he believed, to a hoped-for neutralization of the region, leading to "the withdrawal of American military power to the islands and waters around the coast of Asia. . . ."[34] Whether such an outcome was possible depended on one's view of Chinese behavior. That was a key variable which could determine the future course of Sino-American relations.

The McMahon Lecture was one in a series of lectures which Fulbright planned to give that spring on various university campuses. He had committed himself to doing this in order to build a constituency for peace and because he hoped his views would be communicated to elite opinion makers. As a realist, Fulbright harbored no illusions that speech making would produce immediate results. He knew that it would take a long time to educate people about a situation that in his own mind was as complex as anything he had ever before encountered. In the meantime, like Wayne Morse, he was worried that war with China was a real possibility.[35]

By that same spring, Johnson was already trapped in Vietnam: If he made peace along the lines recommended to him by Fulbright and Mansfield, the Republicans would probably crucify him. If he sought to win the war in such a way as to threaten the political independence of North Vietnam, then he would risk bringing Russia and China into the fray. Either way, he discovered that there was little or no room to maneuver except to escalate the conflict in the South.

Part of Johnson's problem, thought Fulbright, was rooted in the country's singular fear of communism, which had made McCarthyism an always latent and sometimes manifest feature of American political life. Because Johnson had long remembered the damage wrought by the likes of a Joe McCarthy or Richard Nixon to Democratic fortunes in the 1950s, he was afraid that any failure on his part to bring home the "coonskin cap" would unleash a tidal wave of resentment reminiscent of the worst days of that decade. Believing that the enemy was on the right, Johnson felt that he could ill afford to make himself vulnerable to its charges of treason and betrayal. Hence, the war had to be fought, among other reasons, to contain precisely those forces which he thought were most dangerous to him and the most threatening to the stability of the country. Of importance, too, was a point made years later by Stuart Symington: Johnson was determined to avoid the charge that he was the first president to lose a war.[36] It seems, then, that his fear of the right, plus his personal desire for vindication, had come together to make him obsessed with the need to win the war, or at least not to lose it.

Fulbright had long since recognized the emotional commitment that Johnson had made to Vietnam. He also knew that Johnson was a cunning politician who would most likely respond to political pressure, but the next presidential election was still more than thirty months away. At the moment, Fulbright and his fellow critics were more worried about the immediate prospects of war with China, but they felt powerless to do anything about that perceived drift toward disaster. Adding to their gloom was the realization that they did not even constitute a voting majority on the Foreign Relations Committee. As Fulbright admitted, Johnson "is running the show. He has control of this Congress, including my committee. I have a lot of the young members with me, but they are afraid to expose themselves. They know they can be gutted."[37]

Despite this depressing situation, Fulbright moved into high gear in an attempt to mobilize further resistance to White House policies. He gave the Christian A. Herter Lectures at Johns Hopkins University in Baltimore on 21 and 27 April and 5 May in order to discuss the relationship between power and ideology, patriotism and dissent, and revolution and history in the context of the Vietnam War. Thanks to Seth Tillman's writing and analysis, Fulbright's preparation was such that his lectures, as well as a speech he gave in New York on 28 April, succeeded in stimulating discussion and provoking comment across the entire ideological spectrum.

The 21 April lecture was titled: "The Higher Patriotism." For Fulbright, this meant that "to criticize one's country is to do it a service and pay it a compliment. . . . It is not pejorative but a tribute to say America is worthy of criticism." The criticism he had in mind was directed at what he feared was becoming a characteristic of American foreign policy, namely its succumbing "to that arrogance of power which has afflicted, weakened and in some cases destroyed great nations in the past." In order to arrest that development before it was too late, Fulbright called on citizen-patriots to give a "higher loyalty" to the "country's ideals" rather than its current policy. In that vein, Fulbright praised the student opposition to the war, saying that it was "an expression of the national conscience and a manifestation of traditional American idealism."[38] But he warned the students to eschew symbolic gestures like draft-card burnings and urged them to play by the rules.

Fulbright concluded his first Herter Lecture with a discussion and analysis of why Congress, over the years, had lost power to the president in the making of foreign policy. He explored this historic shift in a remarkable passage which all but buried his past remarks about the need to depend

solely on the president-helmsman to steer the ship of state through dangerous foreign waters:

> The cause of the change is crisis. The President has the authority and resources to
> make decisions and take actions in an emergency; the Congress does not. Nor,
> in my opinion should it; the proper responsibilities of the Congress are to reflect
> and review, to advise and consent. In the past twenty-five years American foreign
> policy has encountered a shattering series of crisis and inevitably—or almost
> inevitably—the effort to cope with these has been Executive effort, while the
> Congress inspired by patriotism, importuned by Presidents, and deterred by lack
> of information, has tended to fall in line behind the Executive. The result has
> been the unhinging of traditional constitutional relationships, the Senate's con-
> stitutional powers of advise and consent have atrophied into what is widely
> regarded—though never asserted—to be a duty to give prompt consent with a
> minimum of advice. The problem is to find a way to restore the constitutional
> balance, to find ways by which the Senate can discharge its duty of advice and
> consent in an era of permanent crisis.[39]

Fulbright's 27 April lecture in the Herter series was titled "Revolutions
Abroad," and it built on insights found in both his Dominican speech of 15
September 1965 and his China speech of 7 March 1966. In seeking to explain why violent revolutions in the Third World were likely to persist,
Fulbright advanced the view that the combined problems of endemic pov-
erty and population growth had generated enormous pressure for change
which revolutionary elites would direct for the purposes of "moderniza-
tion" not "democratization." Given that likely development in both Latin
America and Asia, the senator hoped his countrymen would be more understanding of the processes at work in a world so alien to them. He knew,
however, that most Americans, because of their country's stunning "success and good fortune," could not even begin to comprehend, let alone
"empathize with," those demands for change, and this fact worried him.[40]
  At the core of Fulbright's discussion of America's relations with a revolutionary world, especially with China, was his belief that past revolutionary regimes tended to mellow, moving away from a puritanical stage to one
of Thermadorian moderation. This meant, then, an "abatement of fanaticism, a reassertion of human nature and a return to everyday living." His
view of the life cycle of the great historical revolutions, from that of Crom-
well to those of Lenin and Stalin, was taken from Crane Brinton's classic
study of revolutionary "uniformities," *Anatomy of Revolution*, a work
that served his purposes very nicely. By employing the Brinton model, Ful-

bright challenged American policy toward China, suggesting that since history had shown a moderating of past revolutionary zeal, it was in America's interest to wait out the current phase of Chinese "fanaticism." China, like other revolutionary societies, would thus become a "more or less normal society with a more or less normal relation with the outside world." Of concern to him was whether American behavior was simply perpetuating "the extremist phase of the Chinese Revolution" while failing to "encourage progress toward moderation." Fearing that war was a possibility between the United States and China, Fulbright raised an important matter by postulating that American behavior, whatever it was, would at some point be reciprocated by the other side.[41]

On 28 April, Fulbright went to New York to speak on the subject of "The Vietnam Fallout" to the American Newspaper Publishers Association. He said that the war was having a damaging impact on Soviet-American relations, West European–American relations, and American society at home. The status of Soviet-American relations was always a matter of utmost concern for Fulbright, because he could never forget that those two countries held "the power of life and death over all of humanity."[42] Having long supported the policy of détente, Fulbright now feared that the war was undermining efforts to stabilize relations between the superpowers. The only reason the situation was not worse, he argued, was the "restraint showed by the Russians with respect to the war."

In Western Europe, there was a clear expression of alarm and concern over the American escalation in Southeast Asia, indicating to Fulbright a loss of confidence in American leadership. He believed that if Europeans avoided giving any moral and material commitment to the American cause, it was probably due to a fear of being too closely associated with an undertaking that might complicate their security at home.

Fulbright's most sharply stated remarks dealt with the war's impact on American society. The war, he felt, was doing irreparable harm to Great Society programs, while generating a "war fever" in the minds of the American people and their leaders. Congress, he insisted, had become "politically and psychologically" a war Congress. A war fever, abetted by various propaganda mills, was conditioning people's minds to accept the worst about the other side. The developments both at home and abroad forced Fulbright to conclude that

America is showing some signs of that fatal presumption, that overextension of power and mission, which brought ruin to ancient Athens, to Napoleonic France and to Nazi Germany. The process had hardly begun, but the war which we are now fighting can only accelerate it. If the war goes on and expands, if that fatal process continues to accelerate until America becomes what it is now and never has been, a seeker after unlimited power and empire, then Vietnam will have had a mighty and tragic fallout indeed.[43]

When Fulbright presented the last of his three Herter Lectures on 5 May, he addressed the broader philosophical and historical dimensions of the current crisis. That lecture was titled "The Arrogance of Power," which he defined as a "psychological need that nations seem to have to prove that they are bigger, better, stronger, than other nations." As he had already mentioned in New York, American behavior in Vietnam made him fearful that the United States was following a course of action which had brought ruin to other great nations. If America was to avoid a similar fate, it would have to reject the missionary impulse to do good. At the heart of Fulbright's critique of that sense of mission was an alternative view of power predicated on the force of example rather than the example of force.[44]

Fulbright's analysis of American foreign policy stamped him as the leading congressional critic of the war. Also, having been educated by the unfolding tragedy in Vietnam and the recent intervention in the Dominican Republic, he now spoke out on behalf of a new policy toward China, a more sympathetic approach to revolutionary developments in the Third World, and the establishment of a solidly based détente with the Soviet Union. Equally important were his remarks critical of the arrogance and irresponsibility of executive power. He feared that such power was seriously undermining, if not destroying, a balanced relationship between the executive and Congress, as well as threatening democratic values and practices at home. Believing that the quest for Pax Americana was incompatible with the goal of preserving democracy in America, Fulbright had become a serious opponent of the imperial presidency.

On the other hand, Fulbright, despite outward appearances, had not broken with those broader policies which helped to make the Vietnam intervention possible. He still believed that the United States had the primary role to play as the major stabilizing force in world politics, and he continued to advocate the use of air and sea power to contain China. In other words, while Fulbright rejected Johnson's intervention for tactical reasons, he still remained committed to an expansive foreign policy and to strategic goals which did not differ fundamentally from those held by Dean Rusk.[45]

Nevertheless, Fulbright's Herter Lecture and his New York speech elicited an immediate critical response from leading political figures in Washington. Ex-Senator Barry Goldwater remarked on 5 May that Fulbright should resign from his position as chairman of the Foreign Relations Committee for giving "aid and comfort to the enemy." Goldwater insisted that "no American has the right or the justification to level such charges against his own country. . . . And that goes double for doing it in a time of war. . . ." On that same day, Senator Jacob Javits, speaking on the Senate floor, contended that "the acceptance of power, not the arrogance of power" had characterized American foreign policy since World War II. He asserted that Fulbright's thesis was "largely negative" and offered no guidelines for action.[46]

LBJ was also provoked enough to comment. Speaking at Princeton University on 11 May, he noted that "the exercise of power in this century has meant for all of us in the United States not arrogance but agony. We have used our power not willingly and recklessly ever, but always reluctantly and with restraint." The next night, he addressed a congressional dinner in Washington, and he was more pointed and personal in his remarks. Looking directly at Fulbright, he said, "I am delighted to be here tonight with so many of my very old friends as well as some members of the Foreign Relations Committee. You can say one thing about those hearings, although I don't think this is the place to say it."[47]

Newspapers and periodicals joined in the chorus of denunciations or praise. Fulbright was seen as foolish, wise, impetuous, or thoughtful, depending on the particular journal's slant. The *Washington Post*, a pro-Johnson paper, was sharply critical, as were many other newsapers of similar persuasion. An editorial in *Life* was full of biting comment. The *New York Times*, on the other hand, gave Fulbright generous coverage, by either publishing his speeches or lengthy extracts from them. The country's leading dove newspaper, the *Times* supported a negotiating position similar to Fulbright's as the months of conflict lengthened into years of travail.[48]

Not every journal reported Fulbright's views as responsibly as the *Times*, which led Fulbright to complain that his remarks were either taken out of context or misconstrued altogether. In order to set the record straight, Fulbright, on 17 May, spoke to the National Press Club in Washington. There, he admitted regret over remarks found in his New York speech of 28 April, which seemed to liken the American role in Vietnam to Nazi Germany in Europe. As he said, "I neglected to make it clear that I was talking about the extent, not the character of a nation's aspirations; the distinction between

Hitler's design for conquest and America's desire to do good in the world seemed to be so obvious as to be unnecessary to mention." The senator also regretted that he had referred to Saigon in his 5 May speech as an "American brothel." He felt that it received far too much play at the expense of the larger point, namely, that "rich and powerful nations have a strong impact on small and weak ones." And, finally, he reminded his audience that he had not charged any American official with "arrogance in the exercise of power." Of concern to him, he said, were "concepts," not accusations.[49]

Fulbright evidently conveyed similar sentiments in a letter he wrote to Johnson. The president replied on 27 May by agreeing with him that "statements can be taken out of context and interpretations can draw a different meaning than you meant from your words. It's happened to me!" In that same letter, Johnson shrewdly defended his policies by pointing out that there were other historical analogies—such as Munich—that were worth considering in addition to those mentioned by Fulbright in his lectures. He concluded on a friendly note, writing that "I cannot believe our differences over policy have erased the friendship we have shared for so long. I have a fondness for Betty and you that is real. . . . I am sorry that careless people have appeared to paint another picture." Johnson's fondness for Fulbright was manifested in unusual ways, for following the Vietnam hearings, he had placed Fulbright and several other Senate doves under strict FBI surveillance.[50] Apparently Johnson wanted to make certain that his Senate critics were not in the clutches of foreign agents under Moscow's control.

Although Johnson and Fulbright were once more in personal contact, Fulbright knew that he had not a shred of influence with the president. He also knew that it was Johnson, not his advisers, who made policy. Yet those advisers—Rusk, McNamara, and Clark Clifford, men of the center—were as obsessed with avoiding a defeat as was Johnson, a point that Fulbright fully understood. Nevertheless, he continued to do what he could to oppose the war. Carl Marcy remembers that he often met with various senators at lunch or at other times during the day to talk to them and to explain his own position. Yet very few of Fulbright's colleagues were open to persuasion. According to Lee Williams, his administrative assistant, Vance Hartke and Ernest Hollings had shown that they were educable. Fulbright's failure to find many others highlighted a recurrent problem that the doves could not resolve, that is, how to develop a loyal and coherent opposition within the framework of the two-party system, which itself was bound to the rules and traditions of the Senate. Apart from that intractable problem, there was another difficulty as well. As Fulbright admitted years later, it was impossible to bargain on an issue of such magnitude, especially because the war was for so many senators a matter of honestly held conviction, reinforced by a national consensus and mood.[51]

There may have been a good political reason as to why Fulbright worked so hard on the inside to win over his colleagues. He and his aides, explained Williams, were well aware of the dangers involved if he went too far in the direction of Wayne Morse. Aware that most voters in Arkansas supported the war, Fulbright recognized that a slow conversion was necessary if he was to retain his position and influence. Thus fearful, in Williams's words, of "turning off the public," Fulbright did not strike out as aggressively against Johnson, as Williams himself had recommended.[52]

Whatever Fulbright and other doves did at that stage made little difference; Johnson was not backing down. Thus Fulbright knew that if there was to be a change in Johnson's war policy, it would come about only as a result of electoral politics which was still many months removed from the current situation. Nevertheless, he did not retire or just sulk; he kept pressing, going so far as to raise the matter of the Gulf of Tonkin affair, albeit in camera. He had long since known that the incident of 4 August 1964 probably never took place. In an exchange with Secretary Rusk on 30 April 1965, he made reference to an "alleged" attack on 4 August. Whatever Fulbright knew about this situation probably came from George Ball, who had been told by Johnson himself only a few days after the "event" that it was entirely possible that nothing had really happened out there in the Gulf of Tonkin. Fulbright had no way of testing this proposition, lacking access to the cable traffic or other confidential material at the Pentagon and the White House. Then, in March 1966, he received a letter from retired Admiral Arnold True, a distinguished World War II naval officer, who wrote him that the administration's explanation for what happened on 4 August "sounds unrealistic."[53]

That letter encouraged Fulbright to pursue the matter. Consequently, he and his committee queried Assistant Secretary of Defense John T. McNaughton, a close friend and confidant of Secretary McNamara, about this incident in a closed-door hearing on 24 May. This hearing exposed for Fulbright the vast gap separating the administration's claim and the ambiguous reality of that day. Later, after he read the transcript of that 24 May hearing, Senator Milward Simpson wrote Fulbright to express his doubts about the administration's "credibility." In reply, Fulbright said that "I have no evidence regarding the veracity of the Administration, but there is some question that the incident was unprovoked."[54] This particular investigation was kept under tight wraps, as Fulbright knew very well that it was too explosive and dangerous a topic to air at that time. Without far more evidence at its disposal, the committee could never prove, let alone properly argue, that the administration had deceived the Senate about the events in the Gulf of Tonkin in August 1964.

The current situation in Vietnam was depressing enough. After concluding several conversations with Johnson at the White House on 1 and 15 June, Fulbright got the message that he was determined to win the war in the South before the 1966 congressional election. Faced with the prospect of more escalation, Fulbright wrote Chester Bowles that "I am bound to say that the war in Vietnam is having a very deleterious effect upon every other program, domestic and foreign, in which I am interested. I cannot recall when I have felt so depressed about our foreign relations."[55]

Adding to Fulbright's depression was news of the American bombing on 29 and 30 June of the petroleum and oil deposits and sites in and around Hanoi. These were targets which had long been restricted for fear that if they were bombed Russia and China might respond in some way. As those raids signified a new stage in the escalation, they also coincided with an ominous domestic development that Fulbright mentioned in a letter to a constituent: "Vietnam is almost impossible to explain, it is so involved, and yet it carries within it grave possibilities for harm for the foreseeable future. We are going through the early stages of an inflationary period at great cost in life and wealth, and for a purpose I simply do not understand." He remained confident, though, that in time "the people of Arkansas will agree that [the war] is a poor investment."[56]

Meanwhile, Johnson continued to defend that investment. On 12 July, he spoke in White Sulphur Springs, West Virginia, emphasizing the point that the United States was a Pacific power and would seek to use its resources to promote an era based on "cooperation and peaceful competition among nations." Such a happy prospect was possible for everyone, he insisted, as long as "we stand firm in Vietnam against military conquest."[57]

Fulbright responded to Johnson's 12 July speech by telling the Senate on 22 July that his program constituted a "radical departure in American foreign policy in that it is virtually unlimited in what it purports to accomplish and unilateral in its execution." Fearing that Johnson was now embarked on a mission to bring the Great Society to Asia, Fulbright urged his colleagues in the Senate "to consider some of the implications of the 'Asian doctrine' before it becomes an irrevocable national commitment undertaken without the consent or even the knowledge of the Senate."[58]

The Arkansan's attack did not go unnoticed at the White House. That same day, White House Press Secretary Bill Moyers spent considerable time at a hastily called press conference challenging Fulbright's arguments, while remarking that "the President told me he finds it very difficult to follow exactly what the Senator is saying in respect to the Government's Asian policies and disappointing to try to follow what the Senator means." Moyers also cited evidence showing that Fulbright had in the past supported such proposals designed to aid noncommunist Asian countries in their development plans. Having denied that Johnson was offering a new Asian doctrine, Moyers insisted that whatever Johnson had discussed in his 12 July speech had been the product of long-standing congressional support and consultation. It was ironic that Moyers was in this instance Johnson's appointed spokesman, for he and Fulbright had become very friendly after both men came together in late 1965 out of mutual concern over Johnson's escalation.[59] For that reason some people in the White House probably viewed him as a "double agent."

Moyers's rather gentle treatment of Fulbright was not matched by others. Robert Kinter of the White House staff made sure the Moyers "briefing" reached friendly journalists and editors in Washington, including Ben Bradlee of the *Washington Post* who, according to Kinter, was "extremely cooperative." Indeed he was. On 25 July, the *Post* opined that "the Senator from Arkansas had become so querulous and cantankerous a critic that President Johnson could not state the most obvious truth about foreign policy without inviting the Senator's distempered dissection. His fault finding started out with the Gulf of Tonkin Resolution and now he would even repeal the Monroe Doctrine."[60]

After having been savaged by the *Post* during that last week of July, Fulbright wrote to his old friend Lewis Douglas that "I appreciate more than I can say your cordial letter. It is very encouraging to have a word of approval from an experienced man when there is such disapproval and criticism from various quarters." Even more poignant were Fulbright's concluding words: "I do not have any influence with the President, but perhaps you and others in whom he has confidence will have better luck."[61]

That same sense of realism led Fulbright to declare in mid-August that if Hanoi and Peking were counting on an American withdrawal because of the dissent in the United States, they were making a big mistake. He noted that the Congress was even more warlike than the president and that doves carried no political weight in Washington. The hawkish Washington papers praised him, and Vice President Hubert Humphrey informed him that he was a "patriot, statesman and a great Senator." A week later, Fulbright, who had been accused by some doves of "having thrown in the sponge," sought to clarify his stand. He repeated what he had said earlier, namely, that the Congress was more warlike than the president, and he reaffirmed his long-standing position that the country was overcommitted in Asia and that administration policies were likely to lead to a larger and more dangerous war.[62]

That expanding war now seemed to include Thailand, where in the summer of 1966 signs of a communist-backed insurgency could be found. Because he was curious to know what was happening there, Fulbright queried Assistant Secretary of Defense Arthur Sylvester about the matter in an open hearing on 31 August, but Sylvester refused to discuss anything relating to Thailand in public. Fulbright later announced that he would hold hearings on the American involvement in Thailand beginning on 19 September, and he hoped that Secretaries Rusk and McNamara would appear at those hearings.[63]

Johnson was very angry upon hearing that Fulbright intended to move in this direction, especially at a time when bombing raids from Thailand were about to commence over North Vietnam. For this reason, Johnson was prepared to denounce Fulbright publicly "for giving aid and comfort to our enemies." Congressional leaders warned him, though, that if he spoke out, his remarks would further divide the Democratic party before the midterm election. He may have been restrained, also, by the assurances given to him by Mike Mansfield and Russell Long that they would seek to prevent Fulbright from turning his hearings "into another televised attack on Vietnam."[64]

McNamara and Rusk never gave testimony, but the committee met, on 20 September, with Assistant Secretary of State William Bundy. When Fulbright later briefed reporters about Bundy's appearance, he mentioned that Thailand had been a focal point of that day's discussion. He also informed them that he was less concerned about the short-term situation (the use of bases for B-52s) than about the nature of the American involvement in Asia, which he saw growing out of the foreign aid program.[65] Although Fulbright was eager to examine the long-term American objectives in the region, which seemed to be tied to the containment of China, he said that there were no plans for additional hearings.

The senator was clearly baffled about what to do next. In a letter to Barbara Tuchman, the historian, in which he invited her to speak informally to the committe, Fulbright admitted that "I am grasping at straws and do not know what will influence the President."[66] Part of his frustration stemmed from his realization that the president was so able to dominate the news media that it was very difficult for critics to get a sustained hearing. For example, when Johnson announced that he would soon meet with America's Pacific allies in Manila to discuss future plans for the region, full media attention was given to his announcement; Fulbright's remark that this "cosy" gathering of like-minded countries would be better served if India and Japan also attended went unnoticed.

While preparations for the Manila meeting went forward, Congress was preparing to adjourn. It had been a very frustrating year for Fulbright, whose best effort did little to dent Johnson's control of the Senate. In fact, Fulbright believed that the war had further weakened the Senate's advice-and-consent role. And he knew that the war was beginning to do great damage to the domestic political and economic life of the country. He took note of this development in a letter to Lewis Douglas on 22 October. Mentioning the increased political activity of the extreme right, including the John Birch Society and the Liberty Lobby, he expressed concern about their resurgence.[67] Ironically, then, if Johnson was fighting the war to contain the right, it was his jingoism that created for the right a favorable climate.

While Johnson was preparing to return from Manila, Fulbright had to deal with another matter that came up very suddenly. Tristram Coffin, a friend, had written a biography entitled *Senator Fulbright: A Public Philosopher*. Although it was not scheduled for release until mid-November, Fulbright had seen an advance copy and was troubled by what he read. Evidently Coffin had attributed to Fulbright a sarcastic statement about Johnson's war policy that the senator had not made either to Coffin or to anyone else. Embarrassed by that apparent mix-up, Fulbright wrote Bill Moyers about his problem, expressing the hope that he could discuss it with Moyers and if possible with Johnson, too. Fulbright concluded his letter with the remark that "you must know that I wish him success in all his efforts, and our differences of view about the war in Vietnam has [*sic*] not affected my friendship for him."[68]

Fulbright and Johnson briefly referred to the Coffin book when they met on 3 November. Of greater importance was their discussion of Johnson's trip to Manila. Following his meeting with the president, Fulbright told the press that he thought the president was "sincere" in his desire to withdraw American forces and to liquidate American bases as soon as a peace agreement had been reached. And he again recommended that the United States stop the bombing of North Vietnam, accept a cease-fire, and include the Viet Cong as a partner to the negotiations, as a way of augmenting the peace process.[69]

With that conversation behind him, Fulbright now had to face the fact that the new Congress, elected in November 1966, was even more hawkishly inclined than the one which had just retired. The old Congress had not been a haven for doves; in October 1966, only 15 percent of the membership favored a greater stress on initiating peace talks. The results of November, which saw many more Republicans come into the House, meant that LBJ's critics were more isolated than ever. Subsequent to the election, Johnson, ignoring the advice he received from a number of key officials in his administration, unleashed a major attack near Hanoi in early December that effectively undermined a possibly promising peace initiative that had been undertaken by a Polish intermediary.[70]

Despite this latest failure to end the war, Fulbright was surely relieved to learn that the administration planned to submit a consular agreement with the Soviet Union to the Senate in early 1967. Good relations with the Soviet Union were for him a matter of the highest importance, and it may explain why he sought to conciliate Johnson about the material in the Coffin book. Meanwhile, he and his committee were making their plans for the coming year. A major review of American policies and commitments was under consideration, as was a proposal from Alfred Landon, a good friend of George Aiken, to hold hearings on executive commitments. And theologian Reinhold Neibur's recommendation that hearings be held on the subject of America's responsibility as a world power seemed attractive.[71]

After disposing of committee business, Fulbright then flew to Stockholm to give a lecture to the Swedish Institute for Cultural Relations. In his prepared remarks, he attempted to define the requirements for survival in an age ridden with murderous ideological conflict, dangerous national rivalries, and an unparalleled arms race in nuclear weapons. He posed the problem in the form of a question: "Can we devise a course of action toward the building of an international community which is both bold enough to eliminate or reduce the danger of nuclear weapons and modest enough to be within the limits of tolerance imposed by prevailing fears and prejudices?" He had no answer per se, but he felt that any "effort" to restrain competition among nations was worth making, simply as a civilizing act on its own terms. Fulbright's tool for change was education. He recognized that "it might not be fast enough to save us from catastrophe but it is the strongest force available for that purpose and its proper place therefore, is not at the periphery but at the center of international relations." This exercise in conflict resolution led him to conclude that "international education should try to change the nature of the game, to civilize and humanize it in this nuclear age."[72]

This speech, when coupled with the earlier Herter Lectures, added to Fulbright's reputation as a leading spokesman for de-escalation. But what few understood at the time was that his opposition to the administration's Vietnam policies did not then constitute a basic challenge to mainstream thinking about overall American foreign policy goals. He and Dean Rusk agreed that the United States had a fundamental role to play in the search for world order and international stability. Where the two men basically differed was over the issue of Vietnam. Fulbright took the strongest exception to Rusk's argument that Vietnam was a vital interest of the United States and that America's continuing commitment to global stability was dependent upon American resolve in Vietnam.

Because Fulbright was fearful that the war would undermine the Great Society at home and damage the country's standing abroad, he was now desperate to change the policy before matters got out of hand. By the time he returned to Washington in December, Random House was about to publish a manuscript that Seth Tillman had prepared for him. Titled *The Arrogance of Power*, it contained Fulbright's program for achieving peace in Vietnam, as well as a general statement of his evolving views on American foreign policy since the appearance of his last volume in 1964. With the publication of his new book, Fulbright would again try to persuade readers that the pictures in their minds needed changing.

5 DEADLOCK: I

On 16 January 1967, the Foreign Relations Committee met in closed session with Secretary Rusk to discuss Vietnam. Afterward, Senator Fulbright informed reporters that little had changed since the secretary's last visit back in October. He told them that committee members were now asking thoughtful questions, but that Rusk was giving them the same old answers.[1] One problem facing Fulbright was to find some way to bring Rusk into a public session so the differences between them could be ventilated in a more useful way.

Despite Rusk's constant refusal to appear in open session (Johnson would not sanction it), Fulbright had another vehicle for presenting his views on Vietnam. His new book, *The Arrogance of Power*, was published on 23 January, and it provided him with a fresh opportunity to argue his case against the war. The book's title was derived from one of the Herter Lectures, and its contents came from those lectures which he had given at Johns Hopkins University and elsewhere during the spring and summer of 1966. Thus, included in this volume was a discussion of Sino-American relations, the Vietnam War, Latin America, and the psychology of international relations. Although the material and discussions were pitched to a fairly sophisticated reader, the point of view throughout was one which had the ordinary Arkansas voter in mind.[2] As Fulbright was seeking to educate that voter, he included in the book an eight-point peace program to provide the reader with a constructive alternative to Johnson's policy.

Fulbright's suggestions for peace included an end to the bombing of North Vietnam, recognition of the National Liberation Front as a proper party to future peace negotiations, the neutralization of the region, a pledge by the United States that it would eventually withdraw its troops from Vietnam, and the consolidation of American military forces into fortified defensible areas if negotiations failed to end the conflict.[3]

Fulbright's program combined the Gavin enclave strategy with his own earlier call for the neutralization of the area and the inclusion of the Viet Cong in the negotiating process. Yet this approach was essentially unworkable, doomed by Hanoi's refusal to bargain for less than victory and by Johnson's rejection of the Viet Cong as an independent party to any settlement.

Nevertheless, *The Arrogance of Power* sold well both in hard and paper copies; for a few weeks it was listed on the *New York Times* best-seller list, and by June 1967, 100,000 copies had been bought. By the end of the year it was listed as the sixth-best seller in paperback trade books. And soon there were also Italian, Spanish, German, Japanese, and Swedish editions, further reaffirming Fulbright's worldwide reputation as a leading, albeit moderately inclined, dove. Fulbright had to be pleased with those sales, for the more the book sold, the more discussion it was likely to provoke, and vice versa. Ultimately, over 400,000 copies were purchased, making *The Arrogance of Power* a widely known work for its time.[4]

Fulbright's appearance on "Today" as well as on "Meet the Press" helped to call attention to the book. On both occasions, he spent time discussing his peace program and the overall situation in Southeast Asia. As expected, though, the White House completely ignored his proposals. But I. F. Stone, the maverick Washington journalist, who would in time become a friend of Fulbright, thought that "its good sense, its moderation, and its humanity provide a common platform to which men of good will can rally. To have this program set forth by the chairman of the Foreign Relations Committee is a political asset. This is a moment which should be seized upon." Former Senator Barry Goldwater, speaking in New York, attacked Fulbright's proposals as "foolishness."[5] He urged more bombing, not negotiations.

Reviewers found the book worthy of comment and discussion. In a front-page review in the *New York Times Book Review*, Max Frankel, the *New York Times* diplomatic correspondent, remarked that Fulbright's new book "gropes for a doctrine of dissent that transforms mere criticism into bitter condemnation. It portends, or perhaps already bespeaks, the alienation of a great many thoughtful citizens from their government." He also noted the change in Fulbright's perspective since the publication of his last book: "From disagreement with the national policy, the Senator has escalated to an indictment of the national character. Where once he blamed ignorance, he now finds arrogance. And he offers psychological as well as political judgment and testimony to make his point." But while Frankel felt Fulbright's book was "an invaluable antidote to the official rhetoric of government," he contended that it "is not a satisfying prescription for alternatives to the policies it condemns." Nor was he satisfied with the arrogance of power thesis, saying that "it is one thing to suggest that unnecessary pride and belligerence have compounded error in Vietnam and quite another to describe them as symptoms of messianic zealotry."[6]

Frankel's critical review disappointed Fulbright, who wrote to Bennett Cerf, editor in chief at Random House, that Frankel "seems to take as negative an approach as one can without condemning it out of hand. However, I have found that there is room for difference of opinion, and I am hoping others will be more sympathetic."[7]

More sympathetic to Fulbright was Ronald Steel's review in the *Book Week* of the *Washington Post*. Steel sensed the book's importance by observing that "The Arrogance of Power marks the passage of Senator Fulbright from a relatively orthodox supporter of the liberal line on foreign policy to a spokesman of the post-cold-war generation. It is a book which could not have been written two year ago, before the Dominican hearings and the expansion of the war in Vietnam, for it is a direct response to them." But like Frankel, Steel also felt the book did not adequately explain "the terrible sacrifices we have undertaken on behalf of our clients, or the relative benevolence and restraint with which America has exercised her enormous power. The reality is more complex, more puzzling, and perhaps more elusive than that." In his concluding remarks, however, Steel captured well the book's value and utility: "There may be arrogance in our attitude toward power, but there is also deep anguish throughout the nation over the use of power. Senator Fulbright has helped to focus and channel this anguish into constructive criticism that may lead to the changes he desires. Therein lies the courage of his dissent and the importance of this book."[8]

Both reviewers, having been caught up in the "arrogance of power" theme, neglected to discuss the significance of the more important point, namely that Fulbright was not proposing a radical departure in American foreign policy. In fact, his global outlook was quite conventional in character, combining as it did a realist's concern with power and a conservative's desire for stability and order. Vietnam, of course, was the key issue, as Steel observed. Both he and Frankel failed to note that Fulbright's opposition to the war was rooted in a tactical, not strategic, disagreement with current American policy.

Shortly after *The Arrogance of Power* was published, the Foreign Relations Committee, beginning on 30 January, initiated a fresh series of hearings to explore, in Fulbright's words, "the general theme of the responsibilities of a great power." Fulbright hoped to examine in the course of those hearings the meaning of such words and phrases as "the free world," "the communist conspiracy," and "indirect aggression," in order to determine whether their meanings had changed since the time they first came into vogue. As a spokesman for the post-cold-war generation, it was clear that he was now widening his investigative lens to encompass an intellectual landscape beyond what he would have entertained just two short years previously. That larger shift in his world view was, as Steel suggested, a response to the Vietnam War as well as a realization that containment militarism had structural flaws and was in need of either a major overhaul or a replacement.[9]

When George Kennan spoke to the committee on 30 January, he discussed the implications of the Sino-Soviet split for American policymakers. Referring to the American involvement in Vietnam as "unfortunate," he endorsed a bombing halt "whether or not there was reciprocity." The next day, Edwin Reischauer, former American ambassador to Japan, recommended a "prudent de-escalation" of the bombing despite the gloomy prospects for negotiations. He also insisted that the United States had greatly overestimated the military threat of China "to our interests and its neighbors." On 2 February, Harrison Salisbury of the *New York Times* reported on his recent trip to Hanoi, where he had conferred with Ho Chi Minh. Witness to the destruction wrought by the American bombing, Salisbury shared his discoveries with the committee. Despite his findings, he refused to support a unilateral suspension of the bombing. (Years later he complained about Fulbright's sarcastic "questioning," calling his manner "embarrassing.")[10]

A White House aide was also embarrassed by those questions, but for reasons different from Salisbury's. On 3 February, Robert Kintner informed the president that "these hearings are excerpted in Huntley-Brinkley, Cronkite, and Jennings and also on the Today Show and they have a terrific impact." Thus worried by the preponderant dove influence on the committee, he wondered what could be done to produce witnesses favorable to the administration. If Johnson did not completely control this committee, as he did others in Congress, he was still well represented by Democrats such as Lausche, McGee, Sparkman, and Symington, and most Republicans were not about to cross him. Moreover, he had other resources. As Mike Manatos, a White House aide, remembered years later, both Mike Mansfield and George Aiken kept him and the president abreast of what was going on, so Johnson was never out of touch and could influence the committee's activity at all stages.[11]

The fact that Mansfield was so cooperative is not surprising. Although he was a staunch dove on the inside, he could never compromise his leadership position in the Senate or higher loyalty to Johnson, which may be why Fulbright, years later, referred to him as "Johnson's alter ego." According to Carl Marcy, Mansfield was no favorite of the committee, as he often received information from the White House which was not shared with his colleagues. Frank Church confirms that there was "tension" between Fulbright and Mansfield, despite their similar positions on the war.[12] Whatever the precise reason for it, the two men did not work at all well together in those years, as they would once Lyndon Johnson left the White House.

Despite these manifold political obstacles, Fulbright continued to struggle against the war. He interceded with Johnson to have State Department doors opened for two old friends, journalists Harry Ashmore and William Baggs, who had recently returned from Hanoi after having spoken with Ho Chi Minh. Reporting that the situation seemed more fluid and hopeful than one might have imagined, they tried to see Johnson but he refused, sending them to the State Department. Escorted there by Fulbright, they received assistance from William Bundy and Averell Harriman in composing a friendly and conciliatory letter to the North Vietnamese president. But that effort was undermined by Johnson, who sent his own letter to Ho, which, according to Ashmore, destroyed any chance of negotiating a settlement short of Hanoi's unconditional surrender.[13]

Shortly after Ho replied to Johnson's letter, another wide-ranging debate on the war broke out in the Senate. It was prompted by Senator Joe Clark's amendment to a Vietnam supplemental appropriations bill, which called for a ceiling of 500,000 American troops in Vietnam plus a cessation of the bombing of North Vietnam unless Congress first approved a formal declaration of war. Not surprisingly, Fulbright and his old friend Richard Russell found themselves on opposite sides of the issue. The two of them, who were most responsible among senators for preparing the Gulf of Tonkin Resolution for floor consideration in August 1964, debated long and hard over the question of whether that resolution had given LBJ all the authority he needed to wage a "limited war" in Southeast Asia. Russell claimed that Johnson had the necessary legal basis to continue the struggle, rejecting Fulbright's efforts to draw him into a colloquy over constitutional issues. Fulbright surely had to be discouraged by Russell's stand; he knew, better than anyone else in the Senate, that the Georgian did not desire or want a land war in Southeast Asia. Some days after their exchange, Mike Mansfield managed to have the Clark amendment withdrawn from floor consideration, fearing that it would be rejected by such a wide margin that Johnson would consider the vote another endorsement of his policies.[14]

In the midst of these proceedings, Fulbright had another duty to perform, one which was replete with sadness and a sense of profound loss. After his good friend Bernard Fall had been killed in Vietnam, Fulbright participated in a memorial service for him at Howard University on 6 March. His remarks that day were particularly poignant and also revealing of the inner journey he himself had taken since late 1965, in no small measure because of Fall. Fulbright praised Fall's intelligence and courage and his willingness to persevere in the search for truth. As Fulbright put it, "we have suffered a great loss. Those who knew and admired Bernard Fall will be joined in the future by others who seek the truth and who will thus come to realize what he has bequeathed us all."[15] Such was Fulbright's tribute to an exceptional individual, one who had educated him as he was now seeking to do with others in a climate not congenial to such an undertaking.

Robert Kennedy was also familiar with Fall's work. He had grown dovish wings, but was finding it difficult to take flight. When he finally spoke out on 2 March to denounce the bombing and to offer his peace proposals, Fulbright was among the few senators who publicly supported him. With Kennedy now publicly embracing the views of the dove current, Johnson proceeded to defend his policies with even greater intensity and passion. He spoke before the Tennessee General Assembly on 15 March, where he offered three reasons to continue the bombing. They included the need "to back our fighting men by denying our enemy a sanctuary; to exact a penalty against North Vietnam for her flagrant violations of the Geneva accords of 1954, 1962; and to limit the flow or to substantially increase the cost of infiltration of men and material from North Vietnam." Johnson's speech in Nashville, plus his recent trip to Guam to embrace the Saigon leadership, now convinced Barry Goldwater that the president meant business. It was clear to him that LBJ had disregarded "the words of Bobby Kennedy and Bill Fulbright who would pull out at any cost."[16]

Long before Goldwater's remarks, Fulbright had been subjected to an attack from his own colleagues, who suggested to him that his dissent was prolonging the war. Angered by this charge, Fulbright wrote a friendly constituent in Arkansas that "demagogues are more at home in Washington than anywhere else." The opportunity for renewed demagoguery was enhanced by General William Westmoreland's brief return trip to the

United States in late April. Westmoreland was scheduled to speak to the Congress on 28 April, but before going to Washington, he told a New York audience that the dissent at home was encouraging the enemy in Vietnam to continue the fight.[17]

On 25 April, the day after Westmoreland spoke in New York, George McGovern addressed the Senate. Saying that he could not "remain silent in the face of what I regard as a policy of madness," McGovern attacked all aspects of Johnson's war policy, thereby triggering a wide-ranging debate on the subject. Fulbright, pointing to Westmoreland's New York remarks, said that they "will lead to the charge of disloyalty . . . and from that to treason." In Fulbright's mind, there wasn't the slightest doubt that "all the pressure is now on and that this war is going right on to military victory."[18]

When General Westmoreland addressed Congress on 28 April, he was greeted with a standing ovation after assuring the lawmakers that the United States "will prevail in Vietnam over the Communist aggressor." But in the course of his remarks, he asserted that the "enemy believes our Achilles heel is our resolve." Immediately following Westmoreland's speech, CBS ran a live television special for the purpose of discussing it. Appearing on this program was Fulbright, who commented that his difference was not with Westmoreland or the troops in Vietnam, but, rather, with the policy which sent them there. Those troops were, after all, only doing their duty. Fulbright knew, of course, who was orchestrating this attack on dissent. Writing to Carl Reiner, the actor, Fulbright lamented that the "Administration's drive at total consensus, climaxed last Friday by General Westmoreland's appearance at the Joint Session, is leading us into a frenzy of chauvinism."[19]

Fulbright's frustration and unhappiness burst forth while he was being interviewed by a reporter from *Newsday*, a Long Island newspaper then edited by Bill Moyers, the former White House Press Secretary. Not knowing that his remarks would later be published, Fulbright told the reporter that he no longer believed what Johnson, Rusk, or McNamara said about the war; he thought that Johnson was seeking a military victory, not a negotiated settlement; and that Johnson was far more concerned about avoiding the charge he was "soft on communism" than about losing popularity due to his war policies. None of these comments was particularly newsworthy insofar as Washington insiders were concerned; but what did produce a stir was Fulbright's assertion that heavy Pentagon spending in states such as Washington, South Carolina, and Georgia may have had something to do with the support Henry Jackson, Mendel Rivers, and Richard Russell were giving to the war. Congressman Rivers was so indignant that he asked Fulbright to explain his statement. In a letter to Rivers, Fulbright simply pointed out a political fact of life, that in states where Pentagon spending was high, interests in the form of jobs and careers were created, which politicians could no more ignore than he, Fulbright, could disregard the views of poultry or cotton producers in Arkansas.[20]

A letter which Frank Church sent to Ho Chi Minh was far less controversial. Cosigned by fifteen other senators, including Fulbright, McGovern, and Morse, it made the point that all the signatories were opposed to any unilateral American withdrawal from Vietnam and that they favored a negotiated settlement. Perhaps aware that the idea for such a letter came from Johnson himself, Eugene McCarthy refused to sign it, saying that the whole thing was nothing more than an "election cover" for doves facing reelection battles in 1968.[21] Although Fulbright was not a scared dove, he did face the prospect of a serious primary challenge in 1968 from either Orval Faubus or Sidney McMath, both former governors and staunch Johnson supporters. McCarthy himself, it should be noted, did not face a reelection challenge until 1970.

In June 1967 the blowup in the Middle East, occasioned by war between Israel and the forces of Egypt and Jordan, diverted attention away from Vietnam. That conflict forced Fulbright to suspend plans to hold fresh hearings on Vietnam, but he thought that if the war in the Middle East could be resolved, then it might also open possibilities for ending the one in Vietnam. In other words, if Johnson took this latest crisis to the United Nations and managed to obtain Soviet support for a cease-fire, Fulbright hoped this could lead to significant developments elsewhere, including the creation of a more suitable diplomatic climate for a breakthrough in Vietnam. For this reason, he again urged the White House to "stop the bombing and to call on Russia and Britain to reconvene the Geneva Conference before the war gets out of hand and involves the Chinese."[22] Johnson gave his advice short shrift.

Fulbright and Johnson did discuss Soviet Prime Minister Aleksei Kosygin's visit to the United Nations. And Fulbright, in contact with Johnson via telephone and letters, urged him to meet with Kosygin in order to develop "a new working relationship between the Soviet Union and the United States." A policy of patience and conciliation, argued Fulbright, could "create opportunities" leading to the "resolution of outstanding issues." The Johnson-Kosygin meeting at Glassboro, New Jersey, laid the groundwork for a nuclear nonproliferation agreement, but there was no evidence that anything had changed with regard to Vietnam. Because Johnson refused to compromise his position, Fulbright and the other doves were now back to square one. As Fulbright put it, Johnson "is looking toward '68 and believes that Nixon and Reagan may attack him as being soft on communism if he gives an inch."[23]

While Johnson worried about Richard Nixon and Ronald Reagan, his 1964 consensus was coming apart, damaged by the combination of war, urban riots in Detroit and Newark, and growing political polarization inside the Democratic party. By the middle of July, then, Fulbright detected a change in the attitudes of a few colleagues not known for their dovish proclivities. In some cases, that change resulted from individuals making a cost-benefit analysis; in other cases, individuals were beginning to see that the war was, in Fulbright's words, "a highly immoral operation."[24]

The support Fulbright received for a proposed National Commitments Resolution, which he introduced on 31 July, was suggestive of a fresh current flowing through the Senate. Hoping, in his words, to arrest the "gradual erosion of the role of Congress, particularly of the Senate, in the determination of national security policy," Fulbright offered the following resolution: "That it is the sense of the Senate that a national commitment by the United States to a foreign power necessarily and exclusively results from affirmative action taken by the executive and legislative branches of the U.S. Government through means of a treaty, convention, or other legislative instrumentality specifically intended to give effect to such a commitment." To avoid the charge of partisanship or the accusation that he was seeking to link this resolution to the Vietnam issue, Fulbright told the Senate that "this resolution in no way tries to interfere with the day-to-day conduct of our foreign affairs. It does not attempt to restrict the constitutional responsibility of the President or to revoke any past decisions. It does not respond to any current crisis situation abroad, and it is not a measure directed against any single administration in this century—or against anyone at all."[25]

Motivating Fulbright to act was LBJ's dispatching of three C5A cargo planes and 130 servicemen to Zaire without first consulting with Congress; it was a move he took to help the Mobutu government quell an uprising of white mercenaries. But because both Fulbright and Russell feared that this step could mushroom into something far bigger and more unmanageable, they agreed to work together, hoping in this way to send Johnson a message. Thus Fulbright drafted the resolution and presented it, while Russell endorsed his action, not just because of his pique over the C5As, but also because of his frustration with and concern over the prolongation of the Vietnam War.[26] Russell seemingly feared that the war of attrition that Johnson was fighting in Vietnam was draining the country of needed resources for other, more important contingencies.

Fulbright had long been concerned about excessive American commitments, ever since the Vietnam hearings. And following Johnson's October 1966 trip to the Philippines, it seemed to him that the United States was now more deeply involved in the affairs of Southeast Asia, either through bilateral agreements or in the verbal assurances given by the president, vice president, or the secretary of state about which the Senate knew very little or nothing at all.[27] Because he questioned that process, Fulbright scheduled for mid-August a series of hearings to examine American overseas commitments, as those commitments related to his resolution.

While the Senate debate over the war began to crescendo, Fulbright went to Honolulu to address members of the Bar Association on 8 August. There, he delivered his most trenchant speech to date on the subject of the war. "The Price of Empire" spelled out in no uncertain terms Fulbright's conviction that the Great Society was now a sick society and that the violence and mayhem found in the jungles of Vietnam were psychologically connected to the riots and rot of America's inner cities. Vietnam, he said, was "poisoning and brutalizing our domestic life."[28]

That dual violence, both at home and abroad, was, in his view, a reflection of the "grotesque inversion of priorities" which saw the Pentagon receiving almost $76 billion for fiscal year 1968, while only $15 billion was alloted to what were called "social functions." That situation compelled Fulbright to remark that "priorities are reflected in the things we spend money on. Far from being a dry accounting of bookkeepers, a nation's budget is full of moral implications; it tells what a society cares about and what it does not care about; it tells what its values are."[29]

"The Price of Empire" was a powerful speech which both updated and extended the analysis Fulbright had first offered in the Herter Lectures and later in *The Arrogance of Power*. He had spoken out because of his belief that the critics knew what policymakers did not: "that it is ultimately self-defeating to fight fire with fire and that you cannot defend your values in a manner that does violence to those values without destroying the very thing that you are trying to defend."[30] Long before Watergate, he recognized that the Vietnam War was doing more damage to the country's finest traditions than anything that the country's most implacable enemies could ever achieve short of nuclear war itself.

Among those critics Fulbright praised were "students, churchmen and professors," whose opposition he felt was necessary in order to prevent the wholesale corruption of democratic institutions and values by an imperialist war. Recognizing, in particular, Dr. Benjamin Spock's vital role in the antiwar movement, Fulbright wrote him that "I very much appreciate what you have done and I know that it has been very influential in bringing to the American people the seriousness of our situation."[31]

Fulbright's support of the protestors was in keeping with his commitment to the democratic process and, above all, his desire to find an appropriate strategy to put political pressure on Lyndon Johnson. Yet Fulbright did not approve of all facets of antiwar activism. He deplored the violence and trashing which sometimes accompanied student demonstrations. And he opposed draft resistance, counseling young people to serve in the Army and to work for change inside the system or otherwise risk the consequence of such opposition for a period extending far beyond "the duration of the present war." On the other hand, Fulbright acknowledged that he, too, would go outside the law "if I were convinced that we were actually following a course similar to that of Hitler's Germany. It is only to suggest that by my personal standards we have not reached that point and hopefully will not reach it."[32]

Fulbright also feared that demonstrators who carried Viet Cong flags and shouted obscenities simply gave their political opponents on the right the pretext to smash all dissent.[33] Since he wanted, above all, to see organized opposition to the war develop inside conventional political institutions, he may have wondered whether massive mobilizations of the sort that took place in front of the Pentagon in October 1967 contributed anything important to that cause.

While the president was still obsessed with his search for victory, there was no organized opposition to him inside the Democratic party. Hence Fulbright realized that nothing would change for some time to come. He had already bemoaned the lack of alternatives and the lack of leadership. Like many others, he was hoping for someone to emerge to make a case for a change in direction and policy: but the likelihood of that happening seemed poor. Meanwhile, he despaired over the size of the military budget, which seemed to him to be "so large that it is incomprehensible." And he predicted that "its impact will begin to show up within the year—taxes, inflation, and unrest." Consequently, he joined four other senators in a floor vote on 22 August in support of Wayne Morse's amendment calling for a 10 percent reduction in the $70 billions the administration had asked for the Department of Defense for the next fiscal year.[34]

As the war remained deadlocked, pressure was building among hawks for an even more intensified aerial assault on North Vietnam. A Senate Preparedness Subcommittee, headed by John Stennis, was meeting in closed-door sessions throughout August to hear testimony about that bombing campaign from Secretaries Rusk and McNamara, among others. By this time, McNamara had long since become disillusioned with the bombing, and he made his views known to that committee. But the Joint Chiefs, who opposed McNamara, privately warned Johnson that they would resign en bloc if the bombing of the North were halted. It seems obvious that Johnson was responding to pressure from the right when he authorized, in early August, fresh bombing raids near the Chinese border, a move which Fulbright called "very dangerous and extremely stupid."[35]

While the Stennis Committee took testimony and prepared its report, the Foreign Relations Committee also was meeting to consider Fulbright's National Commitments Resolution. At the opening session, which began on 16 August, Fulbright read a brief statement that captured well his recent change of heart on the question of what role Congress should have in the making of foreign policy:

Having now experienced the frenetic mobility of the 1960s, the overheated activism, the ubiquitous involvement and the mounting sense of global mission—often referred to as the "responsibilities of power"—I now see merit that I used not to see in occasional delay or inaction; I now see how great the Executive's foreign powers are and how limited the Congress's restraining powers are; and I see great merit in the checks and balances of our eighteenth-century Constitution.[36]

On both 17 and 21 August, Fulbright, along with the rest of his colleagues, listened to Under Secretary of State Nicholas Katzenbach, no hard-line hawk, defend the administration's position. He argued that there was no need for such a resolution. But, more important, he claimed that the Tonkin Gulf Resolution had given the president all the authority he needed to wage his war in Vietnam. That resolution was in so many words a "functional equivalent" of a declaration of war. Katzenbach spelled out his position in a forthright exchange with the chairman:

MR. KATZENBACH: A declaration of war would not, I think, correctly reflect the very limited objectives of the United States with respect to Vietnam. It would not correctly reflect our efforts there, what we are trying to do, the reasons why we are there, to use an outmoded phraseology.

THE CHAIRMAN: You think it is outmoded to declare war?

MR. KATZENBACH: In this kind of context I think the expression of declaring war is one that has become outmoded in the international arena. . . .

THE CHAIRMAN: They (the Administration) did not ask for a declaration of war. They do not have one yet.

MR. KATZENBACH: That is true in the very literal sense of the word.

THE CHAIRMAN: It is quite true, not only literally, but in spirit. . . .

MR. KATZENBACH: . . . didn't that Resolution authorize the President to use the armed forces of the United States in whatever way was necessary? Didn't it? What could a declaration of war have done that would have given the President more authority and a clearer voice of the Congress of the United States than that Resolution?

MR. CHAIRMAN: . . . it was presented as an emergency situation; the repelling of an attack which was alleged to have been unprovoked upon our forces in the high seas. It looked at the moment as if it was wholly unprovoked, unjustified, and an unacceptable attack upon our armed forces. . . . The circumstances partook of an emergency, as an attack upon the United States which would fall within the procedures of the principles developed in the last century of repelling attacks temporarily as opposed to a full-fledged war like the one which we are in. . . .

MR. KATZENBACH: . . . Now the language of that Resolution, Mr. Chairman, is . . . as Congress knew full well, a very broad language.

THE CHAIRMAN: Yes.

MR. KATZENBACH: As it was explained in the debate. You explained it, Mr. Chairman, as head of this Committee.

THE CHAIRMAN: But I misinterpreted it.

MR. KATZENBACH: You explained that Resolution, and you made it clear as it could be what Congress was committing itself to, and that Resolution provides—

THE CHAIRMAN: No, I didn't.

MR. KATZENBACH:—That it stays in existence until repealed by a concurrent resolution.

THE CHAIRMAN: I not only didn't make it clear, but obviously, it wasn't clear to me.[37]

Few knew that this exchange contained a hidden element. Back in 1964,

Johnson had told Fulbright that the resolution itself applied only to the specific incident in the Gulf of Tonkin. And Fulbright believed him. Now, in 1967, Katzenbach's remarks so aroused Fulbright that he gave permission to William Bader, a committee staffer, to investigate further the allegation that the 4 August 1964 incident involving the *Maddox* had not occurred.[38]

On 18 August, the day after Katzenbach's first appearance, the president, at his press conference, was asked about the Gulf of Tonkin Resolution. Johnson claimed that Congress knew very well what it was doing in August 1964 when it approved that resolution. For that reason, he said, "we think we are well within the ground of our constitutional responsibility. We think we are well within the rights of what Congress said in its resolution."[39]

Knowing that Johnson was unmovable, Fulbright endorsed Mike Mansfield's nonbinding resolution, introduced on 28 August, that called on the United Nations to take action to help end the war. Yet Fulbright fully recognized the difficulties with that approach. He understood that if the Security Council were to recommend the reconvening of the Geneva Conference and a cease-fire, it would be necessary for the United States to compromise its position in advance in order to avoid a Soviet veto. There was no evidence that the White House was prepared to do any such thing. Thus viewing the scene from the capital, Fulbright felt, in late September, that "Washington becomes more like 'Alice in Wonderland' every day, and I can see no hope for the better."[40]

That gloomy outlook notwithstanding, Fulbright went back to Arkansas to test the political waters of his home state preparatory to the 1968 campaign. Aware of the difficulties facing him in a state that supported the war, Fulbright presented a well-publicized speech at the Lion's Club in El Dorado. There, on 26 September, he reaffirmed his opposition to the war, telling the audience that Arkansas had not sent him to the Senate to be a "rubber stamp." He noted, too, the enormous expense of the war, for which Arkansas voters were paying not only in lost lives but in higher taxes and reduced government services. If his reception in El Dorado had been cool and correct, at least Fulbright had made his point. In fact, he was eager to campaign on his record, believing that his constituents would eventually end up supporting his stand. After several trips back to Arkansas, Fulbright sensed a changing attitude among the voters; they now seemed to him to be more "questioning" and less hawkish than he had formerly thought.[41]

Returning from Arkansas, Fulbright spent time working out a compromise with his colleagues in order to obtain committee approval for his nonbinding commitments resolution. After several weeks of discussion, the committee agreed that this resolution would apply to future action only, thereby excluding the current situation in Vietnam. With that compromise in language, the committee, on 16 November, sent Fulbright's resolution to the floor, thereby giving the Senate a chance to debate the issue if it so chose. Accompanying the resolution was a report that traced the history of executive-legislative relations in the area of war-making powers. After pointing to the vast discrepancy that existed between the two branches, the report recommended steps that could be taken if the Senate wanted to seek a more balanced partnership with respect to war powers.[42]

On 16 November, the committee also sent to the floor Mike Mansfield's resolution calling on the president to request the assistance of the United Nations to end the war. It was approved by a vote of eighty-two to zero on 30 November.[43] Because Johnson had no intention of altering the American position, there was little hope that the Security Council would take up the Vietnam issue.

On the same day that the full Senate gave its approval to the Mansfield resolution, Eugene McCarthy, a member of the Foreign Relations Committee, declared that he was going to challenge Johnson for the party's nomination. Fulbright welcomed this move, saying that McCarthy was a man of ability and intelligence.[44] Though he admitted it was altogether premature to endorse him, Fulbright was obviously very pleased with the fact that a challenger had arisen who shared his general outlook on the war.

News of McCarthy's candidacy heartened Fulbright, but word of Secretary McNamara's resignation, coming at the end of November, caused him considerable concern. Fulbright had long since known that McNamara had become a voice of restraint inside the administration, and now he feared that his departure meant that Johnson was possibly planning to escalate the war, up to and including an invasion of North Vietnam.[45]

Worried about what McNamara's departure might mean, Fulbright and his colleagues tried again to bring Secretary Rusk before the committee in open session. Rusk had not appeared publicly to discuss Vietnam since 18 February 1966, and his persistent refusal was probably tied to Johnson's unwillingness to give his critics another opportunity to challenge him on national television. Demanding action on this matter was Albert Gore, a staunch committee dove, who wanted the committee to write a letter to Johnson requesting him to authorize Rusk's appearance. But Mansfield,

DEADLOCK: I

Aiken, Lausche, and Hickenlooper managed to stall Gore's initiative for the time being.[46]

While the committee debated the issue, Fulbright was busy making fresh speeches on the Senate floor detailing his ever more pessimistic assessment of the war's impact on American society and the peoples of Southeast Asia. On 8 December, he spoke out in an effort to rebut Secretary Rusk's recent defense of the American commitment to Saigon. At a press conference on 12 October, Rusk had derided all talk about a bombing halt or calls for a new Geneva conference, and he repeated his longstanding argument that if the United States failed in Vietnam, it would do very great damage to American credibility in the world.[47]

Fulbright confronted Rusk in the following way:

> Far from proving that wars of national liberation cannot succeed, all that we have proven so far is that even with an army of half a million men and expenditures now approaching $30 billion a year, we are unable to suppress this particular war of national liberation. Far from demonstrating America's willingness and ability to save beleaguered governments from Communist insurgencies, all that we are demonstrating in Vietnam is America's willingness and ability to use its B-52's, its napalm and all the other ingenious weapons of "counterinsurgency" to turn a small country into a charnel house. Far from inspiring confidence and support for the United States, the war has so isolated us that, despite all our alliances and the tens of billions we have spent on foreign aid, we cannot, according to the administration, get nine out of fifteen votes to put the Vietnam issue on the agenda of the United Nations Security Council. Far from demonstrating America's readiness to discharge all of its prodigal commitments around the world, the extravagance and cost of Vietnam are more likely to suggest to the world that the American people will be hesitant indeed before permitting their Government to plunge into another such costly adventure.

And he added:

> In recent weeks, General Westmoreland and other administration spokesmen have been making optimistic statements about victory being in sight. This is not the first time that optimistic predictions have been made, but it is of course, possible that this time they may be right, that Ho Chi Minh will surrender or die or the Vietcong will collapse or just fade into the jungle. Even in that event, it should not be supposed that the American commitment would be at an end; we would still be the sole military and economic support of a weak Saigon regime, at a cost of perhaps $10 billion or $15 billion a year. This of course would assume— as we cannot safely assume—that the Chinese and Russians would do nothing to

prevent the collapse of the Vietcong or of North Vietnam. But even if these most optimistic prospects should be realized, grateful for peace though we would be, we would still have little to be proud of and a great deal to regret. We would still have fought an immoral and unnecessary war; we would still have passed up opportunities which, if taken when they arose, would have spared us and spared the Vietnamese the present ordeal, and done so, as Professor Reischauer says, "with only trifling costs, if any, to American interests."[48]

Long before Fulbright gave this speech, he had spoken out about the costs of the war. But never before had he challenged so specifically and so cogently the administration's case for making its war in Vietnam. It was a major critique of Rusk's worldview and Johnson's political obsession.

Fulbright pointedly rejected Rusk's defense of credibility as a justification for continuing the war, believing simply that the war had been a tragic mistake, resulting in a serious loss of confidence in American leadership both at home and abroad. Unlike Rusk, then, he favored the principle of "selectivity" in the choice of commitments as one way of reducing the intolerable burden now on the back of the American economy.

Fulbright had been perceptive about developments at home and abroad, but speechmaking was one thing, influencing policy was another. Like other congressional doves, Fulbright could not abide the continuation of the war or the likelihood of its escalation, but like them, too, he publicly opposed any unilateral American withdrawal. Such a stand could have politically ruined him in Arkansas. Having no influence on the inside, he could only await developments with unease and fear, believing that the war might yet lead to a Chinese or Russian intervention.

6 | CONTAINING THE CENTER

William Fulbright was depressed by the continuing poor prospects for peace in the early weeks of 1968. The war seemed endless, and LBJ was determined to achieve a military victory. The problem, as Fulbright saw it, was that "the President, unfortunately, seems to have closed his mind to the consideration of any alternative, and his Rasputin—W. W. Rostow—seems able to isolate him from other views, and the Secretary happens to agree. I regret that I am unable to break this crust of immunity." But after President Johnson appointed Clark Clifford to replace Robert McNamara as secretary of defense, Fulbright seemed to see a ray of light. Although Clifford was a Johnson confidant, he was also a "close personal friend" of Fulbright as well. Perhaps already knowing or sensing that Clifford's position on the war was more fluid than it appeared in public, Fulbright asked his good friend Lewis Douglas if he and Generals James Gavin and Matthew Ridgway could privately discuss the situation with Clifford.[1]

Fulbright was eager to recruit the newly designated secretary of defense to his side because he knew "that, if the war continues, restrictions on policy for domestic programs will cause further serious disruptions throughout our economic and social order." But given his helplessness in the face of the current reality, he wrote Erich Fromm that there is "literally a miasma of madness in the city, enveloping everyone in the administration and most of those in Congress. I am at a loss for words to describe the idiocy of what we are doing."[2]

Because Johnson's support in the Senate was still solid, Fulbright and the other Senate critics were unable to mobilize further opposition to him. Nevertheless, the Arkansan continued to offer suggestions for an ending of the war. In his 21 January appearance on "Meet the Press," as well as in the 5 February edition of *U.S. News and World Report*, he spelled out his program for peace making.[3] It included a unilateral ending of the bombing of North Vietnam, the implementation of a cease-fire, and a reconvening of the Geneva Conference for the purpose of getting the United States out of Indochina as expeditiously as possible.

The administration ignored all such proposals coming from Fulbright and others, like McGovern and McCarthy, but it could not quell the sharpening debate about its policies resulting from the Tet offensive, an offensive that marked a decisive turning point in the war. At the end of January, Hanoi and its Viet Cong ally launched a major military undertaking in the South in the hope that it would spark an uprising of support in the cities and the countryside. At first it appeared as if Hanoi and the Viet Cong had won a substantial military victory, but in reality both had suffered a staggering loss of trained cadre and personnel, and there was no uprising to match their effort. On the other hand, Tet was a profound psychological defeat for the Johnson administration, as it disillusioned millions of Americans who, contrary to their former expectations, now believed that the war was not being won.[4]

Tet sparked a new round of debate in Congress and the country over American war aims and objectives in Asia, and that controversy was soon reflected inside the Foreign Relations Committee, which voted twelve to four on 7 February to have the chairman write a letter to the president requesting that he authorize Secretary Rusk to appear before the committee in open session. While Johnson took this request under advisement, the committee also decided to look once more into the Gulf of Tonkin affair. Inspiring it to move in this direction was a twenty-page staff report about the August 1964 incident which William Bader had prepared after examining documents provided by the Pentagon. Because the committee hoped to clarify the points in dispute between this report and testimony that Secretary McNamara had given in August 1964, it invited him to discuss the matter. After giving the committee a difficult time, McNamara finally agreed to appear on 20 February.[5]

The executive session posed a delicate problem for committee members, for they did not want to destroy Johnson's capacity to govern. Yet they surely knew that it was Johnson himself who had ordered those destroyers to approach and penetrate North Vietnamese waters, with the intent of provoking an incident which could then be used domestically and internationally. But because the hearings focused largely on the events themselves (probably the result of prior arrangements), nothing was said that day which would explicitly point the finger of culpability at LBJ. Although command and control procedures were ostensibly what the hearing was all about, Wayne Morse indirectly raised this matter in his usual outspoken way when he reminded his colleagues that "I don't think we have been talking all day about what we ought to be talking about, the Tonkin Bay Resolution."[6]

Although the committee did not dig deeply into that aspect of the story, its hearing produced enough in the way of fireworks to make it worthwhile. McNamara was kept busy answering questions about whether American ships had violated North Vietnamese waters, and he was pushed hard by Fulbright, Gore, and others who wanted him to discuss the appearance of an operational connection between OPLAN 34-A and the DE SOTO mission.[7] By taking this tack, the committee sought to challenge the case the administration had made back in 1964 when it claimed that there had been an unprovoked and certain attack on American ships then situated in international waters.

I. F. Stone later pointed out that the committee hearing failed to pursue leads which he thought would have proven that the affair had been both planned and provoked. In fairness to Fulbright, it should be noted that his mandate to investigate the incident was probably limited by a committee consensus to take this investigation only so far. To have pushed beyond a certain point might have threatened not only Johnson, but Fulbright's ability to discharge his business as committee chairman, and (who knows?) his own reelection chances as well. In short, Fulbright and the committee tried to make their point without, at the same time, playing Samson inside Johnson's temple. Years later, he mentioned that it was, after all, "a critical time," which largely explains why the committee hesitated to do much more with its investigation.[8]

When Fulbright appeared on the 25 February edition of "Issues and Answers," he emphasized that his main objective in holding this hearing was to promote a general discussion of the administration's policy objectives in Vietnam. While Fulbright and other doves tried to open up the issue, LBJ, following Tet, was launching his own "A-to-Z" review of the situation, a review that had been prompted by General Westmoreland's request for another 206,000 additional troops for South Vietnam.[9] Undertaking that study for him was Secretary of Defense Clark Clifford, who would soon be caught up in his own reappraisal of the American war policy.

As Clifford went to work, the Foreign Relations Committee was preparing to welcome Secretary Rusk, who had received Johnson's permission to appear in open session on 11 and 12 March. Johnson allowed Rusk to speak because he surely realized that unless there was a positive response to the committee's letter of 7 February, his foreign aid bill might be shelved or deferred. Before Rusk appeared, Johnson met with Fulbright and several other members of the Foreign Relations Committee at the White House on 6 March.[10] Whatever Johnson said that evening, it is clear that his words failed to mollify Fulbright, for the next day Fulbright joined a full-scale Senate debate on the war by offering his own critical remarks about current developments in Vietnam.

Fulbright told his colleagues on 7 March that it was vital that there be full executive-legislative consultation in advance of any decision to send more troops to Vietnam. Obviously worried about such a prospect, as it could have led to an invasion of North Vietnam, he repeated that point several times. Of special interest, then, was his brief exchange with Mike Monroney, a staunch Johnson supporter. Monroney asked him to reveal his source for the rumor that more troops were destined for Vietnam. Fulbright refused, saying only that certain figures were under consideration. Among those numbers he mentioned was 206,000, a precise figure he may have received from Richard Russell, Carl Marcy speculated years later.[11]

By the time Secretary Rusk finally appeared before the committee on 11 March, news of General Westmoreland's request for 206,000 troops had been published the day before in the *New York Times*. That story provided the context for the committee's discussion with Rusk. Aware of the high stakes involved, Fulbright and his colleagues tried to obtain from him a commitment that there would be prior consultation with the Congress before any decision on troops was made. Rusk said only that "if more troops are needed, we will, as we have in the past, consult with the appropriate members of Congress." Although Rusk managed to survive his two days of televised testimony, he did not do very much else. From the reaction of several senators to him, it was now clear that Stuart Symington and even Karl Mundt were no longer willing to support the administration's cause. Their shift away from the administration was a clear indication that Johnson's consensus had unraveled.[12]

That shift was also reflected in the results of the New Hampshire primary, where Eugene J. McCarthy, by winning 42 percent of the vote, demonstrated that Johnson was indeed politically vulnerable. Although a good deal of McCarthy's support came from hawks, not just doves, it was enough to convince Robert Kennedy that now was the time to run for the presidency. With both McCarthy and Kennedy in the race, Fulbright— who earlier had despaired over the choice of Johnson versus Nixon— thought that the political pressures were finally building for some kind of change in American policy, "if not this spring, then certainly next November."[13]

Meanwhile, Secretary Clifford, alone of Johnson's advisers, was advocating, in the words of Herbert Schandler, that "the direction and level of effort be changed, that our objectives be modified and that different methods be used." Now committed to de-escalation, Clifford was uncertain that his effort would bear fruit, especially because Johnson was in no mood to change either the direction or objectives of American policy. Operating apart from Clifford was Secretary Rusk, who himself was making a case for a partial bombing halt without conditions, as a means of rallying public opinion behind Johnson; it was a tack which Johnson would eventually find to his liking.[14]

While the White House was considering various options, Fulbright publicly recommended that the president appoint a special negotiator with cabinet rank to seek a solution to the conflict. His proposal was reminiscent of Senator Robert Kennedy's earlier suggestion which the president had already rejected. Several days later, Fulbright flew to Cleveland to deliver a major speech on Vietnam. Before leaving Washington, he had been told by Clifford that Johnson had agreed to a bombing halt and would make it public when he delivered a speech to the country on the same night as Fulbright was to speak in Cleveland.[15] Because of the keen interest in Johnson's address, Fulbright interrupted his own speech to join the audience there in listening to the president.

Johnson's speech announcing his retirement and a partial bombing halt was of historic magnitude, while Fulbright's was consistent with his own recent speeches on the subject of the war. Spelling out once more his reasons for opposing it, he rested his case on legal, moral, political, and strategic grounds. He was aware that not everyone who was now opposed to Johnson's policies would agree with his analysis; many recently hatched doves had emerged from their shells only because America's war machine had bogged down in Vietnam. No Johnny-come-lately, Fulbright had long believed that "there was always something about this war that has gone against the American grain. The dissent was not born of something alien to American life and experience: it was born of traditional American ideas about decency and fair play and the sanctity of life." If the country was to learn from this war, it was necessary, he said, to define the term "vital interests" in such a way that the domestic well-being of the American people was the key consideration of policymakers. As he put it, "only when we have made a clear, conscious decision that vital interests have to do with the kind of society we live in, with the kinds of society other people live in, will it be possible to be comfortable in the face of diversity and to distinguish clearly between that which is menacing and that which is merely unfamiliar." And he added that "the most pressing of needs and the greatest of opportunities await us not in foreign relations but in our own country. We have been preoccupied with foreign wars and crises for a generation and, in our preoccupation, we have scarcely noticed the revolution wrought by undirected change here at home."[16]

Fulbright's words left him aware that he might be open to the charge of being "an advocate of neo-isolationism." Seeking to head off such criticism, he said that "no designation could be more inaccurate." What he favored was not a withdrawal from the world but the application of the principle of selectivity with regard to American commitments. He contended that the principle of selectivity would be based on "our own needs, our own capacities, and a healthy respect for the right of others to make comparable judgments for themselves. If accepted, this general view of vital interests must lead to a reevaluation of American strategy in Asia."[17]

Fulbright's evolving views coincided with those offered by Ronald Steel, Hans Morgenthau, Edmund Stillman, and William Pfaff, among others, who, in response to Vietnam, had been developing what Eugene Brown calls a "limitationist" critique of American foreign policy. According to Brown, the key elements of that critique included the repudiation of the ideology of globalism tied to a reflexive and indiscriminate anticommunism; the recognition that local situations and histories, not communist aggression per se, determined political developments in the Third World; and the recommendation that the United States not only cut back on its excessive overseas commitments and curb its appetite for military interventionism but begin to think in terms of interests, not ideology.[18]

Morgenthau, in particular, was interesting. A leading academic realist, who had been a long-time sympathetic critic of American foreign policy, he now believed that it had lived too long on the "intellectual capital" of the Truman years. As a result of Vietnam, it was time, in his view, to commence "a radical rethinking of the issues and of the policies adequate to them." Consistent with that argument was his belief, virtually identical to Fulbright's, that instead "of embarking upon costly and futile interventions abroad, the United States ought to concentrate its efforts upon creating a society at home which can serve as a model for other nations to emulate."[19]

That critique, which Fulbright, Morgenthau, and others had been fashioning since 1966, became more respectable by March 1968. Because of

Tet, and the changed political and economic situation both at home and abroad, Johnson's center had collapsed, and with it his political prospects for 1968. He was now compelled by circumstances to remove himself from the presidential race and to offer Hanoi and the American people a partial bombing halt.

Upon his return to Washington, Fulbright called Johnson to congratulate him for his statesmanlike speech, and he publicly praised him for making a change in policy. But on 2 April he disagreed with fellow doves Mike Mansfield and John Sherman Cooper about the meaning of Johnson's action. Admitting that his initial praise of Johnson had been based on the understanding that all air attacks had been suspended except for the area just north of the Demilitarized Zone (DMZ), Fulbright said that in actuality those attacks would continue over a wide area, ending just forty or fifty miles south of Hanoi. Given that reality, Fulbright did not think that Hanoi had been given a strong enough inducement to come to the conference table, and Wayne Morse agreed with him. On the other hand, both Mansfield and Cooper felt that although Johnson had made a significant move, it was necessary for him to clarify his terms so as to obviate any confusion about his recent speech.[20]

Much to the surprise of some, Hanoi accepted Johnson's invitation to open talks with the United States. Fulbright was enormously pleased by this development, a point he made at a press conference on 3 April, a day after his floor discussion with Mansfield and Cooper. He went on to explain that after his conversation with Secretary Clifford on 30 March, it was his impression that the bombing halt would be more substantial than it turned out to be. After deciding that those concessions had been only minimal (as both Russell and Stennis tried to suggest), Fulbright then made his critical remarks on the Senate floor, remarks which evidently angered Clifford, who felt that Johnson had indeed made a genuine concession.[21]

Although Johnson's policy shift had opened a door to a diplomatic conference, the difficulty in finding a suitable site for those proposed talks concerned Fulbright. After Washington had rejected Phnom Penh and Warsaw, he wrote one correspondent that "I share your reaction to the Government's refusal to meet in Warsaw or, for that matter, in Phnom Penh. It leads one to believe that the whole thing was a ploy to throw the opposition off balance and to stop criticism preparatory to the coming election."[22]

Fulbright was justifiably skeptical about Johnson's motives, but he was relieved to learn that both sides had finally agreed to hold their first formal meeting in Paris on 13 May. But at the same time, he did not know whether this arrangement would produce positive results. Earlier, Secretary Rusk had testified before the committee on 10 April, and he made it clear that the key to a settlement was tied to the principle of reciprocity.[23] That is, he affirmed that there would be no complete cessation of the bombing of North Vietnam unless or until Hanoi promised to stop infiltrating troops and supplies into the South, a position which Hanoi had categorically rejected more than once.

Fulbright also had additional evidence of the administration's hard-line attitude. This time it came from his old friend Harry Ashmore, who had been in Hanoi the night of Johnson's 31 March speech. Ashmore confided to him that upon his return to Washington he had tried to contribute to the peace process only to discover that the doors of the White House had been closed to him, and at the State Department he found that the Rusk position on reciprocity was beyond challenge.[24] Based on such evidence, it is no wonder, then, that Fulbright had little confidence that anything substantive would come out of those Paris meetings. In short, he properly sensed that Johnson—despite his speech—was hoping somehow to produce a military victory or, at the very least, preserve a stalemate which the next president might yet resolve in America's favor.

As the Paris talks dragged on into the summer of 1968, Fulbright was busy with his election effort in Arkansas. In a concerted effort to reach the voters in that Democratic primary, he zigzagged across the state, concentrating his attention on the three candidates opposing him, including State Supreme Court Justice Jim Johnson. Fulbright was fortunate in that neither Orval Faubus nor Sidney McMath decided to challenge him, and he was aided by the statewide feeling that he had done the right thing in standing up to Johnson. Many voters who were hawkish evidently took pride in his dissent even though they disagreed with him. While Secretary Clifford tried hard to avoid more escalation, and while Eugene McCarthy tried to rally support from Democrats in the aftermath of Robert Kennedy's tragic death, Fulbright made headway in his battle to keep his Senate seat. On 30 July, he won just under 53 percent of the vote in the state Democratic primary, thereby guaranteeing that he would meet Charles T. Bernard, the Republican candidate, in the November election.[25]

Several weeks after that primary victory, Fulbright resigned as a delegate to the Democratic National Convention, leaving the favorite son designation to someone else. It was a piece of good fortune for him that he didn't attend the Chicago convention, as Arkansas voters might have linked him with the violence there, thus damaging his reelection hopes come November. Years later, he said that he stayed home because nothing could be gained by going to Chicago. He also revealed that in choosing between two dove candidates, McCarthy or McGovern, he favored McGovern, who sought to carry Robert Kennedy's banners and supporters into a convention that nominated Vice President Hubert Humphrey for the presidency.[26]

Fulbright did appear before the Platform Committee of the Democratic National Committee that met in Washington on the eve of the Chicago convention. Addressing that group on 20 August, he spelled out his position on the war and offered a plank for the Platform Committee's consideration. Before moving on to his specific proposal, he sought to explain the American intervention as a product of an arrogance of power and a mindset that allowed policymakers to assert that Ho Chi Minh was "similar to another lunatic Hitler," or to view Asian communism "as a centrally directed conspiracy for the conquest of territory." He also pointed to "the factor of pure circumstance"—that is, "the gradual cumulative, and in some respects accidental way in which we came to be doing something we said we would never do, fighting a land war on the continent of Asia." Because of that intervention, he said, old allies, like Britain and France, had refused to offer support to the United States, the Great Society was now in shambles, and there had been a further centralization of power in the hands of the executive. The existence of such concentrated power— which he believed was a product of a generation of war and cold war—led him to conclude that the United States was virtually an elective dictatorship in the area of foreign policy as well as in "those vast and expanding areas of our domestic life which in one way or another are related to or dependent upon the military establishment."[27]

After having analyzed from his perspective the causes and consequences of the American intervention, Fulbright offered his model plank: he recommended that the United States endorse the goal of self-determination and neutralization as the most reasonable basis for ending the war. And he asked that the Platform Committee include a specific reference to a bombing halt and a cease-fire in its plank. Finally, he called attention to his National Commitments Resolution which had been shelved by the Senate for the current session out of deference to Johnson's peace initiative. Fulbright supported its endorsement as a step to restoring Congress to its rightful place in the constitutional scheme of things. Yet he was well aware that "no legislative enactment can assure the survival of constitutional government. A nation chronically involved in war and crisis abroad must almost inevitably become a nation ruled by centralized executive authority."[28]

Fulbright's statement to the Platform Committee could have been his political valedictory unless he won reelection in November. Going into September, he had reason to be worried about the situation; he had not been given a strong endorsement in the primary, which saw him win less than 53 percent of the vote against three weak opponents, and his Republican opponent, Charles T. Bernard, had promised to make Vietnam a major campaign issue. Adding to his nervousness was Ernest Gruening's defeat in the Alaska primary. Fulbright wrote him to praise his fine service to the nation and to express his "great sadness" over the result. In that vein, Fulbright remarked that "I have a rough Republican campaign coming up so I may join you."[29]

Bernard never ignited the Vietnam issue, so Fulbright managed to build a comfortable lead in a state where anti-Humphrey sentiment was very strong, perhaps out of resentment over his identification with civil rights. Such was not a problem for Fulbright. A well-known supporter of racial segregation, his views were popular with many voters in that state. On election night, Fulbright retained his Senate seat, George Wallace carried the state for the American Independent Party and the Republican Winthrop Rockefeller was elected governor. Far more important was the fact that Richard Nixon had been elected president of the United States. Years later, Fulbright mused that if Hubert Humphrey had worked harder as a dove, he might not have lost the election, and he strongly believed that if Humphrey had won, the war would have ended much sooner than it did.[30]

Humphrey lost, but so did the Democratic doves Wayne Morse and Joe Clark, both members of the Foreign Relations Committee. Nevertheless, the Democrats retained control of Congress, meaning that Fulbright would return as chairman of his committee at a time when a Republican would occupy the White House.

The results of that election set the stage for Lyndon Johnson's retirement from public life. After Johnson returned to Texas, he remained bitter at the thought of Fulbright, referring to him during a 1970 television interview with Walter Cronkite as "this Rhodes scholar."[31] He felt that Fulbright had betrayed him by attacking his Vietnam policies, policies which Fulbright had both supported and endorsed in 1964 and part of 1965. LBJ had a point, but then so did Fulbright, who had gone along with the administration's slowly evolving escalation for personal reasons and in the mistaken belief that it would prevent a land war in Asia. Only after Johnson turned on him did he publicly break with the policy. Subsequently, both men came to view each other with intense mistrust and dark suspicion, though evidence cited in this study suggests that their fractured friendship caused Fulbright more pain and a greater sense of loss than that felt by Lyndon Johnson.

Fulbright never had any positive feelings about Richard Nixon or his supporters. When he spoke in Ann Arbor, Michigan, on 24 November, Fulbright sought to explain Nixon's victory as a product of a middle-class fear of violence and anarchy. Or as he put it in a remarkably sharp-edged way: "The election of 1968 showed that middle class fear is a far more powerful force in America than the combined forces of black and student rage, of the NAACP and the Women's Strike for Peace, and of all the miscellaneous dissenters from the United States Senate to the Berkeley campus." And he reminded his audience that "all but forgotten are the days—really only a few months ago—when it seemed quite possible that Kennedy or McCarthy would be taking the presidential office in January 1969 on a platform of peace and reform."[32]

With the election of Nixon, was peace within reach? Fulbright, like most everyone else, had no idea what policy the incoming Nixon administration would follow in Vietnam. During the campaign, Nixon claimed that he had a "plan" to end the war, but he never revealed precisely what it was. Nixon was astute enough, however, not to make tactical mistakes even before he was sworn in. Consequently, he called Fulbright shortly after the election—a conversation described later by Fulbright as a friendly chat— to say that "he was looking forward to working with Mr. Fulbright and that the two had many areas of common interest."[33]

Of common interest was Nixon's appointment of William Rogers, former attorney general in the Eisenhower administration, to the position of secretary of state. Fulbright was very pleased with this news because he had known Rogers for years and liked and respected him very much. In Fulbright's words, "he is a man of unquestioned integrity and ability . . . and his common sense and good judgment will serve the country well." After his "prickly" relations with Dean Rusk, the prospect of working with Rogers had to appeal to him.

More important was the reality that Nixon would soon be president. Over the years, Fulbright had had little in common with him. Each had a political style and an intellectual perspective that the other detested. Yet as 20 January 1969 approached, Fulbright was hopeful that Nixon would find it in his interest to end the war as soon as possible. Otherwise, Vietnam would remain the issue on which everything else would pivot.

7 | A GAINST MILITARISM AND VIETNAMIZATION

As Richard Nixon was preparing his inaugural address, Senate doves, including William Fulbright, thought that the incoming administration would move quickly to end the war. William Rogers, the secretary of state designate, encouraged this hope, for he told the Foreign Relations Committee in a closed-door hearing on 15 January 1969 that he desired to move quickly to expedite negotiations in Paris. He also made it clear that the seeking of good relations with Moscow was high on his agenda. Pleased with what he heard, Fulbright told a news conference that Rogers "is a broad-gauged man, not doctrinaire and is capable of adjusting to change."[1]

After the Nixon administration settled in and sought to get its bearings, various doves advanced their views as to how best to end the war. Mike Mansfield favored the phased reduction of troops, but Fulbright advised that the first priority should be securing a cease-fire. He contended that "once you stop the major fighting and killing of people, I think tempers, feelings and emotions tend to calm down a bit and we can be a little more rational in approaching the political solution."[2]

Because Fulbright thought that the Nixon administration was eager to find a "political solution," he remained quiet while hoping for a breakthrough. Meanwhile, he delivered a signal of sorts with his vote against the confirmation of Alexis Johnson as under secretary of state.[3] Johnson, a career diplomat, had been an ardent defender of the war, but Fulbright's opposition did not prevent his overwhelming endorsement by the Senate.

On 3 February, Fulbright announced that an ad hoc subcommittee had been created to undertake "a detailed review of the international military commitments of the United States and their relationship to foreign policy." In a shrewd move, he selected Stuart Symington to serve as its chairman because he had the unusual distinction of being a member of both the Foreign Relations Committee and the Armed Services Committee. Symington, a former hawk, had been gradually educated by Fulbright into seeing that the extraordinary price the country was paying for that war was without justification.[4] With this assignment, Symington emerged as one of Fulbright's strongest supporters on the Foreign Relations Committee, creating a working partnership that would open the Pandora's box containing the secret American intervention in Laos.

Even as that partnership was forming, both men sensed that something important had happened when they discovered that certain foreign policy functions were being transferred from the State Department to the White House, where National Security Adviser Henry Kissinger was ensconced. This news led Fulbright to remark that "in our view taking matters out of the hands of official agencies and putting them in the hands of individuals with executive privilege could be interpreted as a move to deprive Congress of information." Symington noted that other national security advisers, specifically McGeorge Bundy and Walt Rostow, had earlier avoided appearances before the committee on the grounds of executive privilege. Neither senator had any idea at the time of what was really happening: namely, that this move constituted an enormous shift in power and planning away from the State Department, thereby allowing Nixon and Kissinger to control and manage the foreign policy apparatus of the United States government. Even before Nixon had been sworn in, he and Kissinger had agreed to take such a step.[5] Now they were at work implementing their program.

As the Symington subcommittee prepared its agenda, Fulbright and other committee doves, including Albert Gore, were critically evaluating the administration's case for an antiballistic missile (ABM) system. With attention focused on that issue, little was heard of Vietnam until Fulbright spoke out on 14 March to remind the country that there seemed to be little or no activity in Paris. Having said that much, Fulbright expressed his fear that there could be a re-escalation of the war. Several days later, George McGovern suggested that the Nixon administration had failed to show "moral courage" in reversing LBJ's war policy; but he was admonished by both Mike Mansfield and Edward Kennedy, who felt that the president needed more time, not criticism, to implement his peace plan.[6]

Fulbright was not swayed by any such plea for patience. On 21 March, he urged Secretary of Defense Melvin Laird "not to delay too long in bringing about this change in the policy which this administration inherited," adding that, "if this administration continues and escalates the war, it will soon be Mr. Nixon's war and there will remain little chance to bring it to a close short of a major catastrophe." Laird, who was appearing before the committee to discuss the administration's ABM proposal, sought to assure him of the administration's good intentions, remarking that "this administration is committed to end the war in Vietnam. We are presently engaged in very important peace talks in Paris." But if those talks failed, Laird warned that "we will have an alternative other than the present conduct of the war."[7]

Fulbright also inquired about the current state of military activities in Vietnam. He asked both Laird and General Earle Wheeler whether the United States had intensified the conflict since the bombing halt. They both assured him that since 20 January (the day Nixon became president), nothing had happened in Vietnam to suggest unprovoked American belligerency. That point was debatable, but their statistical evidence seemed convincing. On the other hand, they said nothing about the bombing attack on a Cambodian sanctuary occurring on 18 March. That mission—and those that followed—had been undertaken in secret because the White House did not want to precipitate an international crisis or give the committee cause for protest. As these raids continued in the spring of 1969, many on Capitol Hill were aware of what was happening. The critics, including Fulbright and Mansfield, said nothing; they remained quiet out of fear that a public disclosure would give Nixon an opportunity to attack them for undermining the security of American troops in the field.[8]

When Secretary Rogers appeared before the committee on 27 March, he assured it that "we are not seeking a military victory, nor do we want military escalation." The administration, said Rogers, sought a "mutual withdrawal of forces and military respect for the demilitarized zone." In short, the administration's objective was an "honorable peace" in Vietnam. According to Rogers, "no other objective and no other problem is of greater importance."[9]

Fulbright, agreeing with Rogers on the importance of the problem, shared his views with President Nixon and Henry Kissinger that same day, as the three men discussed Vietnam in the Oval Office. During the course of their hour-and-a-half meeting, both Nixon and Kissinger assured him that they would move quickly to end the war and would not repeat Johnson's mistakes. At the conclusion of that meeting, Fulbright presented Nixon with a memorandum outlining his views as to how the United States might best proceed with negotiations in Paris. In it he expressed concern that the resumption of military activities in Vietnam meant that "the military war has regained a momentum which threatens to defeat the political approach to a settlement." Such a development, he feared, could limit Nixon's options, making it more difficult to end the war in a quick and decisive manner. To bring the war to a prompt close, Fulbright recommended the acceptance of a coalition government in Saigon, which might evolve in the context of the "natural interplay of indigenous forces within Vietnam." He further advised that the United States not "take any further military action beyond the requirements of American security."[10]

Despite what these two key policymakers told Fulbright about their intentions, he had to wonder whether his message got across to them. The next day, he appeared at a symposium entitled "Military Budget and National Priorities," which was held on Capitol Hill. There, he revealed a depth of pessimism about Vietnam that probably shocked his audience. While discussing what action Congress might take to end the war, Fulbright remarked that the votes were not available "to do anything substantial about Vietnam." Hence he did not know what else to do other than to complain and to try to persuade policymakers to change their course. Because the administration was bent on achieving "an honorable peace," Fulbright now feared that the current period was "probably the calm before the storm." For that reason, he said that "unless something happens soon, we face a bad time."[11] Fulbright did not know for certain what the administration planned to do about Vietnam, but he sensed that what Nixon and Kissinger had in mind was not very different from what Johnson had wanted—a military victory or, at the very least, the avoidance of political defeat.

Fulbright believed that there was a strong connection between the war and the institutionalized militarism which was so deeply embedded in American society. Consequently, he found to his liking an article—"The New Militarism"—which General David Shoup, a retired Marine Corps commandant, had published in the April 1969 issue of the *Atlantic*. So impressed was Fulbright with Shoup's stinging analysis of the power and influence of the military that he sent copies of that piece to a number of his Senate colleagues, hoping in this way to educate them about a situation that desperately needed such treatment.[12]

On 18 April, Fulbright delivered a speech, "Militarism and American Democracy," at Denison University in Granville, Ohio. After alluding to the "unreality" of the Senate debate over the ABM, and after noting the emergence of a "glorious new invention known as MIRV [multiple independently targeted reentry vehicle]," he remarked that "violence has become the nation's leading industry." According to Fulbright, this meant that "millions of Americans have acquired a vested interest in the expensive weapons systems which provide their livelihood and indirectly therefore in a foreign policy that has plunged the United States into a spiraling arms race with the Soviet Union . . . and committed us to the defense of 'freedom'—very loosely defined—in almost fifty countries, including Vietnam, Spain, and Greece with their freedom-loving regimes."[13]

Because the military services had such economic clout and social acceptability, Fulbright viewed them as "ardent and dangerous competitors for power in American society." Their reach inside both the executive and Congress had given them, he believed, an extraordinary opportunity to politicize a point of view few presidents had the courage to challenge in the public realm. Fulbright insisted that peace was essential and democracy indispensable if the influence of the military was to be checked and contained. In line with the indispensability of democracy, he admitted being encouraged by such recent developments as "the dissent on Vietnam, the opposition to the ABM, and the new willingness on Congress's part to examine the hitherto sacrosanct military budget."[14]

If the Department of Defense constituted a major power block within a larger system of power, this did not mean that Fulbright saw the problem as solely or uniquely one of militarism per se. As he pointed out in an interview with Philip Geyelin of the *Washington Post*, the problem of militarism was inextricably tied to the very character of American foreign policy. He suggested that the military establishment could be cut in half without threatening American security,"assuming we follow a reasonably decent policy in international relations. We cannot go about threatening people and keeping bases all over the world without provoking things. Assuming we concentrate upon the United Nations—it doesn't cost much. This takes brains and attention and conviction."[15]

Fulbright's general discussion of militarism—however thoughtful and insightful—failed to take into account an underlying reality: that is, that foreign policy was made by a civilian elite, led by the president, for the purpose of advancing and protecting American political and economic power in a global setting. That this elite used force, or threatened its use, was obscured by Fulbright's emphasis on the military's role in policy-making.[16]

Still, his speech critical of militarism captured something of a changing mood in the country about the Pentagon as well as the Vietnam War. And it was the war itself that, in Fulbright's words, "poisons our political life."

He had hoped that Nixon would move quickly to end the conflict, but it was turning out otherwise. Writing to R. B. McCallum, Fulbright remarked that

> my greatest disappointment with Nixon is his tendency to follow the established policies and practices and, in many cases, rely on the same advisors. I assumed he would make a point of adopting a new approach, especially in the foreign field. It is possible he may yet, but I see few signs of this. Up to this moment, I see little or no progress to settling the war although there has been much talk.

During a "Face the Nation" interview on 27 April, he publicly commented on the lack of progress. Part of the problem, he thought, had to do with the Nixon administration's desire to keep the Thieu regime in power. That position made it difficult to find a "solution," insisted Fulbright, who himself continued to oppose any large-scale unilateral withdrawal. He thought "that we ought to do this with a conference. I am not very taken by unilateral action as a dignified and intelligent way, even traditional way, of settling these matters."[17]

Nixon, aware of the growing demand for action, decided to make a major statement about the war. Addressing the country on 14 May, he offered a dollop of hope for everyone but Hanoi, saying, "we have ruled out attempting to impose a purely one-sided withdrawal from Vietnam, or the acceptance in Paris of terms that would amount to a disguised American defeat." And he reaffirmed "our willingness to withdraw our forces on a specified timetable. We ask only that North Vietnam withdraw its forces from South Vietnam, Cambodia and Laos into North Vietnam also in accordance with a timetable."[18]

Only a few isolated critics took exception to Nixon's remarks. Among them was Frank Church, who observed that "all of the shopworn proposals were reiterated and no departure was apparent from the static stance of the Johnson-Rostow-Rusk triumvirate." It looked to Church "like the same Johnson wine poured from a Nixon bottle." Mike Mansfield, however, was "impressed" because the speech appeared to leave a lot of room for "flexibility, compromise and give and take." Fulbright, though privately recognizing that the Johnson policy remained largely intact, said that he was "pleased" with the conciliatory tone but thought that Nixon's words did not go far enough.[19]

As the country waited to see what Nixon's speech would accomplish,

Fulbright and other doves continued to work hard to defeat his ABM proposal. Fulbright was convinced that its construction was an unnecessary and futile undertaking, as it would only intensify the arms race while wasting valuable economic resources. Its defeat, he hoped, might also make it possible to challenge "the military forces in Congress and in other areas." Nixon believed otherwise. He saw the ABM system as a useful "bargaining chip" that would help to promote an arms control agreement in defensive weapons systems with the Soviet Union.[20] Consequently, he decided to strike out against those who challenged his authority on national security issues.

Speaking at the Air Force Academy on 4 June, the president defended the cause of military preparedness in terms which left no doubt about whom or what he had in mind. As he saw it, the basic problem was one of defining America's role in the world, and determining its responsibilities as a great nation. One school of thought favored, in his words, "a downgrading of our alliances and what amounts to a unilateral reduction of our arms." According to Nixon, it believed that "the United States is as much responsible for the tensions as the adversaries we face." Contending that this criticism of American power stemmed from an "isolationist" orientation, Nixon declared that he would no more sanction a global American retreat than he would countenance a recommendation for "unilateral disarmament." And he refused "to pose a false choice between meeting our responsibilities abroad and meeting the needs of our people at home. We shall meet both or we shall meet neither."[21]

The same day Nixon spoke, Fulbright appeared before the Joint Economic Committee of the Congress to discuss the subject of the military budget and national priorities. Like Nixon, he, too, addressed the large philosophical issues associated with military spending:

Your hearings focus on the question all Senators and Congressmen should have uppermost in their minds in approaching their responsibilities—what do we want our Nation to be? Do we want it to be a Sparta, or an Athens? Do we want a world of diversity where security is founded on international cooperation, or do we want a Pax Americana? Do we as a people place a greater value on trying to mold foreign societies than we do on eliminating the inequities of our own society? I believe that, contrary to the traditions which have guided our Nation since the days of the Founding Fathers, we are in grave danger of becoming a Sparta bent on policing the world. The budget tells the story. . . . It reflects the present distribution of power among the bureaucracies of Washington.[22]

In the discussion which followed this presentation, Fulbright expressed his concern that the Vietnam War would be prolonged as long as Nixon was intent on preserving the Thieu regime. Fulbright also told the committee that "to accuse the Senator from Missouri [Stuart Symington] and me of being isolationists is nonsense. We are not isolationists. None of us is saying that we should withdraw into a shell and have nothing to do with the world. It is a matter of balance." After alluding to the riots, the trouble in the country's schools, and now, the rise in the prime rate to 8 percent, Fulbright reiterated the point that the greatest problem facing America was internal. Speaking as a political realist, he insisted that "our security lies in trying to bring back into balance our economic and political system."[23]

Interestingly, both Nixon and Fulbright spoke that day as realists. Nixon emphasized that the keeping of American global commitments was a matter of the highest national importance. Behind Nixon in spirit stood Dean Acheson. Fulbright, seeing that the war was causing acute damage to the United States both at home and overseas, urged that the American commitment to Vietnam be ended. Behind him stood that archetypal eighteenth-century rationalist, John Quincy Adams, who long ago had warned his countrymen of the dangers inherent in the act of going abroad "in search of monsters to destroy."[24]

Fulbright also saw somebody lurking in the shadows. He remarked at a press conference held subsequent to his appearance before the Joint Economic Committee that he was "offended" by Nixon's speech, suggesting that it was "a form of demagoguery that was fashionable in the days of his friend, Joe McCarthy." He accused Nixon of misrepresenting critics like himself and Symington, who were not attacking the military but the political judgments of the civilian leadership. Of greater concern to him was evidence that Nixon was now preparing to stay in Vietnam either directly or through his proxy, Thieu. Following the president's recent speech at the Air Force Academy, and his embrace of Thieu at Midway Island, Fulbright saw him as the reincarnation of Lyndon Johnson.[25]

Realizing that a political solution was now far off, Fulbright quickly endorsed Clark Clifford's suggestion, found in an article in the June 1969 issue of *Foreign Affairs*, that 100,000 troops should be brought home at the end of 1969 and that all combat troops be removed by the end of 1970. Nixon responded to that same suggestion by stating that he "was hoping to beat Mr. Clifford's timetable."[26] Almost immediately after he spoke, the White House backed off from this statement. Nixon was gong to push for Vietnamization his way and according to his own schedule.

That meant Nixon needed time to build up the Thieu regime, while he continued to look for a breakthrough in Paris. He was under growing pressure from Secretary Laird to remove those troops as fast as possible, a move that would go far to satisfy the desire of the American people to end an active American military role in that war.[27] On the other hand, Nixon could ill afford to appear weak or vacillating; consequently, as soon as American troops began to return home in numbers, he intensified the bombing of Indochina to strengthen his hand in Paris and Saigon. In short, his policy of Vietnamization did not end the war; it merely changed the way the war was being fought.

While Nixon worked to piece together a viable Vietnam strategy, the Senate was debating Fulbright's National Commitments Resolution, which the Foreign Relations Committee had approved on 12 March by a vote of twelve to one. That resolution was virtually the same one Fulbright had submitted on 31 July 1967, but the earlier version had been shelved in April 1968 because the Senate leadership did not want to do anything to embarrass Johnson after Hanoi had agreed to open negotiations. In addition, Fulbright himself had been too involved with politics in Arkansas to give the matter the attention it needed.[28]

Like Fulbright's 1967 resolution, this one sought a nonbinding Senate endorsement for the proposition that a "commitment" made by the executive to a foreign power would not be viewed as a commitment unless it had received congressional approval. Although Nixon thought the resolution might tie his hands in a fast-moving situation, the administration did not use its clout to oppose it, knowing that Fulbright had solid support behind him in the Senate. That support was confirmed on 25 June when the Senate voted seventy to ten to endorse his resolution, but only after its language had been further tightened and its objectives clarified by John Sherman Cooper.[29] As everyone knew, this action would not hamper or impair the president's ability to make foreign policy, but it was a move in the direction of restoring the Senate's pride, and it also served as a vehicle for educating the Senate to the fact that the constitutional relationship in foreign policy had been one-sided for too long. In its limited way, Fulbright's resolution sensitized the Senate to its responsibilities, preparing for the coming of war powers legislation at a later stage.

As the commitments debate was ending, Fulbright was seeking to hold public hearings on Vietnam, but because he failed to convince Clifford to appear in open session, that opportunity was lost. Concurrently, ominous news came from Wichita, Kansas, where, on 1 July, Vice President Spiro

Agnew, addressing the Midwestern Governors Conference, lashed out at "self-professed experts" on Vietnam whose opposition was "undermining our negotiations and prolonging the war." The next day, Fulbright declared that Agnew's remarks reminded him of the Johnson administration's policies and style. But what made Agnew's assault so "offensive" in Fulbright's eyes was that it came from someone "with so little background and so little experience in the field he is talking about."[30]

Fulbright was well aware that Agnew had spoken out because he had been encouraged by the Nixon White House. His remarks had been designed to intimidate the doves, while gathering support for Nixon's ABM proposal. And that support was forthcoming, so much so that on 19 June Nixon predicted victory whenever the issue came to a vote on the Senate floor. And Fulbright agreed, sensing only a "slim" chance to defeat this proposition. Nixon's victory on 6 August was as close as possible, with the administration winning on a fifty-one to fifty vote.[31] It was a very disappointing result for those, like Fulbright, who were hoping to rein in military spending.

Adding to Fulbright's despair was the continuing conflict in Vietnam. When he spoke to Secretary Laird about the war, Fulbright emphasized the need for a far faster rate of withdrawal as "the only way to clear up the horrible and tragic mess in which we are involved." Although Laird seemed sympathetic to this approach, Nixon was determined to move only at his own pace and for his own reasons. As Fulbright put it, Nixon "seems to be too much of an ideologue, committed to last-ditch opposition to Communism, than is Laird."[32]

As if to confirm this point, Nixon rejected requests from Fulbright and others that he send a representative to Hanoi for Ho Chi Minh's funeral. Fulbright made that proposal in early September in the belief that it would serve as a gesture of reconciliation, as would an American acceptance of Hanoi's proposed offer of a three-day cease-fire. Conciliation with Hanoi was the last thing on Nixon's mind; conciliation of sorts with the American people was very much part of his strategy to contain doves such as Fulbright, Church, and McGovern. Therefore, he authorized the return home of 35,000 more troops, and reaffirmed that he would seek a reduction in the number of men drafted, which could do much to lessen student protests against the war. News of these fresh initiatives caused Fulbright to remark that they seemed like "a nice opiate" designed to "calm everybody down."[33]

That calm abruptly disappeared on 25 September, the day Senator Charles Goodell introduced an amendment to the foreign assistance bill requiring a complete suspension of funding for military activity in Vietnam after 1 December 1970. That proposal, claimed Goodell, would "help the President and Congress develop a workable plan for ending American participation in the war and the slaughter of American servicemen in the near future." It produced an immediate response from the White House, the Defense Department, and Senate doves. Nixon characterized proposals such as Goodell's as "defeatist in attitude," adding that "they inevitably undercut and destroy the negotiating position we have in Paris." Secretary Laird called on the country to support Nixon's approach, saying that "it is the thing that Hanoi will understand." Fulbright warmly welcomed Goodell's initiative, suggesting that it was an original and workable approach. And he announced that because his committee had jurisdiction over this amendment, he planned to hold hearings on it. Having waited a long time to see what Nixon had in mind, Fulbright was at last ready to speak out against the White House, at a time when the polls showed that the president was vulnerable on this issue.[34]

Fulbright, speaking to the Senate on 1 October, declared with biting sarcasm that "it has been nine months since the President took office, the normal period of gestation for humans to bring forth their issue. No one expected a miracle, but many of us did expect the President to make progress in delivering on his campaign promises to give birth to his plan to end the war." After mentioning that 10,000 Americans had died in Vietnam since Nixon took office, Fulbright affirmed that what was now needed was not a moratorium on criticism, but rather a moratorium "on killing." "It is time," he said, "for Americans to leave Vietnam; it is time for the Vietnamese to fight their own war."[35]

Hugh Scott, the late Everett Dirksen's successor as Republican minority leader, responded pointedly to Fulbright's challenge. He asked Fulbright that day whether he favored an immediate American withdrawal, knowing that this would lead, in Scott's view, to the slaughter of Catholics and the further endangerment of the American prisoners of war. Fulbright replied that a Geneva-style conference would be the best way to end the conflict; but given the Nixon administration's refusal to disavow the Thieu regime, all moves toward peace were blocked, all exits from the battlefield closed. Or as Fulbright put it: "the words 'Vietnamization of the war' seem to mean that we will support the Thieu government as long as it is necessary for them to establish firmly their control in South Vietnam."[36]

Fulbright had given his speech to support the Vietnam Moratorium planned for mid-October. He was hoping that this mobilization would generate a widespread national constituency for peace at a time when his committee was planning to hold open, possibly televised, hearings on 27 October to consider a number of antiwar proposals, including the Goodell amendment.[37]

Much to Fulbright's delight, the Vietnam Moratorium of 15 October turned out well because, in the words of Fred Halstead, "millions of ordinary Americans were out in the streets demonstrating, canvassing door to door, picketing, leafletting and so forth." Significantly, a variety of events associated with the Moratorium took place across the country, extending from college campuses to Wall Street, without a sign of violence or nasty confrontations. Later, Fulbright informed a correspondent that "I am sorry that you thought the demonstrations of October 15 were 'subversive and hysterical.' They seemed to me to be extremely well-behaved and a very serious demonstration of disapproval of the tragic mistake . . . in Vietnam."[38]

Meanwhile, the Symington Subcommittee on Military Commitments was already at work looking into the problem of Laos. Using material provided by the subcommittee's resourceful staff investigators Walter Pincus and Roland Paul, Symington and Fulbright tried to pry open the workings of a hidden war in Laos, which the United States had been waging for years. The CIA, as the subcommittee discovered, had had a large role in directing that war, which Nixon supported as one way of preventing a communist victory in Laos. Such an outcome, Nixon feared, could undermine Saigon's willingness to fight, and thus ruin his Vietnamization program, which was designed to remove, by stages, all American ground troops from Vietnam.

Fulbright, too, saw the connection between the two fronts, but he feared that there would be an even greater American military involvement in Laos unless the war in Vietnam was soon concluded. Subsequent to a closed-door hearing of the Symington Subcommittee on 20 October, he expressed the hope that Nixon, who was working on a major address on Vietnam, would seek to wind down the war throughout all of Indochina.[39]

While Nixon was preparing his statement, Mike Mansfield and George Aiken, the senior Republican on the committee, asked Fulbright to defer his scheduled hearings until after the president had spoken to the country. He complied with their request as a matter of courtesy, but there may have been another reason why he took this step. Cyrus Vance, a former Johnson emissary to the Paris peace talks, turned out to be a very reluctant witness, and Clark Clifford, who also had been scheduled to testify, had already publicly declared that he did not favor the Goodell amendment, describing it as "unrealistic and impractical."[40] He feared that it would lead to a "bloodbath" and bring about the collapse of the Saigon regime. It was indeed ironic that Clifford had taken this position, for he had been the chief proponent of a major withdrawal of American combat troops by the end of 1970, and now he opposed a proposal which Fulbright saw as the only available alternative to an otherwise prolonged struggle. Continuing deadlock, Fulbright feared, would further debilitate the political and economic institutions of the United States.

Fulbright's worst fears about the current impasse were confirmed by Nixon's speech on 3 November. It was a Nixon tour de force, offering the country a prospect for Vietnamization but little else. By adroitly playing on fears of a "bloodbath" resulting from any "precipitate withdrawal," he called on a "silent majority" to join him in protecting American honor and in opposing the "vocal minority." And they did. Nixon's speech was a smashing success, providing him with the political clout he needed to put the doves on the defensive while continuing the struggle to protect the Thieu regime from its "external" enemy.[41]

Nixon was now in a good position to implement a strategy which included elements from left, center, and right. He lifted from the left the language of de-escalation, which was used to justify Vietnamization; he retained the center's commitment to the Thieu regime; and he appropriated from the right a more aggressive and expansive policy via the use of air power and rhetorical bluster.

The following day, Fulbright expressed his dismay with the tenor and substance of Nixon's speech, contending that Nixon had now "fully and truthfully taken upon himself Johnson's War." He again expressed the desire to hold public hearings for the purpose of presenting "the real facts" about the war to the American people, who, he believed, would then recognize the truth and reject Nixon's propaganda. But because there was such widespread and deep support for Nixon, Fulbright now saw the need to appear "responsible and careful," and not "antagonistic." He joined other members of the Foreign Relations Committee, excluding Mansfield and Church, in opposing open hearings.[42]

Fulbright was worried that those hearings, occurring during the period of the New Mobilization's planned "March against Death" in Washington on 15 November, would only exacerbate an already tense situation and play into Nixon's hands. In other words, he sensed that Nixon was now eager to promote a confrontation with his critics. In a letter to Professor George Wald of Harvard University, he wrote that "with an Attorney

General such as we have and all the other difficulties of controlling provocateurs, I have stated from the beginning that I do not think it would be a useful exercise to bring vast numbers of students to Washington. In fact, it has the great danger of discrediting the protest movement." Fortunately for the doves, that march of 15 November was generally peaceful, with only a few incidents marring the day. Fulbright took note of that situation, and he later praised the Mobilization for displaying such good sense and dignity.[43]

In the meantime, Nixon's success had left Fulbright with a feeling of despair. As he wrote to Tristram Coffin, "it is very distressing, indeed, to think that we eliminated LBJ only to end up with this, which is almost more than the human spirit can endure." Fulbright's gloom was not lifted when Secretary Rogers told the Foreign Relations Committee on 18 November that prospects for a negotiated settlement were poor. And Secretary Laird did not help as he refused to reveal to the committee anything new about either the rate of withdrawals or their timing. After hearing their testimony, Fulbright and Church admitted that, yes, the United States was on its way out of Vietnam, but it was Fulbright's view that because the administration had displayed such little interest in a negotiated settlement, it had given the committee "a prescription for a very prolonged war."[44]

The shocking revelation of the My Lai Massacre, exposing the fact that American troops, in early 1968, had wantonly killed many civilians, revived Fulbright's interest in the hearings. He had been profoundly upset by that story, saying that "it is a matter of the greatest importance and emphasizes in the most dramatic manner the brutalization of our society." This incident, he felt, made it imperative that the United States move toward a negotiated settlement, and he endorsed a thorough investigation of the event, fearing that otherwise it "can cause grave concern all over the world about what kind of country we are, what people think we are." On 1 December, Fulbright asked his committee to examine the My Lai incident in the broader context of investigating the war's impact on American morality. The committee decided to shelve the proposal for at least the time being. As Fulbright explained to George Kennan, committee members already burdened with work "seem to be interested in exploring this matter after the first of the year in connection with an examination of our policy in Vietnam."[45]

Although the Foreign Relations Committee had delayed action on Fulbright's My Lai proposal, he continued to discuss this incident. At the annual luncheon of the Salvation Army in New York on 3 December, he said that the "recent reports of atrocities in Vietnam suggest that the war in Vietnam has had the effect of brutalizing America in ways we would not have thought possible." He insisted that those reports "must be taken as a warning and a symbol of what can happen to a whole society" that could not disengage from "an unjust and unnecessary war." While arguing that the price the United States was still willing to pay for that war was morally, politically, and economically prohibitive, Fulbright also told his audience that "it is not a matter of being defeated or of surrendering anything, but of acknowledging a terrible mistake, and, even more important, of returning to our primary responsibility, which is the welfare and happiness of the American people."[46]

Upon his return to Washington, Fulbright was quickly drawn into the debate over Laos, which was now the subject of Senate concern. Although the veil of secrecy had long concealed the full extent of the American involvement there, Fulbright sought to publicize those details during a Senate debate on 15 December. By using materials drawn from the secret Symington subcommittee hearings on Laos, he was able to ask such sensitive and pointed questions that the Senate agreed to his suggestion that they move the entire discussion into executive session in order to make use of classified information. During the executive session, Mike Mansfield supported the American bombing of Laos as a way of stopping Hanoi's push into the region. Fulbright opposed it, especially in northern Laos, where the situation had "very much the aspect of a civil war."[47] Despite their disagreements, both men still endorsed the Cooper-Church amendment to a military appropriations bill, forbidding the use of American ground troops in Laos without Congress's approval. As the Nixon administration did not oppose this measure, it cleared Congress and became law.

Fulbright and other doves raised the matter of Laos because it gave them a chance to challenge the administration at a time when its Vietnamization policy had pushed them into a corner. Much earlier in the year, Fulbright had thought that Nixon would move quickly to end the war, but Nixon's refusal to divorce himself from the Thieu regime meant that all hopes for a prompt settlement were dashed. Meanwhile, Nixon realized that it was necessary to protect himself from the kind of political pressure that had led to Johnson's defeat; so he latched onto Vietnamization, which was designed to buy him time while he continued to seek "peace with honor." To expose that ploy as a deliberate delaying tactic would prove to be an enormous challenge to Fulbright and other doves as the decade of the sixties ended.

C AMBODIA: THE CHALLENGE FROM THE SENATE

As the Foreign Relations Committee prepared to hold its long-delayed hearings on Vietnam, William Fulbright confessed in January 1970 that "the President seems to have lulled the people into the belief that the war is practically over. I find it more difficult to deal with the situation than I did with the preceding Administration, since the issues seemed more clear-cut then." Despite his frustration, Fulbright did admit, however, that "whatever may be the eventual limits of the President's Vietnamization program, it does have the immediate beneficial effect of cooling down the temperature of the country."[1]

Fulbright's own deep skepticism about the Vietnamization process had been substantially reinforced by a staff report which Richard Moose and James Lowenstein had prepared for the committee in January 1970. After spending several weeks in Vietnam investigating the situation, they concluded that if Vietnamization was to work, it would require a successful military effort by Saigon, plus the stabilizing of the regime, which in turn required that Hanoi not disrupt its operations. They ended their somber assessment of current conditions by suggesting that "the prospects for a successful outcome of any of the aforementioned three factors, much less all three, must be regarded as, at best, uncertain. Dilemmas thus seem to lie ahead in Vietnam, as they have throughout our involvement in this war that appears to be not only far from won but far from over."[2]

Just after that report was released, the Foreign Relations Committee met on 3 February to begin hearings on a number of proposals bearing on the Vietnam conflict. Fulbright opened the session with a statement in which he acknowledged that Nixon's policy was indeed "far preferable" to the escalation policy of the Johnson administration. But that improvement notwithstanding, he thought it advisable that the committee investigate Vietnamization in order to determine how much time would be needed to complete the process, and he also wanted to examine the alternatives the

White House had in mind in case its present policy failed to work. Then taking note of the current impasse in Vietnam, Fulbright wondered if the prospects for peace would not be better served by a renewed diplomatic effort in Paris.[3]

As Fulbright surely knew, whatever action the committee took would do little to dent Nixon's protective armor. With dovish Republicans such as George Aiken and John Sherman Cooper endorsing Vietnamization, it was impossible to forge a committee consensus for any proposal critical of the current policy; only Charles Mathias's resolution calling for the repeal of the Tonkin Gulf Resolution seemed to have sufficient committee support to ensure a likely floor vote later in the current session.

Despite these poor prospects, the committee continued its work by focusing attention on the operation of the Phoenix program, which had as its objective the "liquidation" of pro-Hanoi supporters and cadre in the villages of South Vietnam. The committee's interrogation of William Colby and other officials connected with the Phoenix program produced the admission from them that there had been aberrations in the administration of the program on the lower levels. These same officials insisted that the moral standards guiding their operations were no different from standards guiding the "average American." (Fulbright earlier had characterized their work as a program of assassination, which he also thought was symptomatic of the war's brutalizing impact on American society.)[4]

Those hearings, coupled with others which followed in March, had no visible impact either on Congress or the country at large. The news media, sensing that most people were not interested in the story, gave very little publicity to the committee's revelations about this exercise in counterintelligence. Still Fulbright and like-minded colleagues persisted in their efforts to keep the discussion of the war alive, hoping by this tactic to put pressure on Nixon to end it quickly.[5]

Laos became the focus of that attempt at public education. Fulbright joined Stuart Symington in calling for the public release of the transcripts of the recent Symington subcommittee hearings on Laos. And he denounced on the Senate floor the escalating air war over Laos that now extended beyond the Ho Chi Minh trail to include the Plain of Jars.[6] Fulbright feared that this latest round of conflict could lead to the commitment of American troops there and possibly to Thailand as well. Any such escalation, Fulbright knew, would make it exceedingly difficult to end the war, which he had long argued was responsible for the "corruption of our national life," the chief object of his concern and worry.

That criticism coming from the Senate ostensibly galvanized Nixon to act. On 6 March he released a long statement about Laos for the purpose of defending his policy. After admitting that the bombing campaign in Laos had been intensified in response to North Vietnamese moves, he announced that American troops would not be sent to Laos without congressional approval, and he made known his desire to reconvene the Geneva Conference in order to deal with the crisis in Laos. Fulbright was not placated by Nixon's move. Therefore, on 11 March, he offered a resolution opposing combat "in and over Laos" without congressional approval. But there was no chance that it would pass, as even Majority Leader Mike Mansfield supported the bombing of the Ho Chi Minh trail.[7]

While attention was riveted on Laos, a far more significant development was taking place in Cambodia. On 18 March, Prince Norodum Sihanouk, while vacationing in Europe, was toppled from power, a victim of a coup d'etat led by General Lon Nol. Subsequently, Fulbright, along with Mike Mansfield, declared that the United States should stay out of Cambodia in order not to complicate the task of peace making in Vietnam. In a closed-door hearing on Cambodia, which was held on 2 April, Secretary Rogers assured the Foreign Relations Committee that it was Washington's desire to preserve Cambodia's neutrality. Nevertheless, Fulbright had good reason to worry that Nixon would give military help to the new regime, thereby enlarging the scope of the war.[8] As events soon showed, his concern was not unfounded.

The situation in Laos and Cambodia served as the backdrop for the most critical speech Fulbright had yet made on the Vietnam War. Speaking to the Senate on 2 April, he sought to dispel some old myths about Vietnam with what he called new realities. For him "the master myth of Vietnam— that is, the country as distinguished from the war—is the greatly inflated importance which has been attached to it." Fulbright sought to counter the myth with the argument that "it simply does not matter very much for the United States, in cold unadorned strategic terms, who rules the states of Indochina." After pointing out that "North Vietnam is the paramount power of Indochina," he emphasized that he did not fear a communist-dominated Indochina; he proposed accepting it "if it arises from the local power situation, as something unwelcome but tolerable, and most emphatically not worth the extravagant costs of a war like the one we are fighting."[9]

Turning to what he called "the myth of Vietnamization," Fulbright pointed to recent events in Laos and Cambodia as confirming the failure of

Nixon's policy. With the war now encompassing all of Indochina, there was, in his opinion, no chance that Vietnamization could offset the strategic advantage Hanoi currently possessed unless the United States were prepared to take new military steps to counter it. Opposed to escalation, Fulbright counseled Nixon to pursue with celerity a diplomatic settlement in order to avoid both a military defeat in Vietnam and a resultant political disaster at home. In order to facilitate such a breakthrough, he urged the administration to accept a neutralist regime in Saigon, while making a commitment to withdraw American forces.[10]

Fulbright's solution for ending the war appeared reasonable, but it was completely unrealistic. Hanoi would not at this time settle for a neutralist regime in Saigon any more than it was prepared to accept a coalition government that included Thieu, and Nixon would never forsake the Thieu regime. (Carl Marcy reflected years later that Senate doves did not have a well-conceived proposal for ending the war. According to him, they had simply decided that the war was doing terrible damage to the United States, and it was now time to get out. The precise details of that departure could best be left for others to handle.)[11]

Fulbright's speech made it clear that he did not believe Nixon when he told Congress on 18 February that Hanoi was demanding a unilateral American withdrawal and the toppling of the Thieu regime as "conditions for just beginning negotiations." What Fulbright did not then know is that Henry Kissinger had already commenced secret talks in Paris, where he discovered that Hanoi had indeed made the demands that Nixon had accurately passed on to Congress. It is understandable that Fulbright was skeptical of Nixon's claims after his experience with LBJ.[12] He simply did not trust Nixon enough to believe he would accurately spell out Hanoi's bargaining position. It would be some time before Nixon would successfully expose that public/private game which Hanoi was playing so skillfully— telling doves one thing and Kissinger something else.

Fulbright's speech provoked an angry response from Nixon supporters. The *Indianapolis News* labeled his critique of current policy as "Fulbright's Munich," and the *Richmond Times Dispatch* attacked him similarly. The once hawkish *Washington Post* responded to his speech with a lengthy editorial that was both respectful in tone and thoughtful in its commentary.[13]

Although Fulbright managed to reach the *Post*, he hoped, also, to reach the business community and thus the president by having prestigious businessmen speak out against the war. One such spokesman was Louis Lundbourg, the chairman of the board of the Bank of America, the country's largest banking institution. On 15 April, Lundbourg appeared before the committee and said, "The war in Vietnam distorts the American economy. It is a major contributor to inflation—our most crucial domestic economic problem. It draws off resources that could be put to work towards solving imperative problems facing this nation at home. And despite the protestations of the new left to the contrary, the fact is that an end to the war would be good, not bad, for American business." Lundbourg's testimony was precisely what Fulbright had wanted to receive. He subsequently distributed this testimony "to more important financial publications." In the weeks to come, Fulbright gave other prominent businessmen an opportunity to speak out against the war; their comments reflected the larger view of 1,100 corporate officials who now believed that the United States had become too "militaristic and aggressive."[14]

While the committee tried to focus attention on the economic, social, and political costs of the war, news from Cambodia increased the anxiety of Senate doves that a new front was fast developing there. On 16 April, the Arkansan issued a statement expressing his alarm upon hearing that Americans in South Vietnam were paying "protocol visits" inside Cambodia. Because he was fearful that this was another example of the inching process which had first led to the Americanization of the war, Fulbright could only hope that Nixon would remain calm and avoid any entrapment in Cambodia. On 23 April, an even more significant story appeared in print suggesting that the administration was planning to give assistance in the form of military supplies to the Lon Nol regime. That same night, while Henry Kissinger was meeting informally with committee members at Fulbright's home, a very agitated Richard Nixon called him three times.[15] Now, Kissinger surely sensed that the president was about to make a major decision regarding Cambodia, but this was something he did not reveal to committee members.

On 26 April, Fulbright again expressed his fear that the United States might yet move into Cambodia. He made this point at a press conference in North Dartmouth, Massachusetts, where he was scheduled to give a speech at a local college. In his speech, Fulbright implored the students not to use violence as a vehicle of protest, because such a tactic "might succeed in bringing on something resembling a counterrevolution from the right, inflated by support from great numbers of honest and decent and frightened citizens." Sensing how volatile was the current situation, Fulbright went on to predict that "if American democracy is overthrown in our generation, it will not be by radicals flying the Vietcong flag but by other radicals flying the American flag."[16]

Fulbright then urged those students to continue to work against the war, reminding them that past dissent, especially when placed in the political context of the 1968 New Hampshire primary, probably prevented the situation in Vietnam from becoming any worse. And if escalation had been replaced by Vietnamization, it happened, according to Fulbright, because President Nixon had a "political incentive" to do so. For that reason, Fulbright said that he "would hate to see that incentive taken from him."[17]

After advising his young audience to speak the language that politicians understand, "the language of votes," Fulbright observed that

> discouraging though it may seem at times, peaceful dissent is the most powerful incentive our policymakers have for bringing the war in Indochina to an end. If, indeed, the war is a single step closer to its end now than it was in 1967 or 1968, it is only because of sustained public dissent and political opposition. The real impact of orderly, democratic dissent in America is not on the policymakers in Hanoi, as the people who support the present course are fond of asserting, but on the policymakers in Washington. That, no doubt, is why they object to dissent, and that is why those of us who oppose this war must sustain it.[18]

Little did Fulbright know that because of the rapidly developing situation in Cambodia, his words would take on added significance and importance in just a few days.

On 27 April, Secretary Rogers appeared before the committee to discuss a proposed arms package to Cambodia, but he did not reveal that the Nixon administration was ready to plunge into Cambodia. It is possible that his reticence was not rooted in mendacity or the desire to deceive; he may not have known at that precise time just what Nixon planned to do. In any event, the committee made known to him its opposition to any such involvement with Cambodia. On 28 April, however, the pace of events quickened as South Vietnamese troops moved into Cambodia with obvious American help and assistance. Fulbright and Mansfield both denounced that move, as did the other members of the Foreign Relations Committee. On 30 April, the committee issued a statement that referred to the deepening American involvement as "a grave development." Fulbright mentioned to reporters that there was nothing Congress could do to stop Nixon from sending advisers and equipment into Cambodia. As he noted, the president "has the power to do it."[19]

That same evening, Nixon appeared on national television to announce that he had sent American troops into Cambodia. This action was taken, he said, to "protect our men who are in Vietnam and to guarantee the continued success of our withdrawal and Vietnamization program." And he declared that once Hanoi's troops were driven out of their Cambodian sanctuaries, and once their military supplies had been destroyed, American troops would be withdrawn. Nixon sought to justify his action by saying that "if, when the chips are down, the world's most powerful nation, the United States of America, acts like a pitiful, helpless giant, the forces of totalitarianism and anarchy will threaten free nations and free institutions throughout the world."[20]

The Foreign Relations Committee was so incensed by the president's action that on 1 May it authorized its chairman to request a private meeting with him "at his earliest convenience." As this was the first time since 1919 that such a request had been made, it was an indication of how seriously the committee viewed the latest developments. After sending his letter, Fulbright then went to Indianapolis, where on that evening he delivered a speech to a rally sponsored by Hoosiers for Peace. Following his opening remarks, which were critical of planned deployment of Multiple Independently Targeted Reentry Vehicles (MIRVs), the expansion of the ABM, and the military-industrial labor complex, Fulbright turned to the Vietnam War, describing it as the primary cause of the nation's moral decay and economic troubles. Stating that Nixon's Cambodian intervention was "a clear, calculated, and utterly ill-advised decision to widen the war," he added that the policy not only opened a new front but had the effect of reversing and discrediting "the Vietnamization program." Nixon had taken this step, Fulbright explained, out of fear of suffering "humiliation and defeat" and because he still hoped to achieve victory by keeping Thieu and Ky as the undisputed rulers of South Vietnam.[21]

As the Cambodian pot boiled over, the committee continued to protest Nixon's action. Fulbright well knew there was nothing it could do to stop him. He not only had the power to act, but his action was approved by a substantial majority of Americans.[22] That was the sad fact facing the committee when it met with the president at the White House on 5 May. At that session, each side repeated arguments the other had already heard and rejected. Although Nixon promised to remove all troops from Cambodia by 30 June, the committee felt that the damage had already been done.

The Cambodian invasion, coupled with the shocking news from Kent

State University, where the Ohio National Guard had killed four students and wounded nine other people, provided the immediate backdrop for a hearing which the committee held on 7 May. In an attempt to call attention to the moral cost of the intervention in Indochina, Fulbright and his colleagues heard testimony from three religious figures: Dr. John C. Bennett of the Union Theological Seminary, Dr. Irving Greenberg of Yeshiva University, and Bishop John Dougherty of the United States Catholic Conference. They described the Vietnam War as a "moral disaster" for the American people, agreeing that in human terms the price for that intervention had been very high. Fulbright found their presentation "powerful and important" and full of "depth and perception." He agreed with them that the Vietnam War had not only corrupted the American political and economic system, but also damaged the country's psychological well-being, leaving it, he feared, vulnerable to demagogues and right-wing authoritarianism.[23]

On 8 May, Fulbright released a statement designed to coincide with a massive student demonstration against the war scheduled for Washington the next day. After expressing his sadness about the Kent State tragedy, he again advised student demonstrators not to resort to violence. Peaceful dissent, he insisted, is a "reaffirmation of democracy, of youth's commitment to it and of the desire of people of all ages to save American democracy from becoming another casualty of war."[24]

While congressional doves embraced the many protestors who came to Washington, Vice President Spiro Agnew was in Boise, Idaho, where on 8 May he delivered a tirade against Fulbright. Employing his well-known rhetorical skills to full advantage, Agnew accused Fulbright of trying "to rekindle the debilitating fires of riot and unrest," and he damned him for making "the baldest and most reactionary plea for isolationism heard in the Senate since the heyday of the America firsters."[25] Agnew asserted that people like Fulbright, who constantly criticized Nixon's Vietnam policies, were playing into Hanoi's hands at the Paris peace talks.

As if Agnew's vituperation were not enough, Fulbright also had to face a challenge in Arkansas, where political enemies of long standing, outraged by his continuing dissent and by his recent vote against Nixon's Supreme Court nominee, G. Harrold Carswell, had organized a recall campaign against him. Led by Jim Johnson, a Fulbright opponent in the 1968 Democratic primary and later a Wallace supporter, the sponsors of this recall movement wanted to put on the November ballot a referendum directed against Fulbright.[26] Although the chances were slight that such a movement would succeed, it was a form of political harassment that came at a time when Fulbright and other doves were busily at work on legislation designed to restrain Nixon's hand in Cambodia.

The proposed Cooper-Church amendment to the military sales bill was the most significant piece of legislation attracting attention. A far-reaching measure, it sought to bar all American military activity inside Cambodia. After the committee voted nine to five on 11 May to tack this amendment onto the military sales bill, the White House moved into high gear to block its passage. Consequently, whatever hopes Fulbright and Mansfield had of bringing this amendment to the floor for a quick vote were now dashed; by mid-May, it appeared that a protracted legislative struggle would take place. Aware of that development, Cooper and Church sought to placate Nixon by altering the language of their amendment so as to suggest that it was in full accord with the president's decision to remove American troops by 30 June.[27] Undeterred, the White House continued to rally Senate support behind a series of amendments designed to scuttle the intent of this particular piece of legislation.

Meanwhile, the battle inside Cambodia continued. Although Nixon had set a twenty-one-mile limit to the American troops' movement into the sanctuaries, there was no such limit placed on bombing attacks by American planes, a point Secretary Laird conveyed to the committee in testimony on 19 May. Two days later, on 21 May, the committee was briefed about the situation in Cambodia by its staff investigators, Richard Moose and James Lowenstein, who had just returned from Indochina. According to their report—which was formally released by the committee on 6 June—Nixon had obtained "short-term" military success with his attack, but because of his decision to go into Cambodia, they foresaw both a prolongation of the war and a serious challenge to the Vietnamization process itself." Fulbright foresaw something else, namely, the destruction of Cambodia resulting from the demise of Sihanouk and the subsequent American intervention.[28]

On 27 May, Fulbright appeared on "Today" to discuss the current situation in Cambodia. He pointed out that because Russia and China had promised to replace weapons seized by American troops, the sweep of the sanctuaries made no sense to him. He also noted that Lon Nol's takeover had been "a great mistake for the poor Cambodians," as it had cost the country its precious neutrality. Turning to the home front, he said that the United States "is coming apart at the seams. The economic downturn is the worst since 1932; young people are disenchanted."[29]

CAMBODIA

It was one thing to recognize the problem, another to do something about it. Nixon's shrewd use of television was making it difficult for the doves to mobilize opposition to him. As Fulbright put it, every time Nixon appeared on television, he made the people feel that "victory is just around the corner. This has been going on now for five years, and apparently we haven't reached the end of it." Another side to the media story was the deliberate campaign by officials of the administration to harass and intimidate its media critics and to challenge their professional competence. No one played that game more deftly or with greater flair than Vice President Agnew. Fulbright, aware of the threat to democratic norms inherent in Agnew's attack, wrote Walter Cronkite of CBS News to praise him and his colleagues for their refusal to bend to administration pressure. It was Fulbright's view that "never before have our democratic institutions—whether the Congress or the free press—been so seriously threatened by an Administration experienced in the techniques of mass advertising and uninhibited in presenting inaccurate or misleading information in order to sell official policies."[30]

Fulbright was not intimidated by the likes of Agnew. On 28 May, he told the Senate that the administration was propping up "the feeble Lon Nol military government in order to wage a proxy war" there, and he went on to refer to Marshal Ky of South Vietnam as an "Asian Agnew" because Ky had attacked in "colorful" language those Americans who favored the withdrawal of South Vietnamese troops from Cambodia along with the troops Nixon had sent in.[31]

That speech was part of an intensifying Senate struggle over the Cooper-Church amendment. Among its opponents was Senator Sam Ervin of North Carolina, for whom Fulbright had high regard. In an attempt to clarify the issue, Fulbright wrote him on 3 June that

> I see no substantial difference between President Nixon's policies and those of his predecessor, and I think they are undermining the security of our country. I realize that you do not share this judgment, but I can assure you it is simply a difference in judgment as to how best to serve this country. Not only are we imperiling the security and the safety of our own people, but we are destroying the lives and property of the people of Indochina in an unprecedented manner, and for a purpose which is so vague that hardly any two people agree as to what it is.[32]

Fulbright's letter spoke to the new mood of opposition that had been developing in the Senate since Nixon had moved into Cambodia. Thus when Senator Robert Byrd sought to give the president the authority to take whatever action he felt was necessary in Cambodia after 1 July, his proposal was defeated on 11 June by a vote of fifty-two to forty-seven. Even Henry Jackson and John Pastore, both long-time hawks, voted against the Byrd amendment, apparently because of pressure from their constituents back home. As both men were facing reelection in November, their votes could be construed as an attempt to protect their liberal flanks.[33]

After this defeat, the administration struck back hard. On 20 June, Agnew, while speaking to the party faithful in Cleveland, unleashed a furious attack on leading Democrats, including Fulbright, Edward Kennedy, Clark Clifford, and Averell Harriman. Not only did Agnew accuse them of being "sunshine patriots," he declared that Kennedy and Fulbright were "apologists" for Hanoi. About Fulbright, Agnew also said that

> in 1964, when the winds and the tides were favorable, the military outlook promising, the American ship of state sailed on with the enthusiastic backing of Senator Fulbright and his contented crew. But when the seas became choppy . . . one could soon glance down from the bridge and see Senator Fulbright on the deck demanding that the ship be abandoned and staking out a claim to the nearest life boat.[34]

Agnew's fulsome rhetoric was a clear indication to Hanoi that the administration had no intention of compromising with its critics in the Senate.

Agnew notwithstanding, the legislative process was working. The Senate was moving closer to a final vote on Cooper-Church, a vote which the administration had successfully delayed for weeks, while waiting for American troops to leave Cambodia by the scheduled date of 30 June. On 22 June, the Senate approved an amendment offered by Robert Byrd declaring that the Cooper-Church amendment would not infringe on the president's power as commander in chief.[35] Fulbright was one of the few to vote against this amendment, out of fear that it was a device to make it easier for Nixon to obtain funding for future operations in Indochina. He was joined in opposition by Republicans Javits and Goodell and Democrats McGovern and Hughes.

More distasteful to Fulbright was the introduction of Robert Dole's floor amendment calling for the repeal of the Gulf of Tonkin Resolution. The Foreign Relations Committee had earlier endorsed such a proposal, and it was expecting floor action in the near future. The White House, aware of strong Senate support for that committee-backed proposal, sought to defuse the issue by having Dole sponsor his amendment to the military sales bill. With this action, Nixon could claim—as he later did—that his authority to act in Indochina rested not on that resolution, but in his position as commander in chief. The Dole amendment was approved on 24 June by a vote of eighty-one to ten, with Fulbright joining nine other senators in opposition. Like others, he objected strongly to this breach of Senate decorum and the circumvention of normal Senate routine.[36]

That vote, plus several others, set the stage for the final showdown on the Cooper-Church amendment. As both sides sought to win last-minute converts, Fulbright struck back at Agnew. On 26 June, he addressed the Senate to take exception to a *Washington Post* editorial rebuking Agnew for his recent speech in Cleveland. The *Post* contended that Agnew's speech was very much like Joe McCarthy in style and tone, but Fulbright disagreed, contending that Agnew reminded him of Joseph Goebbels, the master propagandist and hate merchant of the Hitler regime. Fulbright was saying, in short, that McCarthy was a mere senator, unlike Agnew, whose pronouncements carried with them the ominous implication that he had official state power on his side. The *Post* later stated that Fulbright's argument was overwrought, which was true.[37] Yet the point Fulbright made was exactly correct. Agnewism was potentially an even more sinister and pernicious phenomenon than McCarthyism, because it appeared to have the blessings of the White House. In short, Agnewism was more than the loud trumpeting of a demagogue on the loose; it was really the rhetorical aboveground accompaniment to the dirty tricks and White House horrors yet to come.

If Agnewism was an expression of a White House under siege, the vote on the Cooper-Church amendment on 30 June did not help Nixon's equanimity. On that day the Senate voted seventy-five to twenty to approve this amendment. With this action, the Senate sent the military sales bill to a House-Senate conference committee. Because the House refused to authorize its conferees to accept the Cooper-Church amendment, the bill languished in that committee for almost six months.[38]

Fulbright believed, in early July, that the passage of the Cooper-Church amendment was a fresh indication that the Senate had started to move, albeit very slowly, away from its traditional supine and subservient role in the area of foreign policy. Additional good news arrived on 3 July, the day the backers of the recall movement in Arkansas announced that they had failed to obtain the requisite signatures to challenge Fulbright with a recall vote in November.[39]

Unlike his foes in Arkansas, Fulbright had the votes he needed to revoke the Gulf of Tonkin Resolution. On 10 July, the Senate voted fifty-seven to five to repeal it, so as to ensure that there would be a separate measure available for House consideration in case the House refused to approve the military sales bill. (The Gulf of Tonkin Resolution was repealed after the military sales bill, to which the Dole amendment was attached, cleared the House and became law on 12 January 1971.) Before that vote on 10 July, John Stennis taunted Fulbright by saying that the resolution was being "repudiated by its own father, the senator from Arkansas." Fulbright replied tartly that "Lyndon Baines Johnson was the father, I was the midwife to an illegitimate child. I repudiate any suggestion that I was the father." After Fulbright had properly settled the matter of the resolution's paternity, Jacob Javits, a sponsor of a recently introduced war powers bill, contended that the Senate had now given Nixon a mandate to end the war and withdraw the troops.[40]

Few senators believed that the situation in Vietnam would change because the Senate passed the Cooper-Church amendment or repealed the Gulf of Tonkin Resolution. Fulbright—like other doves—knew that the key to peace lay in Paris, and unfortunately, that diplomatic front was stalemated. The reason for that continuing impasse was simple: Nixon remained implacably loyal to Thieu, and Hanoi demanded his removal as a precondition for the start of negotiations. In short, both sides were committed to the politics of deadlock.[41]

The domestic, social, and economic costs of that deadlock were considerable, a point that Cyrus Eaton, the Cleveland financier and industrialist, sought to make when he appeared before the Joint Economic Committee on 13 July. It was his opinion that the war was playing havoc with the country's economic institutions, producing inflation and rising interest rates, while causing serious damage to the bond markets. Eaton's words had no appeal for Richard Nixon; he had his own reasons for continuing the war. According to Fulbright, they were tied to his "attitude toward victory and national honor, coupled with a fear of communism." It could also be argued that for reasons of presidential politics, he would only accept an agreement compatible, in Henry Kissinger's words, "with our values, our international responsibilities and the conviction of a majority of the American people."[42]

While impasse prevailed in Paris, the situation in Washington, in the summer of 1970, was fraught with bitterness and antagonism between the Foreign Relations Committee and the administration. The committee received short shrift from the administration on matters of concern to it. In fact, that policy of noncooperation seemed so deliberate that Fulbright charged that the State Department was attempting "to neutralize if not destroy the influence of the Committee." He did not remain quiescent in the face of its hostility. When the opportunity arose, he protested loudly that the administration had made an executive agreement for the use of military bases in Spain without first clearing the agreement with the committee.[43]

Arkansas's leading dove also took another tack. On 4 August, Fulbright appeared before a Senate Subcommittee on Communications to speak on behalf of his resolution calling for greater congressional access to television. After declaring that "communication is power and exclusive access to it is a dangerous and unchecked power," he decried the president's ability to dominate the television medium so as to preempt virtually all public discussion of a major national issue such as Vietnam. For that reason, he recommended that Congress pass legislation requiring the television networks to grant Congress the right to have their spokesmen appear four times a year to state their views.[44] His proposal won little support from television moguls, but it raised a very important question, to wit: how does one generate political opposition in a democratic culture to a policy that is successfully advanced by a president simply because he is a persuasive television performer? Fulbright may not have had the right answer for this problem, but at least he tried to generate discussion of an issue most politicians would rather avoid.

Despite Nixon's domination of the media, Senate doves continued to press their case. Many of them rallied behind the McGovern-Hatfield amendment to the current military procurement bill, an amendment designed to remove all American troops from Indochina by the end of 1971. Because this proposal was more far-reaching than anything contemplated by the Cooper-Church amendment, it did not attract widespread support even among doves. Only twenty-three senators served as cosponsors, excluding Fulbright and many other members of the Foreign Relations Committee, who viewed the proposal with skepticism. As McGovern mentioned years later, Fulbright did not want to coerce Nixon, thinking that there had to be a more "civilized way" of dealing with the matter. (And he also mentioned that Fulbright later told him that he, McGovern, had been right to push for this amendment.)[45]

The vote on the McGovern-Hatfield amendment, which the White House staunchly opposed, was scheduled for 1 September, but on the evening of 31 August, NBC, in response to pressure from the Federal Communications Commission, granted a half hour of prime-time television to both Fulbright and McGovern to answer the president. Each took advantage of this opportunity to spell out his reasons for opposing the war. After adding up the domestic and international costs of this conflict, Fulbright emphasized, as he had been doing for months, that Vietnamization was no answer to the problem; peace would come only if the president were prepared to drop Thieu's veto over American policy and only if the United States were prepared to make a commitment to a withdrawal from Vietnam by a specified date. McGovern spoke similarly, stating that it was time to end the conflict because it was damaging the United States in a manner that could only benefit Russia and China.[46]

The next day, 1 September, the Senate voted on the McGovern-Hatfield amendment. Not surprisingly, it was defeated by a vote of fifty-two to thirty-nine. When the final bill, minus this amendment, was approved, only Fulbright, McGovern, Hatfield, Goodell, and Nelson opposed it.[47] With this victory in his pocket, Nixon was now home free for at least a few more months, until a fresh crisis, centering again on Laos, erupted in February 1971.

In the meantime, the midterm election fast approached. Aware of that fact, Nixon, on 7 October, spoke to the country about the war. He made another appeal for peace in Vietnam, sounding statesmanlike and reasonable in manner and substance. Since he still insisted on a mutual withdrawal, nothing fundamentally new was placed on the table that would interest Hanoi. Fulbright made this point in a letter to David Bruce, the new American peace negotiator: "I thought the President's speech represented a considerable improvement in our position with regard to a settlement and certainly a great improvement in tone, but I regret to say that I do not think that it is an offer the other side will accept."[48]

That improvement in tone which Fulbright saw in Nixon's speech was not carried over into the fall campaign. Nixon occasionally used strident rhetoric in his appeal for votes. And Agnew was particularly harsh and pointed in his remarks, often singling out Fulbright for abuse and attack, as he campaigned across the country for Republican candidates to the Senate.[49]

Despite that effort, the White House had to be disappointed with the way things turned out. Although two leading doves, Albert Gore of Tennessee and Charles Goodell of New York, were defeated, many others kept their seats. As neither side achieved any real gains, the election of 1970 was a standoff.

In the face of those results, Fulbright wrote Alfred Knopf that "I am not at all sure the Congress will be able to do anything more than we have done in the past, but we can hope there will be a turn in the tide." In a letter to Tristram Coffin, Fulbright was more direct and caustic: "As for the Democrats allowing Nixon to sneak out of the Vietnam issue, just how do you think we could have prevented it? And with his extensive command of television and capacity to tell fairy tales, what are we going to do about it? Most of us expressed our reservations about Vietnamization, but the country prefers to believe what it would like to see occur, even though there is little foundation for it. In any case, Nixon didn't run away with the election, and that's something."[50]

Upon his return to Washington after the election, the senator announced that he bore no "grudges," adding that "nobody has ever taken me so seriously or given me so much free publicity as the Vice-President and Martha Mitchell."[51] (Like Agnew, Mrs. Mitchell, the wife of the Attorney General, had been attacking Fulbright for months.) But soon thereafter, Fulbright was again involved in conflict with the administration, this time over its request for a substantial military aid package for Cambodia and its renewal of the bombing of North Vietnam.

Fulbright viewed Nixon's request for more aid with skepticism, and he strongly criticized the administration's resumption of the bombing of North Vietnam. His stand on the bombing was spelled out in a committee session with Secretary Laird, who justified that attack on the ground that Hanoi had been violating "understandings" it had reached with the Johnson administration in October 1968. After hearing Laird make his case, Fulbright could only say that "the resumption of the bombing in the north and the reasons they give . . . looks like a replay of something we have been through before, and the whole thing is beginning to look like a nightmare."[52]

Fulbright discussed the bombing on a 29 November edition of "Face the Nation." When asked why Laird, not Rogers, had appeared before his committee on 24 November to defend the bombing, Fulbright said that it indicated that Laird was in charge of policy in Southeast Asia and that the State Department had been relegated to a subsidiary role in this administration. He sought to explain this development by saying that "the military establishment runs nearly the whole country. They dominate Congress. They get anything they like out of Congress. I thought everybody knew that."[53]

In response to Marvin Kalb's suggestion that Laird's influence was a matter of style, Fulbright answered: "Well, I don't think 80 billion a year is a matter of style. In our kind of economy, this is muscle, this is influence, this is power. It controls and influences everything that goes on in our government to a great extent. It is the primary control." Representing the interests of the military establishment in the Senate, observed Fulbright, were Richard Russell, John Stennis, and Henry Jackson, members of the Armed Services Committee, and in the case of Russell and Jackson, the Committee on Appropriations as well. In Fulbright's view, "these are the men who have real influence in the Senate." Compared with them, his position as chairman of the Foreign Relations Committee was "very secondary," in the same sense that the State Department was in relation to the Defense Department.[54]

Fulbright vastly overstated the role played by Laird in the making of Vietnam policy. As Henry Kissinger would explain years later, Laird, like Rogers, did not always agree with the current policy; in some cases, he actively opposed steps which Nixon took in Indochina.[55] Furthermore, despite the Defense Department's budget and the political aid it received from such powerful legislators as Russell, Stennis, and Jackson, "primary control" rested in the White House, not in the Pentagon.

Yet there was no denying that the Pentagon had awesome influence and reach. In his book *The Pentagon Propaganda Machine*, which was published in November 1970, Fulbright tried to explain how the Defense Department, backed by a sophisticated public relations apparatus, was trying to shape public debate across the country on such controversial topics as the ABM.[56] As Fulbright understood the problem, this kind of activity was a form of ideological warfare on behalf of an already enormously powerful and entrenched bureaucracy whose integration into all areas of American society was virtually unchallengeable. He was not advancing a new argument. For years he had attacked the Pentagon's privileged position, viewing it as a threat to the preservation of democratic government as well as to world peace. Only by ending the war in Vietnam and by pursuing a policy of détente with the Soviet Union would it be possible to contain an institution whose growth, in his opinion, had produced such massive distortions in American social and economic life.

Fulbright's long-term objective was getting control of military spending. In the interim, he remained busy with other matters, challenging, for example, Nixon's military aid package for Cambodia. On 10 December, Secretary Rogers, making his first public appearance before the committee in seventeen months, defended Nixon's $255 million request. During his testimony, he also said that American troops would most likely not be sent back to Cambodia, thereby giving a signal to Cooper and Church that a reworking of their amendment might yet be acceptable to the White House.[57] (The original amendment was still tied up in a House and Senate conference committee, where it had remained since July.)

During a nighttime press conference on 10 December, President Nixon also affirmed that American troops would not return to Cambodia. At the same time, he strongly endorsed the aid package to Cambodia as "the best investment in foreign assistance that the United States has made in my political lifetime." It was his view that since Lon Nol's troops were tying down 40,000 North Vietnam troops, they were aiding the Vietnamization process. Nixon also warned Hanoi that he would consider resuming the bombing if those understandings reached with the Johnson administration were violated. According to the president, those understandings included the right of the United States to employ reconnaissance flights over North Vietnam and the willingness of Hanoi not to engage in a troop buildup below the DMZ.[58]

When Secretary Laird appeared before the committee on 11 December, he repeated Nixon's bombing threat and added a wrinkle of his own, suggesting that if Hanoi remained intransigent in Paris, that, too, could lead to the resumption of bombing. Of interest, too, was Laird's insistence that Vietnamization could not be concluded until or unless "there is a resolution of the P.O.W. isssue."[59] Laird's defense of the administration's policy drew immediate fire from Fulbright, who accused the White House of abandoning all hopes for a negotiated settlement. It now seemed to him that this administration was returning to the policy of its predecessor.

While tempers flared over these issues, the Foreign Relations Committee, on 14 December, voted eight to four to submit Nixon's funding request to the full Senate. Only Fulbright, Mansfield, Symington, and Gore opposed it. At the same time, the committee unanimously approved the attachment of a modified Cooper-Church amendment to this special foreign aid bill. This was done after Church had received assurances directly from Nixon himself that ground troops would not be introduced into Cambodia. Unlike the first Cooper-Church amendment, this version would not preclude the use of planes in Cambodian air space or the right of the American command in Saigon to take, in Church's words, "precautionary action" to protect American troops in the field.[60]

Once this bill reached the floor, Fulbright joined Mike Gravel in seeking to strip $155 million from the $255 million Cambodian request. As Gravel put it in defense of his amendment, Nixon's proposal represented "an unwise and open commitment" that was likely to promote more bloody conflict in the region. To support that argument Fulbright placed into the *Congressional Record* the hitherto classified report that Richard Moose and James Lowenstein had prepared on Cambodia. Those staffers agreed with the Nixon administration that Lon Nol needed help if Vietnamization was to succeed, but they also pointed out that the United States was involved in training Cambodian troops and participating in "close air action" with them, an activity which the administration had pledged earlier to avoid. This report notwithstanding, the Gravel amendment on 16 December was soundly defeated on the Senate floor. Commenting on that vote, Fulbright told a constituent that "there is some strange madness afflicting the Members especially where military expenditures are concerned."[61]

Fulbright had taken his stand in opposition to the Vietnamization policy, whether it was applied to Vietnam or Cambodia. He recognized that the Cambodian operation was an integral part of that larger process, and that the policy in both places was designed to retain for the American government a strategic vantage point in Indochina by attachments to client states which could be controlled through foreign aid and military assistance.

As the year ended, the senator feared that Nixon, caught in the coils of Vietnamization, would move back into Laos and, most likely, resume the bombing of North Vietnam.[62] It was a gloomy forecast, but consistent with the Nixon administration's own escalation in rhetoric and behavior. On the other hand, the year of Cambodia had produced some changes in the Senate. The upper chamber saw the emergence of a fairly active dove caucus as represented by the thirty-nine votes for the McGovern-Hatfield amendment, and the modified Cooper-Church amendment placed restrictions of sorts on Nixon's future plans for Cambodia. Not to be overlooked was the repeal of the Gulf of Tonkin Resolution. All this legislative activity indicated that a centrist-liberal coalition was able to give Nixon a good fight on matters affecting the military budget and legislative proposals to end the war. The Senate, it seemed, was finally beginning to assert itself, even though a majority had not yet been formed to oppose the administration's tactics or policies.

To a large degree, that development was tied to the hard work of the Foreign Relations Committee and the persistence of its chairman. But Fulbright's opposition had come at a price. As in the Johnson years, he was scorned by the administration and denounced by the president's supporters in the press. Attempting to answer his many critics, who charged that he had been unreasonable in his opposition to Nixon's policies, Fulbright took to the Senate floor to remark that approving commitments is the Senate's "sacred right, but disapproving them is something else again—it is petty, spiteful, cranky and irresponsible." And he noted that "implicit in this view of things is a touching faith in the goodness of human nature, especially when the human involved is the President of the United States."[63]

In other words, said Fulbright, "just as Henry VIII explained that his desire for a divorce had to be the will of God, or else he wouldn't have desired it, we are now supposed to believe that a foreign policy proposal by the President of the United States has got to be in the best interests of the American people, or else the President would not have proposed it." It was in this spirit that he advised his colleagues to stop their bickering and filibustering and "work in harmony with the administration for air pollution, sonic booms, restraint of trade and a wider war."[64]

9 DEADLOCK: II

During January 1971 both the White House and Capitol Hill doves were absorbed with events in Cambodia. Richard Nixon and Henry Kissinger viewed Cambodia as a major prop of the Vietnamization program. Senate doves saw in Cambodia a reckless and needless expansion of the war. Because of those differing perceptions, it is not surprising that controversy quickly arose over the use of American planes and helicopters in Cambodia for missions other than the interdiction of supplies. Senators William Fulbright and Frank Church argued that such close air support given by American planes to Cambodian and South Vietnamese troops was a violation of the spirit of the Cooper-Church amendment, which had become law on 12 January 1971. As revised in December 1970, it did not expressly forbid close air operations in Cambodia, since administration officials had earlier told Church that such a tactic was not contemplated. Consequently, Church charged that he had been "misled" by the administration at the time negotiations were under way for the purpose of making this proposal acceptable to the administration and doves alike.[1]

The Foreign Relations Committee discussed the matter with Secretary Rogers on 28 January. As he talked, the secretary executed several semantic twists while asserting that the administration was not militarily involved inside Cambodian air space. In addition to Rogers' verbal obfuscation was his concealment of administration plans to attack Laos. Just after his appearance, a massive B-52 assault took place over Laos, but an administration-imposed blackout made it difficult to find out just what was going on. Once it was lifted, the world discovered that Thieu's troops, with American air support, had moved into southern Laos in an attempt to prevent "dry season" buildup by North Vietnam. An exercise in Vietnamization, this invasion had Nixon's complete backing. It was his hope that Saigon would show the world that it had the resolve and will to fight.[2]

On 9 February, Secretaries Laird and Rogers went to Capitol Hill to defend this latest escalation. Laird insisted that "we have not widened the war; on the contrary we have shortened it." He then informed the country that another 50,000 American troops would be withdrawn from South Vietnam by 1 May. Rogers told the Foreign Relations Committee that American troops would "by and large" be out of a combat role in Vietnam by the middle of the year, and he declared that no American troops would be sent into Laos.[3]

After this session, Fulbright told reporters that

there is a feeling of defeat, frustration and resignation up here. This thing is so similar to Cambodia, but the situation has been going on for so long that people are resigned. People become tired and feel they are tilting at windmills. They would rather go after pollution or a number of other things. I feel a sense of futility.

Part of Fulbright's gloom was tied to a recognition that Nixon had mesmerized the voters with the politics of public relations. He vented his frustration in a letter to Alfred Knopf:

It's not so much that I am simply discouraged as it is my inability to think of any concrete project that has any prospect of success after the succession of defeats that we have suffered in the Senate. I am perfectly willing to try anything that would appear to have a chance to attract the attention of the public, but I confess I am somewhat at a loss to know just what to do now, having played the various records over and over again.[4]

As the Laotian incursion continued, Fulbright remained quiet, apparently waiting, as Rogers requested, for the operation to end before speaking out. Meanwhile, other doves took up the challenge of attacking Nixon. McGovern, responding to Nixon's remark that he would place no limits on the use of air power other than to exclude atomic weapons, said that the president was "flirting with World War Three," and Church agreed with him. On 22 February, the Senate Democratic caucus endorsed a resolution calling for a complete withdrawal from Indochina by the end of 1972. On 25 February, Walter Mondale, with eighteen cosponsors, offered a resolution opposing any invasion of North Vietnam.[5]

Fulbright's silence was so conspicuous that when he appeared on the 28 February edition of "Face the Nation" Joseph Kraft asked him about it. Fulbright replied that everybody knew his position, so he was now encouraging others such as Walter Mondale and Jacob Javits to step forward. He then endorsed Javits's recently introduced war powers bill, saying that the committee planned to hold hearings on it.[6]

The senator was also busy with other matters. He consulted with CBS News in the preparation of its special televised report "The Selling of the Pentagon." Based in part on Fulbright's *The Pentagon Propaganda Machine*, this report—which appeared on 23 February—evoked a storm of controversy, as many people, including Vice President Agnew, were outraged by the critical tone employed by broadcaster Roger Mudd in dissecting the Pentagon's propaganda apparatus. Because of the controversy and interest it had engendered, "The Selling of the Pentagon" was given a repeat showing a month later. On 18 April, CBS even devoted an hour of prime-time television for a discussion of the issues raised in its special report. Fulbright appeared on that program and did battle with Arthur Sylvester, a former Johnson administration official, about the role played by the Pentagon in spreading its propaganda wares across the country.[7]

Nixon, too, had had success in spreading his propaganda across the country. Nevertheless, he could not suppress the news that the Laotian operation was a fiasco; after battling North Vietnamese regulars, South Vietnamese troops had been badly mauled, and their retreat was marked by confusion and disarray. Once this operation was concluded, Fulbright no longer felt constrained to keep his silence, as Secretary Rogers had asked earlier. On 30 March, he took to the Senate floor to question an operation Nixon was wont to call a success. In his prepared remarks, Fulbright noted the vast gulf separating the administration's objectives from the actual results of the Laotian incursion. He also charged that the whole affair smacked of either "a massive deception of the American people or a massive misrepresentation on the part of our political and military leaders." He then announced that the Foreign Relations Committee would soon hold hearings on various proposals to end the war, hearings that had been delayed as long as Nixon was still caught up in his Laotian adventure.[8]

When the committee began its work, it considered a reworked McGovern-Hatfield amendment calling for a complete American withdrawal from Vietnam by the end of 1971. Although this amendment, in its latest guise, had nineteen cosponsors, Fulbright was not among them. As in 1970, he did not wish to set any specific date for withdrawal, most likely fearing that if Congress approved such legislation and the president refused to comply with it, a constitutional crisis could ensue. Hoping to avoid such a confrontation, he wanted to persuade Nixon to end the war. Thus, according to McGovern, Fulbright viewed this amendment only as "a drastic last resort solution."[9] For that reason he was probably relieved that the committee did not recommend any specific proposal to the Senate.

Whatever his private doubts about the McGovern-Hatfield amendment, Fulbright was decidedly heartened by the obvious change in the public mood, as evidenced by a Louis Harris poll showing that the public had turned away from the unqualified support it had previously given to Nixon's Vietnamization policy. More specifically, a majority now felt it was morally wrong for the United States to be fighting in Vietnam, and a narrow plurality favored the creation of a coalition regime in Saigon.[10]

As that shift in the public mood was taking place, the committee was also receiving testimony from a number of individuals on the subject of war powers legislation. Among those who appeared were such former Johnson administration officials as McGeorge Bundy, Arthur Goldberg, and George Reedy; each supported the idea of such legislation, as did most other witnesses. Secretary Rogers, speaking for Nixon, opposed it, and his presentation on 14 May sparked an angry outburst from Fulbright. It began innocently enough as Fulbright opened that session with a statement spelling out his own views. After noting that Vietnam had catalyzed interest in war powers, Fulbright went on to say that in undertaking "to assert its war powers, Congress is moving toward a significant turning point in our constitutional history. For its own sake as well as that of Congress and the country, I hope that the Executive will see fit to cooperate with Congress in the restoration of Constitutional balance." Rogers saw no need to place restraints on presidential war powers, and he further suggested that any discussion of what he called "hypothetical constitutional questions" as "too risky and unwise."[11]

Fulbright replied that "I cannot remember when I have been more disappointed at the negative response to what I thought and believed to be a good faith offer . . . to try to make progress in a reconciliation between the Congress and the Executive in this area." Rogers's testimony, he said, reminded him of the line taken by former Johnson administration official Nicholas Katzenbach, who had once suggested that Congress's warmaking authority in the missile age was all but nonexistent. The normally cool Rogers heatedly rejected this comparison, denying that there was any similarity between his views and those of Katzenbach.[12]

As the momentum for war powers legislation continued to build in Congress, Nixon and Kissinger had to deal with the immediate and pressing problem of the stalled Vietnam peace talks in Paris. In an attempt to break that deadlock, Kissinger met with Hanoi's representative, Le Duc Tho, in

Paris in early June. Despite some changes in the American negotiating position, the White House's firm support of Thieu meant that the Paris talks would remain deadlocked. Meanwhile, Fulbright and Symington were trying to focus the Senate's attention on current developments in Laos. They met with no success; most of their colleagues were indifferent to the fact that troops from Thailand were fighting in Laos or that B-52s were regularly bombing northern Laos.[13]

Fulbright found a more receptive audience for other remarks that he delivered on the occasion of a commencement address at Cambridge University on 10 June. There, he discussed the role of "Intellectuals in Government":

> I very much doubt that America's brilliant strategy in Vietnam could have been shaped without the scholarship and erudition of two Rhodes scholars and one former Harvard dean. More recently, we have been served at the highest policy level by an illustrious historian and strategic thinker whose special gift is an ability to shape American strategy in Southeast Asia in the light of the experience of Weimar Germany and Metternich's stewardship of the Hapsburg empire.
>
> Eschewing false modesty, I am bound to confess that my country has solved the problem of drawing intellectuals into government. The problem that remains—and one on which we could use some guidance—is: how do we get them out?[14]

One intellectual no longer in government service was Daniel Ellsberg, a former Defense Department and Rand Corporation employee. On 13 June, the *New York Times* began to publish excerpts from the copy of the Pentagon Papers that he had earlier given to *Times* reporter Neil Sheehan. Fulbright was certainly not surprised by this development, for during a conversation with Ellsberg on 31 March, he had advised him to seek out the *Times* in the hope of finding a public outlet for those papers.[15] After having experienced frustration with the situation on Capitol Hill, Ellsberg took Fulbright's advice and acted accordingly.

Many months earlier, beginning in November 1969, Ellsberg had given Fulbright a set of the papers in the belief that something positive might ensue from his gesture. (In October 1969 he had been invited by Fulbright to testify before the committee subsequent to the publication in the *Washington Post* of a letter he and others had written protesting the war. In the aftermath of Nixon's 3 November 1969 speech, those scheduled hearings on Vietnam were canceled.) According to Ellsberg, Fulbright received the papers with enthusiasm, telling him that they could be used with no risk to the donor. But the chairman soon encountered problems: the committee could not decide what to do with the papers, and Secretary Laird denied his several requests to have them declassified.[16]

In the late spring and early summer of 1970 Ellsberg, based on what he had been told, fully expected that hearings on the papers would proceed. By summer's end, that prospect had disappeared. Ellsberg remembers Fulbright telling him that the "material is only history, was it worth the risk?" He also recalls that Norvill Jones, a committee staffer with whom he dealt, mentioned that if the committee held those hearings it might have its jurisdiction over the military assistance program taken from it and given to the Stennis Armed Services Committee. Years later Ellsberg speculated that Henry Kissinger may have had a role in quashing those contemplated hearings on the papers. When asked whether he and Kissinger had discussed the papers, Fulbright answered, "I don't think so."[17]

Several days after the *Times* began to publish its version of the Pentagon Papers, Fulbright, interviewed in London about this major news event, remarked that

> I think it's very healthy for a democratic country like America to know the facts surrounding their involvement in such a great tragedy as the war in Vietnam. I don't think the documents have any significant effect on our national security; the only effect is embarrassment to a few individuals who were party to the deception of the country.[18]

Upon Fulbright's return to Washington, he discovered that there was a move to have a joint Armed Services and Foreign Relations Committee investigation and study of the Pentagon Papers. He quickly lined up support for a proposal that allowed his own committee to direct and control any such undertaking. After the Senate appropriated the funds for this project, a staff was hired by the committee and put to work evaluating the papers—now released by the Defense Department—in a scholarly fashion. In time, the committee issued several useful publications based on the staff's findings and analysis.[19]

Although the Pentagon Papers story dominated the news, it did not fully eclipse other developments. On 16 June, the Senate voted fifty-five to thirty-nine to reject for the second time the McGovern-Hatfield amendment. (Fulbright, who was in London at the time of the vote, was paired in its favor.) On 22 June, the Senate passed by a fifty-eight to thirty-two vote a Mansfield amendment to a Selective Service bill stipulating that the Senate favored the total withdrawal of American troops from Vietnam within nine months after the POWs had been returned by Hanoi.[20] Fulbright, like many other senators, clearly favored this approach, as it did not contemplate a confrontation with Nixon. Unfortunately for the doves, the House refused to act on the Mansfield amendment, leaving it for the time being in legislative limbo.

With his sponsorship of this amendment, Mansfield stepped forward into an active leadership role, thereby helping to strengthen his working relationship with Fulbright. He and Fulbright had not gotten along well in the Johnson years, as there had been tension between the two men, probably resulting from Mansfield's special relationship with LBJ. Operating, in Fulbright's words, as "Johnson's alter ego," he clearly found it difficult to attack the war, remaining protective of Johnson in his capacity as the Senate's majority leader.[21] In the early months of the Nixon presidency Mansfield seemed to be playing the same role. All that changed, however, as a result of Cambodia. Now the two men found themselves working and voting together inside the Foreign Relations Committee, in a common struggle not only against the war, but on behalf of the troop cutbacks in Europe and arms control.

As Senate doves marshaled their resources, Henry Kissinger was at work in Paris. He made no progress there, but his secret trip to China was such a success that it provided Nixon with the opportunity to announce that he would be going to Peking in early 1972. Long before Nixon or Kissinger sought to open the door to China, Fulbright had advocated a fresh approach to Mao's regime. His China hearings in 1966 had gone far to demythologize the entire subject. Ironically, even as Kissinger was preparing to go to Peking, Fulbright's committee was holding new hearings on China, this time for the purpose of examining the issue of China's admission to the United Nations and the possible repeal of the Formosa Resolution of 1955.

Those hearings reminded Fulbright that the United States had lost a historic opportunity to work out an accommodation with Mao in the mid-1940s. He made this point in a statement that was otherwise supportive of Nixon's gambit. While praising Nixon's move, Fulbright also voiced hope that the administration would display the same sort of flexibility with regard to the recent proposals of the Provisional Revolutionary Government. (Like others of similar persuasion, Fulbright did not know that what Hanoi said to doves in Paris was not the same thing it was telling Henry

Kissinger.) Nixon quickly dashed such hopes by saying that his trip to Peking did not imply that the war would soon end.[22]

It was a correct reading of the situation, as was borne out by political developments inside South Vietnam. A presidential election scheduled for 3 October turned out to be a farce as candidates opposing Nguyen Van Thieu dropped out of the race, thereby ensuring his victory. Both Nixon and Kissinger were happy to settle on Thieu, but by staying with him they may have scuttled an opportunity to end the war. According to Seymour Hersh, Hanoi was prepared to strike a bargain if the election had been won by someone other than Thieu.[23]

Fulbright himself had been critical of the way the election was held. His remarks were contained in a Senate speech that was delivered on 30 September in support of a new version of the Mansfield amendment, shortening the withdrawal period from nine to six months contingent upon the release of American prisoners. Also included in this speech was Fulbright's analysis of the five basic arguments and "rationalizations" which had frequently been advanced to justify the American intervention. They included the exemplary war thesis; the Munich analogy; the need, in Nixon's words, to "play out the game" in order not to lose; the role of presidential politics circa 1972; and, finally, the fear that an American withdrawal would produce, again in Nixon's words, a "nightmare of recrimination."[24]

The Arkansan sought to rebut each of these arguments, but his remarks directed at the "recrimination" thesis were particularly pointed:

For all I know there will be an outcry from the radical Right if the war is ended short of total victory—they usually do make an uproar when the government does something sensible—but is that any reason to continue the killing of Americans and Vietnamese? Are our soldiers to be sacrificed for the appeasement of the lunatic fringe at home? If there is to be recrimination at home, I say let's get on with it; it is better than further and useless killing.[25]

While Fulbright and like-minded colleagues were speaking out on behalf of the Mansfield amendment, President Nixon was making his own moves. On 12 October he announced that a summit meeting would be held in Moscow during the spring of 1972. As Fulbright had long supported the easing of cold war tensions, one might have expected him to greet this news with a public statement of support; but none was forthcoming, largely because he viewed Nixon's exercise in summitry as mostly a public relations exercise dictated by the exigencies of presidential politics. As he wrote George Ball, the main motivation for summitry was to divert attention away from "disarray in our domestic affairs and thereby contribute to a favorable outcome in the election of Mr. Nixon."[26]

Interestingly, several weeks before Nixon made his announcement Fulbright had inserted into the *Congressional Record* a transcript of Nikita Khrushchev's remarks to the Foreign Relations Committee on 15 September 1959. On that day, the Soviet leader made a passionate appeal for détente and an end to the arms race. It was the presence of that idea which sparked Fulbright's later interest in and commitment to the cause of better relations between the two superpowers. Over the years, he had come to believe that because of the American obsession with Soviet communism, "we missed a great opportunity to make progress toward a more rational world when we did not respond to Khrushchev's overture." He also thought that the current "paranoia" about Russia explained why the military establishment was receiving "exorbitant appropriations" and why it "is almost impossible to do anything about it." As Fulbright wrote to Roswald Garst, "The war keeps this feeling alive more than otherwise would be the case, and it still remains the No. 1 priority in my book."[27]

The war also remained a major priority for Mike Mansfield. His first attempt in seeking congressional support for his amendment ended with frustration. The House had so watered it down that virtually nothing was left of its original language. Mansfield's second attempt met with Senate approval on 30 September, but again the House stripped it of its key provisions. Ultimately, a modified Mansfield amendment was attached to a military procurement bill that Congress sent to the White House; but when Nixon finally signed it into law, on 18 November, he declared that this particular amendment was nonbinding and did not constitute official American policy.[28]

Shortly afterward Congress went into a Christmas recess, at which point Nixon unleashed a blistering air attack on North Vietnam. Among those who criticized this action was Fulbright; he commented that the administration "remains as dedicated as were its predecessors to a hopeless quest for military victory in Vietnam."[29] If Nixon had truly wanted to end the war, Fulbright said that he "could have dealt more seriously with the proposals Hanoi and the NLF [National Liberation Front] had advanced in July." Nixon refused to consider these proposals because he wanted to end the war on his own terms. He had taken this position, it seems, because of his fear of alienating the conservative bloc within his own party, or those Wallace supporters he hoped to woo in 1972.

DEADLOCK: II

Nixon's effort to placate the forces on the right worked as long as the House, a stronghold of the center, gave him the latitude he needed to execute his policy. Meanwhile, he and Kissinger had worked hard to keep Hanoi at bay, while at the same time they pushed for détente with Moscow and a rapprochement with China. By deftly moving various chess pieces on a geopolitical chessboard of their choosing, they had, in Kissinger's words, made "the two great communist powers collaborators in holding our home front together."[30]

Thanks to the upcoming election, that home front would be highly politicized in 1972, but whether Vietnam would be a significant issue no one could yet determine. Dovish Democrats hoped that Nixon was vulnerable to public pressure and would move toward a settlement. Certainly, public opinion polls indicated that the country was now tired of the war and wanted it ended.[31] Yet Nixon had proven in the past that he could deflect dove pressure with relative ease. He remained a determined foe, capable of ruthless and shrewd moves to protect both his policy and his political standing.

10 *N*IXON PREVAILS

For years William Fulbright had tried to point out the high price the country was paying for its tragic misadventure and folly in Indochina. He also sought to educate his colleagues and the country about the need to reconsider the goals and purposes of American foreign policy.

Fulbright's views about the war, as well as other matters, were often expressed in the form of speeches and articles which had been prepared for him (after consultation) by Seth Tillman, a trusted and valuable member of the Foreign Relations Committee staff. Of the many pieces Tillman drafted for Fulbright and had published under his name, none was more provocative or as far-reaching as the one which appeared in the *New Yorker* on 8 January 1972.[1]

This lengthy essay, which was based partly on material taken from the Pentagon Papers, offered the *New Yorker* readership a sturdy lesson in revisionist history. It sought to explain the disaster in Vietnam as an outgrowth of ideas and commitments evolving out of the Truman Doctrine, whose universalization or globalization Fulbright now deplored. Coupled with that point was the contention that the ideology of anticommunism had so blinded policymakers to the realities of a more complex world that they lost historic opportunities to deal constructively with the leading communist powers.[2] That is, opportunities were lost to stabilize and manage the nuclear environment.

Fulbright's *New Yorker* essay suggested that he would certainly be receptive to whatever moves Nixon and Kissinger might make to improve relations with Moscow. Apart from that consideration, Fulbright thought it would be a valuable exercise to confront precisely those ideas and doctrines responsible for putting the United States in Vietnam in the first place. Thus he hoped that his *New Yorker* article would spark a debate about the major postwar themes of American foreign policy. Much to his disappointment, there was little or no comment from officials in government.

Except for a brief notice in the press, that essay simply failed to generate the discussion Fulbright had sought on this most urgent issue.[3]

President Nixon's speech of 25 January attracted major attention. Nixon not only revealed that Henry Kissinger had been secretly negotiating with Hanoi ever since 1969, but he charged that those efforts had been constantly frustrated by Hanoi's refusal to deal positively with American proposals. Attempting to appear as reasonable as possible, the president declared that he was again offering Hanoi fresh proposals to break the deadlock. Nixon's shrewd revelation about the nature and extent of the secret diplomacy was designed to put the doves on the defensive, and his tactic worked.[4] He had won another massive public relations victory on the eve of his visit to Peking.

Although Nixon's speech of 25 January sounded statesmanlike, the other face of the White House was strikingly revealed when H. R. Haldeman, Nixon's chief of staff, appeared in a taped interview on the "Today" edition of 7 February to denounce the president's critics. He contended that their recent remarks were virtually treasonable in character. More to the point, Haldeman's attack was directed at Senator Edmund Muskie, who was then both the leading Democratic candidate for the presidential nomination and a sharp critic of Nixon's Vietnam policy. Even before Haldeman's remarks were televised, Secretary Rogers, after having been pressured by the White House, publicly criticized Muskie's recent speech on Vietnam as "inappropriate and harmful" to the national interest. Fulbright, in response, sought to defend Muskie with a Senate floor statement deploring the abusive tone and manner of Nixon's partisans. Assisting Muskie was one thing; effectively overcoming the Nixon counterattack was something else. As Fulbright wrote Muskie, "with the T.V. spectaculars of Peking and Moscow pre-empting the airwaves, what you and I or anyone else has to say is going to be difficult to bring to the notice of the public."[5]

Nixon's trip to China was indeed a television spectacular, but it also impressed a hitherto skeptical Fulbright that there had been a change in Nixon's attitude toward China. While welcoming this development, Fulbright reminded reporters interviewing him on the 23 February edition of "Today" that his committee had opened up discussion of China with a series of hearings in March 1966. Rightfully taking pride in that breakthrough, he also mentioned that in the days of Rusk and McNamara, the war had been "sold to the country on the grounds we were containing China." On the subject of Vietnam, Fulbright suggested a process of disengagement by which both sides might avoid sticky details such as a six- or twelve-point plan. It would be better, he said, if the United States simply made a commitment to get out of Indochina in exchange for the American prisoners in Hanoi's hands.[6] As far as Fulbright was concerned, it was up to the Vietnamese to settle their differences; Thieu was not worth the price the United States had to pay to preserve his regime.

Not surprisingly, then, Vietnam remained very much on the mind of the Foreign Relations Committee in early 1972. A new version of the Mansfield amendment was likely to come to the committee's attention. Because the chances were slight that any legislative consensus for end-of-war proposals could be forged in an election year, Fulbright and his colleagues initially concentrated on other issues, including war powers legislation. Once the Foreign Relations Committee finished its hearings on that subject, it put together a bill from proposals offered earlier by Jacob Javits, Thomas Eagleton, and John Stennis. Although Fulbright had been an early supporter of such legislation, he developed reservations along the way. He was now worried that Congress, by passing the legislation in its current form, would provide the president with an advance grant of power. Remembering what Johnson did with the Gulf of Tonkin Resolution, he offered an amendment that would strike from the measure any enumeration of the emergency powers of the president, but this was defeated as were all other floor proposals that sought to modify the committee's draft. On 13 April, the Senate approved a bill that differed markedly from the one passed by the House. Because House and Senate conferees were not able to compromise their differences, war powers legislation expired in conference committee in 1972.[7]

As the Senate voted to approve war powers legislation, the Vietnam War continued unabated. The United States responded to Hanoi's spring offensive with a massive bombing assault. It soon became clear that Nixon was determined to blunt this offensive—described by Kissinger as Hanoi's "last throw of the dice"—no matter what the cost. That is, he was prepared to cancel the summit meeting in Moscow if it were necessary. Only a virtuoso performance by Kissinger, who had gone to Moscow on 20 April to see Leonid Brezhnev, managed to convince Nixon that the Russians were eager to continue with the summit, wanting to do business with him, not against him.[8]

Even before Kissinger left for Moscow, congressional doves had renewed their criticism of Nixon's Vietnam policy. Fulbright, for one, declared that as long as the White House clung to Thieu, no settlement was possible; others voiced similar sentiments. That conflict between Senate doves and the administration reached a climax of sorts when Secretaries Rogers and Laird came before the Foreign Relations Committee to defend Nixon's bombardment. Rogers's appearance on 17 April was full of tension and bad feelings, as the chairman did not want him to read his full statement into the record, preferring instead that he answer a series of questions about current American policy in Indochina. Following that session, during which Fulbright did much of the interrogation, the committee approved a Church-Case amendment to a State Department authorization bill terminating all funding for the war at the end of 1972, contingent upon the release of all American prisoners held by Hanoi. Among the members of the committee who opposed it was George Aiken, long-time defender of Nixon's Vietnamization policy. Years later, when looking back at Aiken, Fulbright described him as a "cynic."[9]

Melvin Laird appeared before the committee on 18 April, and he not only defended the bombing but declared that unless Hanoi ended its offensive, he, Laird, would not "rule out the possibility" that the United States might have to blockade Haiphong Harbor or mine the channel leading to it. Knowing Laird as well as he did, Fulbright now feared the worst. In a letter to a friend a few days later, he remarked that "with the legal training, Rogers always qualifies his statements and conceals what he really has in mind better than Laird. Isn't it a tragedy to have all this break out again."[10]

On 19 April, Fulbright took to the Senate floor in an attempt to rebut the administration's argument for escalation. He pointed out that the testimony of the past two days "has opened a vast range of possibilities for increased American involvement in the war. Unlimited American bombing of North Vietnam has been threatened and the possibility of blockading Haiphong or mining its harbor has not been ruled out." After having attacked the administration's case for its escalation, current or planned, Fulbright suggested that recent events had shown that, in spite of Vietnamization, the United States had not really moved to end its participation in the war. It was his view that "it is clearly not in the interest of our Nation to continue the wholesale destruction of the lives and property of the Vietnamese people. The entire operation has become barbarous, inhumane, and obscene and is a profound embarrassment to the people of our country."[11]

President Nixon appeared on national television on 26 April to announce further reduction in the American force levels in Vietnam to 49,000 troops, as well as the resumption of public talks in Paris. He refused to terminate the bombing until the North Vietnamese had ended their offensive, claiming that their "one remaining hope is to win in the Congress of the United States and among the people of the United States the victory they cannot win on the battlefield in South Vietnam." Nixon had taken his stand because it was his strong feeling that "all we have risked and all that we have gained over the years now hangs in the balance during the coming weeks and months."[12]

Nixon's speech left Fulbright with a "feeling of sadness for our country." George McGovern, now the leading dove candidate among Democratic presidential aspirants, felt that the bombing was a disaster and was destined to prolong the war. George Aiken opposed them by counseling his colleagues not to play into the hands of the enemy by making critical remarks.[13]

Opposition to Nixon intensified considerably after he publicly announced on 8 May that Haiphong Harbor would be mined in response to Hanoi's refusal to end its offensive. Coupled with that bold and dangerous move—which Lyndon Johnson had always rejected—was a major administration concession: Nixon publicly agreed to a standstill cease-fire, indicating that he would no longer demand a mutual withdrawal of forces as an integral part of any settlement. He also promised to withdraw American forces four months after Hanoi returned the prisoners in its possession. Not everyone in Nixon's administration favored this escalation. Secretaries Laird and Rogers, for example, opposed it, but Kissinger went along, even though he thought that Moscow might yet cancel the summit to protest this latest Nixon maneuver.[14]

Nixon's speech galvanized the Democratic opposition like nothing else since his 1970 incursion into Cambodia. On 9 May, the Senate Democratic caucus voted twenty-nine to fourteen to approve a resolution offered by Fulbright denouncing Nixon's war policy. That same caucus also voted thirty-five to eight to endorse the Church-Case amendment to a State Department authorization bill, specifying that all funds for the Vietnam War would be cut off four months after an agreement had been reached with regard to the prisoners.[15]

As the Senate prepared to debate this amendment, the Foreign Relations Committee was holding hearings—scheduled long before—on the origins and the significance of the Vietnam War. These hearings, using the Pentagon Papers as a point of departure, were designed to provide a historical context for assessing the reasons for the American intervention. Among those who testified from 9 May through 11 May were Leslie Gelb, the former editor of the Pentagon Papers; James Thomson, former member of the National Security Council staff; and academics Arthur Schlesinger, Jr., and Noam Chomsky, whose views on how and why the United States went to war in Indochina contrasted in important ways. Among those who were invited to appear but refused were Robert McNamara, William Bundy, and Dean Rusk—though Rusk told Fulbright he might appear at some other time.[16]

Thomson revealed to the committee that White House officials on 4 August 1964 thought that Hanoi might capitulate once the bombing raids of that night had taken place. Schlesinger, in his testimony, attributed the disaster to policies made out of "ignorance, improvisation and mindlessness." And like Fulbright, he stressed the importance of the ideology of anticommunism, that belief system which went hand in glove with the containment doctrine. Chomsky argued on behalf of a more structuralist approach. He contended that the American opposition to a peasant-based revolutionary movement was not the product of blind anticommunism but rather a form of "rational imperialism." Its goals, he believed, were to prevent "any nibbling away at areas that provide Western industrial powers with free access to markets, raw materials, a cheap labor force, and the possibilities for the export of pollution and opportunities for investment."[17]

When discussing this sharp exchange of views, Fulbright said that each had a point worthy of serious consideration.[18] His political experience and intellectual understanding led him to agree with Schlesinger that the intervention was, in the first place, a product of "ignorance, improvisation, and mindlessness." He recognized, however, the validity of Chomsky's contention that an underlying imperial imperative was at work, too. The urge to dominate and expand one's area of control—for whatever reason—was patently the expression of an imperial outlook which Fulbright, years earlier, had characterized as the "arrogance of power." So his own perspective was not inconsistent with either Schlesinger's or Chomsky's: it depended on the situation and context as to which argument was the most appropriate at any given time.

Chomsky and Schlesinger agreed that Nixon's latest move was extremely dangerous, and they, along with other witnesses, were not sure what could be done to restrain him. Fulbright himself had always felt that Congress could not by itself stop the war. He believed that only the strongest manifestation of disapproval from the public could force the president to change his course. Because that expression was absent, Nixon was able to keep his working majority in the House, and to hold the Senate in check.

Aware of that reality, Fulbright recognized that the Church-Case amendment did not have a bright future. Hence, in a discussion with Leslie Gelb, he asked,

> Aren't we really reduced to an appeal to public opinion and thereby as a political leader the President would respond to it in the near future? Even if we passed such an amendment as you mentioned, and it became law, it would be a long time before it took effect. As a matter of fact, there are so many arms in the pipeline, so much armed strength now deployed in the area that as long as the armed forces obey orders, I don't know what Congress can do.[19]

Fulbright had realistically assessed the situation. Thus when the critical vote on the Church-Case amendment came on 16 May, just a few days before Nixon was scheduled to leave for Moscow, another amendment, calling for an internationally supervised cease-fire—which Hanoi had always rejected—was added to the original amendment by a vote of forty-seven to forty-three. That vote, which nullified the value of the original amendment, disheartened the doves. As Fulbright admitted to Clark Clifford, "I must say, I despair of the Senate ever taking an affirmative attitude on these matters." He also wrote to a constituent that "I agree with you that the present policy is not unlike that recommended by General LeMay—that we 'bomb them back into the stone age'—and that is apparently what is taking place. So far, we simply do not have enough votes in the Congress to effectively cut off the funds, which is the only weapon we have."[20]

At this point, Fulbright was so discouraged that he gave serious thought to retiring in 1974. The war was wearing him down, and he was suffering embarrassing humiliations from an administration that had outflanked and outvoted him on other matters on the Senate floor such as increased funding for the United States Information Agency, which he opposed. Fulbright often lacked the votes he needed because his critical outlook and personal style tended to alienate people who felt that he had no right to challenge the president as often and in the manner that he did. In short, his was a way of doing business which did not sit well with colleagues who objected to his intellectualizing of issues and, above all, to his foreign policy views that were decidedly not conventional or mainstream.[21]

The White House had frustrated Fulbright, but it also helped to revive his interest in politics. The success of the Moscow summit convinced him that the president had been eager to pursue détente. Like other critics, including McGovern, Fulbright had not really expected much to come from

Nixon's trip to Moscow, thinking that it had been largely designed as a public relations gimmick for reasons having to do with domestic politics. Having seen those results, which included an ABM treaty and an interim offensive weapons agreement, Fulbright thought that Nixon had experienced "a change in attitude." Accordingly, he informed the president that as soon as the Foreign Relations Committee had received the treaty and the interim agreement, he would do everything possible "to obtain the approval of the Senate and the country."[22]

Nixon's "change of attitude" had made possible a genuine improvement in relations with Moscow and a historic breakthrough with China. Earlier, Nixon had rhetorically rejected the foreign policy objectives of the limitationists as being isolationist in character, but in practice he had shown himself to be a cunning realist who understood the need to adjust American power to the complex political and economic realities now existing at home and abroad.

Fulbright could surely appreciate the irony of seeing his old adversary begin to pursue policies in line with his own views. What still worried him was that in the face of those Moscow arms agreements, the United States would continue to build new weapons systems. He thought that such an undertaking would demonstrate to the Russians "that we don't mean a word of what we said or agreed to in Moscow." Thus he opposed the construction of the proposed Trident submarine and the building of the B-1 bomber. Otherwise, as he wrote Congressman Dante Fascell, "we'll be right back where we were, only in worse position because instead of contributing to a changed attitude, we would have only reinforced their suspicions that we are determined to dominate through military hardware."[23]

The administration totally disagreed with Fulbright's position, and its spokesmen, led by Secretaries Rogers and Laird, clashed with him when they came to Capitol Hill to defend the Moscow agreements. When Rogers appeared before the committee on 19 June, he insisted that future SALT talks depended upon a continuous arms buildup and that past American success was predicated on the fact that Washington had negotiated from a position of strength. Fulbright believed differently, saying that

more force, greater spending and additional weapons will not make either side more secure. More can only lead to a deepening of the balance of terror which has enslaved this world for more than a decade. A further drive for more to achieve a shifting parity can only heighten the possibilities of a holocaust which neither side would consider thinkable.[24]

The next day, Secretary Laird spoke to the committee, and his remarks precipitated a row with Fulbright, who accused him of seeking to sabotage the spirit of the Moscow agreements. Fulbright also charged Laird with misinforming the committee in 1969 about the extent of the Soviet first-strike capacity. He said to Laird that "you scared everybody to death and got your appropriations, but the intelligence community never agreed with you and records show you were wrong." Laird denied Fulbright's charges, and offered to compare their respective voting records on health and welfare.[25] The intensity of this exchange was such that both men—in an unusual breach of decorum—spoke simultaneously, with one accusing the other of damaging the national security of the United States. Following the testimony of Rogers and Laird, Fulbright wondered just how sincere was the administration in its commitment to arms control and détente.

About George McGovern, Fulbright had no such doubts. Earlier in the year, he did not think that McGovern had much chance to win the nomination, but after Muskie's decline and withdrawal, the South Dakotan made such steady progress that by June he seemed to have the nomination within his grasp. As McGovern's position on the war was close to his own, Fulbright thought that he was a perfectly acceptable candidate, who might just capitalize on Nixon's possible vulnerability on this issue. Although he recognized the great advantage of incumbency, Fulbright believed in June that if McGovern ran a good campaign against the president he "could possibly defeat him."[26]

Besides their common position on the war, there were a number of other reasons why Fulbright liked McGovern. He thought that McGovern was an honest and decent politician who, unlike the "shrewd and devious" Nixon, would not threaten Congress or "the liberties of the ordinary people in the long run." Fulbright also believed that McGovern as president would not only move quickly to end the war, he would seek to reduce the influence of the military establishment "over our entire country, and especially over our resources."[27]

When the Democrats met in Miami, Fulbright was there working on McGovern's behalf. While speaking to the Arkansas delegation, he defended the party's platform, which called for an immediate withdrawal of remaining American troops in Vietnam, and he added that McGovern's nomination would force Nixon to end the war very soon, because it would be in his political interest to do so.[28]

McGovern's nomination meant that the New Politics had triumphed for a season inside the Democratic party. In that same mood and spirit, the convention quickly approved of McGovern's choice of running mate, Missouri Senator Thomas Eagleton, a border-state dove. McGovern had not consulted with Fulbright about the selection, but he later learned that the Arkansan had tried to reach him to recommend Congressman Wilbur Mills for the second spot.[29] After what later happened to Eagleton, McGovern surely had reason to rue the fact that he had not discussed the matter with Fulbright. Yet Mills, then among the most powerful individuals in Washington, would be politically finished in a few short years because of his own serious problem with alcohol.

After the Democratic convention, Congress went back to work, with the Senate taking up end-the-war proposals. On 2 August, it approved by a narrow margin an amendment to a defense procurement bill which "authorized funds to be used only for the complete withdrawal of all U.S. forces from Vietnam, Laos, and Cambodia within four months of the enactment of the bill provided that all U.S. prisoners held by the North Vietnamese and their allies had been released."[30] With this action, the Senate had gone on record for the first time in support of binding legislation to end the war. But the political realities were such that there was little chance that the amendment would win approval from a House-Senate conference committee.

Fulbright himself was well aware of its poor prospects in the House. In a television interview with Martin Agronsky on 2 August, he pointed out that the president's position remained secure: a majority in Congress would rather support him than challenge his policies. For Fulbright those policies were "revolting," particularly the persistent bombing of Indochina:

It is more immoral today than even when we had our 500,000 men there. There is something profoundly revolting about a big country as big as we are using technological superiority to destroy a small people who have no capacity for retaliation. I mean, in the old days of war there was a certain dignity and solemnity about a war in which each side risked its own life. You had to feel fairly strongly about the issue if you were risking your own life. But when you go into the war, when we are not risking the lives of our soldiers, it really becomes revolting to read day after day about the dropping of bombs from five miles up and killing of innocent people, I mean, civilians.

Yes, the bombing was revolting to some people, observed Agronsky, but he declared that an overwhelming majority of Congress, as well as millions of Americans, did not want to think about it and were not upset. Why was this so? he asked. Fulbright's answer was very much to the point:

Perhaps because they sense it's revolting, a lot of people pretend that the war is over and we are no longer engaged, that we are winding it down. This administration is extremely adept in popularizing the use of semantic trickery. I mean, protective reaction strikes has a sort of an innocent antiseptic air about it, instead of bombing and destroying. This sort of thing is used to a great extent. We no longer have nearly the television exposure of the war that we used to have. They don't have television teams taking pictures on live television. They can't, of course, because of what we are doing to the north. Do you remember the old days in Hue when we, on our own television, had actual pictures of many of the horrors of war. Those no longer appear. I have seen very little of that. They have put it out of their minds. It's far away. They have become insensitive to it. They'd like to forget about it and like to pretend that we now have ended the war and we are no longer in it.[31]

Fulbright's remarks, coming exactly eight years to the day after the first incident in the Gulf of Tonkin, were both poignant and insightful. He had offered a persuasive explanation of why Nixon's Vietnamization policy had succeeded so well in containing the doves at home. If his analysis was correct, it suggested that George McGovern, contrary to earlier expectation, had little hope of challenging Nixon on the war-peace issue. The polls reflected that reality all too well: Nixon's standing had been enhanced by his bombing tactics and his repeated call for "peace with honor"—which, in Kissinger's words, "was the name of the game in Indochina."[32]

As Nixon and McGovern sought to win the hearts and minds of the electorate, another struggle had already begun in the Senate over the question of the interim offensive weapons agreement, which Nixon had brought back from Moscow. Leading the floor fight for that agreement, as well as the ABM treaty, was Arkansas's junior senator. Fulbright had no trouble getting the votes for the treaty, but he encountered difficulties in finding a majority to support the interim agreement. The problem arose when long-time Fulbright foe Henry Jackson, a wily and tenacious adversary, introduced in early August an amendment to that agreement declaring that it was the national policy of the United States to maintain the principle of "numerical equality" in intercontinental ballistic missiles (ICBMs) with the Soviet Union in order to offset a decided Soviet advantage in the number of missile launchers. Fulbright argued contrariwise, claiming that the addition of this amendment would violate the "spirit" of the agreement. It was also his view that because the United States commanded a superior technology tied to MIRVs, a large B-52 fleet, and a network of Polaris submarines, there was no danger of falling behind the Soviet Union. Existing now, he argued, was a rough parity or equivalence between the two sides, which would be upset if the United States went ahead and added new strategic weapons to its already overwhelming nuclear arsenal.[33]

The ambiguous role played by the White House complicated Fulbright's task. On one hand, Jackson claimed that he had Nixon's support for his amendment. On the other hand, Fulbright felt that Kissinger was supporting him until Nixon decided to go along with Jackson, probably to ensure Jackson's support for the construction of the Trident submarine. On 14 September, Jackson won the floor fight as the Senate voted forty-eight to thirty-eight to reject Fulbright's amendment establishing the principle of "overall equity, parity and sufficiency" as the negotiating framework for any future SALT agreement.[34] Although the inclusion of the Jackson amendment in the interim agreement was nonbinding, the debate it triggered prefigured the struggle to come over the issues generated by SALT II and Ronald Reagan's challenges to Gerald Ford in 1976 and Jimmy Carter in 1980.

Following this vote, Fulbright wrote Cyrus Eaton that Nixon "has consistently been obsessed by his suspicion and dislike of Russia, up until his recent visit. I have hopes that he had had a change of heart and mind, but after the Jackson amendment, I am not so sure. He is a very difficult man to understand." Nixon's standing in the polls was not at all difficult to understand. He led McGovern by a very wide margin and seemed assured of a landslide victory. Yet despite those polls, Fulbright, in September, worked hard for McGovern, seeking to keep the issue of Vietnam alive as best he could. He reminded Arkansas Democrats that McGovern "was one of the first and most vigorous voices trying to get the President to stop the war."[35] He told them that if McGovern was elected, he would quickly end the war and seek to confront the serious domestic problems it had produced.

Fulbright's support for McGovern coincided in time with publication of *The Crippled Giant*, seen by its publisher as a sequel to *The Arrogance of Power*. Because Random House thought that a market existed for such a book, Seth Tillman put together a manuscript based on material he had prepared for Fulbright going back to 1967. Included in this new book was an updated version of that long piece which had first appeared in the *New Yorker* earlier in the year, material from speeches Fulbright had given on the Senate floor or at Yale and Denison universities, and articles which had been published in such journals as the *Progressive*. All in all, *The Crippled Giant* was an authoritative distillation of Fulbright's current views on the cold war, the Vietnam War, and the impact of militarism on American foreign and domestic policies.

The book did not have the same appeal as its predecessor; sales were far below expectations, and reviews disappointingly few. Years later both Fulbright and Tillman said that the material critical of Israel had contributed to the book's lackluster showing.[36] It may have been that the market for such a book was not there, the second time around. Whatever the reason for its poor showing, *The Crippled Giant* was not a mere trifle or simply a scissors-and-paste exercise. The book addressed the most important national and international issues from a perspective many disillusioned Americans would find attractive. Moreover, as a result of the change in the political climate produced by the Vietnam War, it constituted a significant intellectual challenge to the centrist cold war wing of the Democratic party represented by Henry Jackson and George Meany.

At the heart of Fulbright's realist critique was the argument that the United States had been using its vast power recklessly and irresponsibly— thus "fostering a world environment which is, to put it mildly, uncongenial to our society." This pattern of behavior, Fulbright believed, resulted from the excessive militarization of American foreign policy on the one hand and the globalization of commitments on the other. In a sense, Vietnam was the end product of that combined process, which in turn produced, in Fulbright's view, a serious weakening of the United States abroad and a "material and spiritual drain" at home.[37] By being more "selective" in its commitments and by disavowing ideological crusades—an outgrowth of the Truman Doctrine—the United States could prevent future disasters like Vietnam.

Fulbright's call for retrenchment, combined with his emphasis on the primacy of domestic priorities, was, of course, anathema to globalists like Jackson and Meany, who saw in his approach a foreign policy of retreat and eventual surrender to the forces of communism. As Truman-style Democrats, they were staunch advocates of victory in Vietnam and keen supporters of Pentagon spending programs. They also looked askance at efforts to improve relations with the Soviet Union. For these reasons, they were no doubt appalled that contrary views, similar to those of Fulbright, had become briefly institutionalized inside the Democratic party under the banner of George McGovern.

In the meantime, McGovern's difficulties with the voters were many, and not the least was his policy for ending the war. On 10 October, he spelled out his position by calling for an American withdrawal from Vietnam in ninety days and the termination of all military aid to the Thieu regime. Both Fulbright and Church endorsed his stand, though each questioned the propriety of cutting off aid to Thieu, saying that the matter was negotiable. Secretary Laird, on the other hand, derided McGovern's plan, contending that it "would abandon negotiations in favor of a pure giveaway program with guarantees for absolutely nothing as far as the United States is concerned." He called McGovern's plan tantamount to "unconditional surrender."[38]

Fulbright himself favored a political settlement over any precipitate withdrawal as the best way of bringing about an American disengagement from Indochina, and he thought that if the polls showed McGovern gaining on Nixon, the president would move quickly to end the deadlock in Paris. Those polls showed no such thing, leading Fulbright on 2 October to comment on the Senate floor that

> we have an election coming up. We know what the polls indicate. It may be that the great majority of people of this country believe in and support the concept of victory and to make the North Vietnamese surrender, as the Senator from Kentucky just suggested. Maybe they will have to surrender.
>
> It was not too long ago that one of the candidates for public office in this country suggested that "we bomb them into the Stone Age" . . . with nuclear weapons. At that time, when our people were a little more sensitive to matters of this kind, that suggestion was ridiculed. Now we find ourselves actually bombing them into the Stone Age, and that people approve that apparently. I think that is regrettable.
>
> . . . How the administration can reconcile the continuation of this war against a small Communist country is beyond my comprehension. If there is any reason for continuing it, other than pride and vanity, I do not know what it is.[39]

At the time Fulbright uttered these words, Kissinger was working hard to obtain a settlement before the election; he feared that without one Congress would impose its terms on the administration shortly after the election. If that happened, Hanoi would get a far better deal, because it would not have to concede to Congress what Congress would not demand. Hence he launched his great initiative to end the struggle, and to his delight, Le Duc Tho, Hanoi's emissary in Paris, indicated in early October that he was prepared to deal on terms Kissinger felt were reasonable.[40]

On 26 October, Kissinger announced that "peace is at hand" and hopes were raised that something solid had been achieved. Fulbright, on the other hand, read that same announcement as nothing more than an act of political cynicism, coming only days before the election. Publicly, however, he said that "if President Nixon ends the war on 7 November, it is better than not at all." Because Thieu had rejected Kissinger's initiative, Nixon did not want a settlement with Hanoi either before or on election day. He was concerned that his margin of victory on 7 November could be reduced if such a settlement came about without Thieu's explicit concurrence.[41]

Nixon won a landslide victory over George McGovern, providing him with the personal vindication he had long sought. Nixon's triumph also marked something of a vindication for Fulbright's own foreign policy perspective. As he acknowledged in *The Crippled Giant*, published before the election, the Nixon-Kissinger foreign policy "has represented a significant departure from the ideological anti-communism which so strongly influenced the foreign policy of American Presidents from Truman to Johnson." He added that it was "an enormous improvement on the ideological crusades which it appears, step by step, to be supplanting."[42]

Although Nixon and Kissinger eschewed ideological crusades, they were still very much committed to a containment strategy. But they also recognized that since the domestic political consensus—which had made Vietnam possible—had come apart, it was imperative to cool down the protests at home and to rebuild support for their foreign policy. In time, thanks to the cooperation of Brezhnev and Mao, several important breakthroughs were made, sufficient to give Nixon increased respectibility at home and added stature abroad.

Fulbright could support several items on Nixon's agenda. As a post–cold-war internationalist, he long favored opening the door to China and better ties with the Soviet Union. Moreover, he could welcome the administration's efforts to seek a diplomatic solution to the stalemate in the Middle East. For years Fulbright felt that American interests were too tied up with Israel at the expense of a more balanced and realistic approach to that region. On the other hand, he had always rejected Nixon's prolongation of the Vietnam War as a costly and futile exercise, disdaining completely the policy elite's argument, which went back to the early sixties, that force had to be used in Vietnam to ensure that American power would be seen as credible in Moscow and everywhere else in the Third World.

After the election, Vietnam, as expected, continued to generate controversy. Fulbright urged the White House to submit any agreement reached with Hanoi to the Senate for its scrutiny. He had taken this position because of the news that the United States would be required to spend a large sum to help in the reconstruction of Indochina. Fulbright did not oppose that expenditure per se, believing that "since we have spent billions in devastating much of Vietnam, it does not seem inappropriate that we allocate some funds for rebuilding the country."[43] His objective was to ensure that the Senate, by examining the agreement, would play the role the Constitution had designated for it.

Fulbright's obvious hopes for a quick end to the war were soon dashed, however, as negotiations which began on 20 November came to a halt on 14 December. Two days later, Kissinger announced that an impasse had been reached in Paris. That news was a major disappointment to Senate doves, who—according to Mike Mansfield—had suspended debate and criticism for nearly a month in order not to undercut or damage those sensitive talks in Paris. Now Mansfield, sensing that a "volcanic upheaval" against the war was building up in the electorate, declared that "the final conclusion of this war rests either with the President or the Congress."[44]

Dove disappointment soon turned to outrage, once Nixon ordered massive B-52 raids over Hanoi. Mansfield quickly denounced Nixon's tactics, insisting that they would only prolong the war, and he hoped that Congress would move to end this terrible agony. Fulbright, for one, still doubted that Congress would act; he did not yet believe that the votes were there for any such overt defiance of presidential will. And he soon discovered that Kissinger himself was not about to defy a now determined Nixon. On 19 December, Kissinger told him that he was going along with the bombing to save his job. That conversation, no doubt, reinforced Fulbright's conviction that Nixon was such an implacable ideologue on the subject of Vietnam that he could not bring himself to "compromise" on the issue.[45]

Meanwhile, pressure was finally beginning to build in Congress for some kind of action. Now, for the first time, Fulbright sensed that there was a possibility of getting something done. He wrote a constituent on 30 December (the same day Nixon suspended the bombing north of the twentieth parallel and announced that negotiations would begin on 8 January) that Congress was really ready to begin to move in opposition to the president's policy. Such a step, he thought, would "provoke a bloody and unpleasant confrontation with the president . . . and we can only await the event."[46]

11 *T*HE TRIUMPH OF THE OPPOSITION

When the ninety-third Congress met in early January 1973, congressional doves were in a stronger position than ever before. In both the House and the Senate they were gearing up for battle with President Nixon following his bombing blitz of late December. That change in mood and outlook was so noticeable that Senator Fulbright believed that if Nixon did not soon end the war, Congress would make a good stab at it. And congressional action might be necessary, because he felt that the "President is afflicted with some serious psychological problems. . . . I think he has an obsession with [Vietnamese] communism and cannot bring himself to accept any compromise which could possibly result in South Vietnam becoming a communist country, either by election or any other way, so long as he holds his present office."[1]

On 4 January, Senate Democrats met in caucus to discuss their next move. During that meeting, Senator Edward Kennedy introduced a resolution declaring that it was Democratic policy to immediately cut off funds for the Indochina war, "subject only to the release of U.S. prisoners and the accounting of those missing in action." It passed by a vote of thirty-six to twelve. Interestingly, Fulbright was absent from that meeting, probably because he favored another course, one which would allow Nixon and Kissinger to strike a deal in Paris before 20 January or face the prospect of certain congressional action to bring this conflict to a close. Fulbright's position was shared by a majority of his colleagues on the Foreign Relations Committee. Like him, they did not want to take action that might be construed as inhibiting negotiations between Kissinger and Le Duc Tho. Thus the Foreign Relations Committee took a wait-and-see attitude, hoping that Kissinger could deliver an agreement so that a confrontation with Nixon could be avoided.[2]

On the other hand, Fulbright was nettled by the refusal of Secretary Rogers and Henry Kissinger to appear before the committee to explain

Nixon's policy. Hence he launched another attack on the principle of executive privilege, which the White House was wont to use whenever it sought to protect its policies and personnel from serious legislative scrutiny. Although Fulbright had long since recognized that this abuse of the principle of executive privilege was a by-product of the extraordinary concentration and growth of executive power, he believed that "never before has our system of government been more threatened than it is now." If Congress failed to assert its constitutional rights, then Fulbright feared "for the survival of the system." In that same vein, he wrote a family friend that

> the question of "what Congress is convening for" is a very good one, but if you will recall, we have an inauguration coming up and there has to be an audience for all those important activities—so we will all file in and applaud at the right time, while our leader goes through the motions of being crowned.[3]

Two days after Nixon was sworn in as president, Lyndon Johnson, on 22 January, died at his ranch in Texas. Fulbright quickly issued a statement in which he observed that

> Lyndon Johnson had one of the most outstanding careers in American politics of any man in our history. . . . As a Senator and as a President he was responsible for some of the most significant legislation of our time. . . . I am saddened by his sudden death and by the fact that he did not live to witness the termination of the war for which we all fervently hope.[4]

Ironically, Johnson died the day before President Nixon announced that a cease-fire had been successfully worked out in Paris. Fulbright quickly called Nixon to congratulate him on his achievement and afterward issued a brief statement in which he suggested that "it is premature to attempt a discussion of the details of the agreement, but it is inevitable that many difficulties will arise out of the liquidation of this long and costly and bitter struggle." Elaborating on that point, Fulbright later told a television interviewer that the only way a lasting peace could come to the region "is for the peoples affected to work it out for themselves." He was aware the peace could not be achieved without, in his words, "a degree of violence." Fearing that hostilities could again resume at almost any time, he publicly endorsed a complete American disengagement from Indochina. And for that same reason, he opposed any economic aid to North Vietnam unless it were first funneled through multilateral institutions such as the United Nations or the Asian Development Bank.[5]

In his public discussion of the Paris agreement, Fulbright further declared that neither side had won a victory, and Nixon and Kissinger had made as good a deal as could be had. Yet he also observed that this same agreement could have been reached in October 1972 or even back in 1967. Fulbright said little else about it, even though he was really quite dissatisfied with Kissinger's work. He had long since favored a broadly based settlement. But since Nixon and Kissinger—like Johnson and Rusk before them—had demanded, in his words, "unconditional surrender" from the other side, such an arrangement was out of the question.[6]

Fulbright may have kept his deeper reservations about the cease-fire to himself because he knew that Nixon would be eager to settle scores with his "enemies" at a time when his power had been enhanced by that landslide victory in November. Nixon, always quick off the mark, asserted at a press conference on 31 January that "the least pleasure out of the peace agreement comes from those who were the most outspoken advocates of peace at any price." With those words serving as his cue, Charles Colson, White House counselor, told television interviewer Elizabeth Drew the very next day that the president's critics in Congress had prevented an earlier end to the war. Among those critics who, in Colson's words, constituted "a sellout brigade" were Clark Clifford, William Fulbright, George McGovern, Frank Church, and Edward Kennedy. According to him, those individuals had been the leading advocates of a "dishonorable peace," as they would have left Vietnam "without regard to consequences."[7]

But it was the issue of aid to North Vietnam rather than Colson's words that concerned Fulbright. Eager to see the program internationalized, he wrote Nixon on 5 February that

> such an approach, in my opinion, would be both good policy and good politics. It would make it easier for Congress to support aid for North Vietnam; it would deny the North Vietnamese the opportunity to characterize our assistance as "reparations," and at the same time allay their apprehensions about foreign intervention; and finally, an internationalized reconstruction program would allow the United States to keep a seemly distance for a time from an erstwhile enemy.[8]

Having stated his position, Fulbright then conveyed to Nixon his "hope for a renewal of cooperation between Congress and your Administration now that this unhappy episode is being put behind us."[9]

Yet there were substantive differences between Nixon and his critics on a number of issues, including impoundment, executive privilege, and military spending which prevented the kind of cooperation of which Fulbright spoke. On 3 February, Fulbright appeared before Senator Sam Ervin's Judiciary Subcommittee on the Separation of Powers to discuss the issue of impoundment. He said that impoundment went to the very heart "of congressional power—the power to appropriate." If Congress allowed Nixon to impose policy via impoundment, then Fulbright believed it would be acquiescing in a fundamental subversion of its explicit constitutional function and authority.[10]

Fulbright also attacked Nixon's stand on executive privilege. As in the case of impoundment, the senator pointed out that Nixon's repeated refusal to allow key administration figures to testify on Capitol Hill smacked of intolerable executive arrogance. And he denounced the size of Nixon's military budget, charging that it was a bloated request in need of major trimming. Funds taken from the Department of Defense might be better used, he said, for needy social programs, especially at a time when the economy was beginning to experience fresh difficulties.[11]

Fulbright harbored no illusion about the obstacles he and like-minded colleagues faced in challenging a seemingly all-powerful president. He knew that it was an "uphill battle" because "the President has a great advantage in the contest. The power of television is so great and perfectly adaptable to use by an individual already surrounded by a regal atmosphere, the question becomes whether Congress can develop public support."[12] Such was the state of affairs in Washington several months before the Ervin Committee began its investigation of the Watergate affair.

Although Fulbright continued to criticize Nixon's aggrandizing domestic policies, he remained relatively quiet about Vietnam and silent about the renewal of hostilities in Cambodia. As he wrote Arthur Schlesinger, Jr., on 12 February, "Pending the end of the sixty day period of withdrawal, there does not seem to be much that can be done or said about the situation." Yet he did not hesitate to discuss the matter of aid to North Vietnam. Appearing on "Meet the Press" on 18 February, he linked his support for any reconstruction program to Nixon's willingness to cut back on military spending, and he again insisted that a multilateral framework was necessary in order to facilitate a total American disengagement from the region.[13]

When Secretary Rogers came to the committee to testify in open session on 21 February, Fulbright greeted him with the declaration that the war in

Vietnam "was no longer a divisive issue." Rogers, too, appeared upbeat in his *tour d'horizon* by emphasizing that the recent cease-fire in Laos "was another important step in the overall solution to the Indochina problem." Like Fulbright, he now foresaw a period of cooperation between the committee and the administration. Yet there was still an undercurrent of concern, for Rogers admitted that the situation in Cambodia was proving difficult to resolve. The resumption of hostilities by the Khmer Rouge was complicating the administration's peace efforts, Rogers informed the committee.[14]

Whatever was happening in Cambodia, the time was not yet right for it to become the focus of major congressional concern and inquiry. The issue of aid to North Vietnam seemed far more important, and on that topic Fulbright remained outspoken. In early March, he backed away from any such commitment to Hanoi, saying that it "must first be considered alongside of our domestic priorities." For him, future support was dependent on Nixon's release of impounded domestic funds. Later in March, Fulbright returned home for some active politicking (this coming at a time when talk was growing in the state that Governor Dale Bumpers might challenge him for his Senate seat). There, Fulbright attacked the size of Nixon's military budget, charging that it was vastly inflated and out of line with the country's real security needs. He also touched on the issue of impoundment, saying that the president "had no right to cancel or negate a law." Nixon's behavior was an indication that he had "gone astray" in his effort to intimidate the Congress. At the same time, Fulbright mentioned that he was prepared to forget about the Vietnam War; serious economic and social problems at home required the country's full attention.[15]

Despite Fulbright's earnest desire to put Vietnam behind him, the situation in Cambodia could not be ignored much longer. With the expiration of that sixty-day period of grace, during which the last American troops were withdrawn and prisoners returned, Fulbright once more entered the fray. On 27 March, he informed his colleagues on the Foreign Relations Committee that B-52 raids over Cambodia had been going on for nineteen straight days. Fulbright was "amazed" to learn this and thought that the administration was obligated to explain its action as well as to provide a legal basis for it. That same day, he took to the Senate floor to ask "by what authority is the United States carrying on military activities in Cambodia?" Fulbright wanted to know if Nixon asserted the right "like kings of old—to order American forces anywhere for any purpose that suits him?"[16]

Fulbright's questioning of the legal basis of Nixon's action was seemingly prompted by remarks made on Capitol Hill a day earlier by Deputy Assistant Secretary of State William Sullivan, a close working associate of Henry Kissinger at the Paris talks. When Sullivan was asked about Nixon's authority to bomb Cambodia, he said that two lawyers at the State Department were working on it, adding that "for now, I'd say the justification is the reelection of President Nixon." That night, 26 March, CBS evening news took note of his remark, and the next day reporters asked Ron Ziegler, Nixon's press secretary, about it. Ziegler informed them that the president was responding to Lon Nol's request for assistance; in addition, he said, Article 20 of the Paris agreement—calling for North Vietnam's withdrawal from Cambodia—had been repeatedly violated by Hanoi. Whenever a cease-fire was in place in Cambodia, the United States would adhere to it, avowed Ziegler. On 28 March, as if to answer Fulbright, Secretary of Defense Elliot Richardson also defended the administration, saying that "[because there is a] kind of lingering corner of the war still underway, the United States is continuing to give the kind of support that we were giving up to the point when a cease-fire was negotiated."[17]

Richard Moose and James Lowenstein, two committee staffers, offered a different and more compelling interpretation of Article 20. According to them, "neither Hanoi's continued presence nor our bombing were violations of Article 20 because it had been clearly understood that Article 20 would not be effective until there was a cease-fire in Cambodia." They also argued that the State Department itself confirmed as much when Secretary Rogers provided the committee on 30 April with a legal brief outlining its position.[18]

While the administration was busy defending its policy on the basis of Article 20, Senators Frank Church and Clifford Case were preparing to introduce an amendment, to an as yet unspecified bill, designed to halt the further use of American military forces in and over Indochina. As Church and Case sought to find a suitable legislative vehicle for their amendment, they also argued that, because Nixon had already withdrawn combat troops from Indochina, he now needed a new grant of authority from Congress if his actions there were to be legally grounded. Their position was directly challenged by a Congressional Research Service report which the committee had earlier commissioned. It pointed out that there was no legal bar preventing Nixon from resuming the bombing in North Vietnam, Laos, or, implicitly, Cambodia. This same report also noted that although Congress had never before terminated an undeclared war, it had every right to act in this instance. Fulbright surely had to be unhappy with the aspect of the report suggesting that Nixon would not be operating illegally if he chose to bomb again, but in keeping with its conclusions, he urged his colleagues to act as soon as possible in order to put a legal clamp on the war.[19]

First on the agenda was the committee's reconsideration of a war powers bill which had been introduced in the new Congress after the earlier bill had expired because of a conference committee deadlock in the summer of 1972. When fresh hearings on such legislation opened on 11 and 12 April, Fulbright challenged the legality of Nixon's bombing of Cambodia, re-marking that the Nixon administration "will not be gotten the better of by anything so trivial as a law." He also added that it would have no trouble finding "some specious legal justification for doing exactly what it wishes to do."[20]

Action on war powers legislation was not only timely but politically nec-essary. According to John Finney of the *New York Times*, the emphasis on war powers legislation—a more abstract and future-oriented proposal— allowed the committee to defer action on the Church-Case amendment ending all military activity throughout Indochina. As Finney put it: "The reason commonly given by Senate critics for their inaction is that the 'polit-ical mood is not right' for such a challenge. But there was also concern that the committee might be blamed for the 'loss' of Cambodia if they took steps to stop the bombing and the Lon Nol regime collapsed."[21]

By 15 April, however, the political climate of Washington was beginning to change; Watergate had erupted into a major administration scandal and a personal nightmare for Nixon. His control of the government had been weakened, his power to retaliate was no longer so certain. Fulbright, ever alert to such shifts in power, pointed out during a "Face the Nation" inter-view on 15 April that Watergate had now made it possible to focus atten-tion on less glamorous problems like impoundment, presidential war pow-ers, and executive privilege. Thanks to this development, then, Fulbright thought that the balance of power between the executive and the legislature might be restored. Yet at the same time, he knew that great power remained in the hands of the executive. As he said, Congress had no practical way to halt the bombing in Cambodia, adding that if Nixon "decided to bomb Burma tomorrow, I don't know how we could stop him from it. It is the nature of our government."[22]

In actuality, the exploding Watergate crisis had already gone far to para-
lyze Nixon precisely at a time when Kissinger was urging him to bomb
North Vietnam for its persistent violations of the Paris agreements.
Nixon—himself now shell-shocked—was incapable of acting because he
was tied up in extended consultation with H. R. Haldeman, John Erlichman, and John Dean, while looking for some way to contain that crisis
before it consumed him. According to Kissinger, Nixon's dithering now
allowed North Vietnam to violate repeatedly the Paris agreement by bringing fresh military supplies into South Vietnam.[23]

In the meantime, the B-52 raids continued over Cambodia, where the
campaign to interdict supplies and troops destined for South Vietnam was
in full swing, as was aerial support for the sagging government in Phnom
Penh. Revealing information about that bombing was contained in a report which Richard Moose and James Lowenstein had prepared for the
Symington subcommittee. When they visited Phnom Penh in early and
mid-April, they discovered that American embassy personnel, including
Thomas O. Enders, were intimately involved in directing the bombing
campaign inside Cambodia. They also found, according to a statement
released by Symington's office, that the bombing "is being employed
against the more densely populated areas of Cambodia." In his memoirs,
Kissinger sought to exculpate Enders and, of course, himself, for the deaths
of many innocent civilians. Years later Fulbright defended the accuracy
and reliability of the study which his two top field investigators had prepared for the Symington Subcommittee.[24]

The release on 27 April of that Moose-Lowenstein report on the air war
in Cambodia coincided with the fast-growing congressional opposition to
Nixon's Cambodian policy. In his appearance before the Foreign Relations
Committee on 30 April, Secretary Rogers sought to defuse the opposition.
He read a State Department brief defending the legality and constitutional-
ity of Nixon's activity inside Cambodia, while arguing that Article II of the
Constitution gave the president sufficient authority to act as he did in this
instance. In short, Rogers insisted that Nixon did not need a congressional
mandate to do what he was doing, because the situation was sufficiently
ambiguous that his action could be viewed, elastically, as appropriate and
perfectly defensible from within a constitutional perspective.[25]

Rogers also justified the bombing strictly along policy lines, contending
that the point of the bombing was to force Hanoi to agree to a cease-fire, as
Article 20 of the Paris agreement had envisioned. He said that

if the United States air strikes were stopped in Cambodia despite the Communist offensive, there would be little, if any, incentive for the Communists to seek a cease-fire in that country, and the temptation would doubtless be great for North Vietnam to leave its troops and supply lines indefinitely in Laos and Cambodia.

Rogers, with these words, had tried to make a convincing case for his position. Committee members were not persuaded; Fulbright, Symington, Case, and Muskie took strong exception to the administration's bombing.[26]

Rogers's statement was lost in the uproar resulting from Nixon's address of 30 April, when he announced the resignations of H. R. Haldeman and John Erlichman and the firing of John Dean. Nixon's words produced an immediate response in Congress, where he was now perceived to be in very serious trouble. On 2 May, the Senate Democratic caucus overwhelmingly approved a resolution calling for an immediate bombing halt in Cambodia, and on 10 May, the House, which for years had supported the president, voted to place some restrictions on that bombing.[27]

That shift in mood and perception was tied to Watergate. Without that development, it is hard to imagine that Congress would have had the nerve or courage to move in a direction leading to a showdown with the president. As Fulbright put it in a televised interview with Elizabeth Drew on 19 May, "Watergate is the bursting of the boil" on presidential powers. He further remarked that this scandal "has caused the Executive to re-examine its role and to be more responsive to Congress and public opinion."[28] For that reason, Fulbright now believed that Nixon would "take heed" of any vote in Congress to cut off the bombing.

Frank Church, sensing that the time was right for action, informed the Senate on 14 May that he and Clifford Case had obtained thirty-eight cosponsors for their proposal to cut off all funding for all American military forces involved "in hostilities in or over from off the shores of North Vietnam, South Vietnam, Laos, or Cambodia." Interestingly, Fulbright and Mike Mansfield were not included on that list of cosponsors for the Church-Case amendment, which the Foreign Relations Committee would soon attach to a State Department authorization bill. Church later said he would have "welcomed" Fulbright's cosponsorship, but he thought that the Arkansas senator "might not have" joined the others because he did not wish "to trouble" Henry Kissinger.[29]

That is a point worth discussing. Fulbright had long since recognized and appreciated Kissinger's importance as the architect of détente, which Church thought was at the core of Fulbright and Kissinger's growing friendship. Fulbright also found Kissinger good company, liking his clever talk and sharp wit. Later, however, Fulbright admitted that Kissinger often told him what he wanted to hear: that is the way he did his business. In that vein, Kissinger was surely seeking to manipulate Fulbright and other critics on the subject of the war and, according to Seymour Hersh, he was remarkably successful.[30]

Whether Kissinger specifically passed the word on the need to delay legislative action on the Church-Case amendment is not known. Suffice it to say that while he was talking with North Vietnam and China about the future of Cambodia, the Senate avoided final floor action on the bill containing this amendment. But on 14 June—just as Kissinger concluded his latest round of talks in Paris and just before Leonid Brezhnev flew into Washington to begin a summit meeting with Nixon—the amendment reached the Senate floor for a showdown vote. Although the bill passed by a wide margin, Fulbright did not vote for it, nor was he paired in its favor; he was merely announced as a supporter.[31]

Why was Fulbright's endorsement so weak? Did he take this stand to help Kissinger, who, according to Washington rumor mills, was in trouble with an increasingly depressed and jealous Nixon? Whatever the reason for Fulbright's position, his lackluster effort in this instance hurt Church, who years later remembered well that Fulbright had not voted with that majority.[32]

Still, there were other issues about which Fulbright was outspoken. On the eve of the summit, he publicly denounced plans to increase military spending for strategic weapons. He called instead for a thorough reappraisal of the military budget, contending that all outward evidence now suggested Russian compliance with the terms of the interim agreement on offensive weapons systems agreed upon earlier in Moscow. This fact, he argued, "should weigh heavily in the setting of our national priorities."[33]

In addition to his speech making, Fulbright also arranged for a 19 June luncheon at Blair House for Brezhnev so that he could speak and meet with twenty influential senators, including most members of the Foreign Relations Committee. During the course of that three-and-a-half-hour session, Brezhnev sought to assure everyone there that "the Cold War was as far as we are concerned, over." He tried, also, to allay fears about the issue of Jewish emigration from the Soviet Union, claiming that only a small percentage of those who wanted to leave had not yet received exit permits. Brezhnev tackled this problem directly because he was fully aware of Henry Jackson's efforts to sabotage administration efforts to grant the Soviets most-favored-nation status after the Soviets had agreed to pay a specific sum settling a World War II Lend-Lease debt. (Jackson would have required Russia to grant the right of unrestricted emigration in exchange for that status. His effort to attach an amendment to the current trade bill, requiring such a concession from Moscow, had been cosponsored by seventy-seven senators.)[34]

After the summit ended, Fulbright quickly endorsed its results. During several television interviews he pointed out that Nixon and Brezhnev had signed a number of agreements suggesting a change in attitude which could lead to other, more substantive, agreements in the future. Among the agreements he praised was the mutually agreed-upon code of nuclear conduct that could provide both sides with an opportunity to improve relations and also to cap the arms race. Here, then, was an opportunity, in his words, for the United States to "divert more of our resources—very scarce and badly needed resources—to our internal problems rather than to foreign entanglements, especially in the field of troops and military bases." Despite that symbolic improvement in relations, Fulbright was worried about the possible impact of the Jackson amendment, saying that unless the administration could persuade Jackson to change his mind the entire affair would culminate "in a great tragedy for the country."[35]

Nixon's meeting with Brezhnev provided him with a week's respite from the harrowing ordeal of Watergate. On 25 June—the day Brezhnev left for Moscow—Senator Sam Ervin resumed his Watergate hearings, which had been delayed for a week at the administration's request. Once the president's former counsel John Dean took the witness stand, he mesmerized a national television audience with his testimony. While he talked, Congress was busy passing legislation designed to end the American bombing of Cambodia. As soon as that legislation reached Nixon's desk, he vetoed it, declaring on 27 June that a bombing cutoff would overturn "the fragile balance of negotiated agreements, political alignments and military capabilities upon which the overall peace in Southeast Asia depends and on which my assessment of the acceptability of the Vietnam Agreements is based." The House immediately voted 241 to 173 to override Nixon's veto, but the doves still lacked thirty-five votes needed to send the bill on to the Senate.[36]

Despite that failure, Congress was determined to act, so it added an amendment closing down the bombing of Cambodia to a continuing resolution designed to sustain the budgetary process.[37] If Nixon vetoed this resolution, as he was wont to do, then a major governmental crisis would quickly loom; for if that resolution did not become law, virtually all funding for every government operation would cease as of 1 July.

Because Secretary Rogers recognized the possibility of a deadlock of historic magnitude, he informed the Foreign Relations Committee on 28 June that a compromise was possible, though he did not commit himself either to a date certain for ending the bombing or the exact terms for such a deal. Not all doves favored such a compromise. Mansfield and Eagleton, for example, looked at such a proposal with horror: they construed any talk with the White House that might prolong the bombing as a fundamental betrayal of principle. Fulbright and Church were inclined to go along with it, because both men recognized that stipulating a date certain for ending the bombing was preferable to facing a series of Nixon-like vetoes that would resolve nothing. Fulbright also feared that without an agreement of some kind, a potentially dangerous executive-legislative confrontation might occur, damaging to all parties concerned. With an agreement, there would be a firm settlement to end the bombing, and the government would continue to function. Fulbright admitted that there was an "honest difference of opinion" about the matter, but he saw no other alternative except to negotiate for the best possible terms with the White House.[38]

With John Dean's testimony crashing down on his head, Nixon agreed on 29 June to end the bombing on 15 August, and he informed House Minority Leader Gerald Ford that if Congress passed legislation specifying that date, it would not be vetoed. After Ford told the House of Nixon's decision, it promptly acted by incorporating into a pending bill the 15 August date. The House also added to its bill language declaring that the use of all past and current funding for combat throughout all of Indochina was prohibited. The Senate acted without delay, approving this measure the same day it was received from the House.[39]

Also on 29 June, the Senate took up a Fulbright amendment to a continuing resolution that had already won House approval. (Earlier that day the Foreign Relations Committee had overwhelmingly approved of his draft, which stipulated that the bombing would cease after 15 August and that no funding, past, present, and future, could be used to support American military action in or over Laos, Cambodia, and North and South Vietnam.) What followed was a spirited floor debate, with doves such as Mansfield, Kennedy, and Muskie denouncing the Fulbright amendment on the grounds that it still sanctioned forty-five more days of bombing. Fulbright and Church responded by saying that because Congress lacked the votes to override a Nixon veto, the opponents of the bombing had no way to end it except through a compromise. The Fulbright amendment passed that day by a vote of sixty-four to twenty-six, with Mansfield, Kennedy, Muskie, and Eagleton voting with the minority.[40] When this measure went to conference committee on 30 June, the proviso prohibiting future funding for Indochina was dropped. The bill, minus that one section, was then quickly pushed through Congress. With that action, Nixon now had on his desk two bills that included a congressionally mandated bombing halt. Because he had made his agreement, and because he needed the funds Congress had herewith appropriated, Nixon signed them into law on 1 July.

The results of 29 June prompted two students of executive-legislative relations to declare—some years later—that this day was "the Bastille Day of the Congressional Revolution." And they had a point. After suffering through more than one hundred roll call votes since 1966, the doves had finally prevailed. They succeeded partly because Nixon had been so weakened by the effects of Watergate that—according to Kissinger—he lacked the inner psychological resources and stamina to stand up to Congress. Thus his capitulation came at a time when only Alexander Haig and Kissinger—among administration insiders—supported the bombing policy, or wanted him to resist "force majeure."[41]

Kissinger later argued that the denial of this bombing weapon deprived him of the leverage necessary to force Hanoi or the Khmer Rouge into accepting a cease-fire in Cambodia, thus making possible the return of Prince Sihanouk as the head of a new national government in Phnom Penh. He further claimed that China had been prepared to help him find a solution, but its diplomatic interest waned once the bombing card had been withdrawn.[42] For having left him in the lurch, Kissinger blamed Congress for its short-sightedness and its failure to appreciate the nuances of power. In its rush to judgment, Congress had unwittingly contributed to Pol Pot's murderous rise to power, Kissinger asserted.

Kissinger's suggestion that Congress failed to see the point of his magisterial statesmanship merits further discussion. It should be remembered that from the perspective of the White House, Cambodia was only a pawn that was manipulated for the larger policy, which always had to do with the question of who was to rule in Saigon. Cambodia, to the very end, remained a sideshow for Nixon and Kissinger, who both realized that if they had accepted Sihanouk's return to Phnom Penh, say, before 1973, Thieu would have been toppled in Saigon. If Sihanouk had taken over, it is highly unlikely that Pol Pot would have come to power. Clearly, then, the White House and Hanoi bear responsibility for what happened. Both sides militarized the conflict inside Cambodia and tied the struggle there to the struggle inside South Vietnam. Thus it can be argued that the disaster soon to overwhelm Cambodia was in no small measure precipitated by Vietnamization, which paralleled the rise and growth of the Khmer Rouge. So if Congress, according to Kissinger, misunderstood the situation in the summer of 1973, one cannot forget that Nixon and Kissinger had both rejected the recommendation of seventy-five senators who, by voting for the Cooper-Church amendment on 30 June 1970, had urged that the United States stay out of Cambodia. The administration rejected that advice and soon opened up a second front in Cambodia, thereby exacerbating a political situation that gave life to the Khmer Rouge.

As Nixon and Kissinger fumed over Congress's vote of 29 June, they also had reason to be angry at the Foreign Relations Committee for action it took on 11 July. On that day, the committee voted nine to seven to reject the nomination of G. Murtley Godley as assistant secretary of state for East Asian affairs. Godley, the American ambassador to Laos, had long since directed the secret war the United States had been waging in that mountainous and remote region of Indochina. Because of his role, he had incurred the opposition of Fulbright and Symington. Fulbright personally liked Godley, but he did not countenance someone with such an interventionist outlook in a key policy-making position in the State Department, and eight of his colleagues agreed with him. The rejection of Godley was almost unprecedented, and no one on Capitol Hill could remember the last time when such a thing had happened to an appointee at this level. Fulbright did not have the votes to turn back the nomination of William Sullivan as ambassador to the Philippines. Like Godley, Sullivan had been deeply involved in the covert Laotian war; but in this instance, only two of Fulbright's colleagues—Symington and McGovern—were prepared to join him in opposition.[43] Fulbright also took exception to the nomination of Graham Martin as the new American ambassador to South Vietnam. Martin, a longtime career diplomat known for his activism in earlier assignments, first in Italy and later in Thailand, was strongly boosted for this appointment by Kissinger, and that evidently was enough to ease him through the confirmation process.

Nixon was sufficiently upset by what had happened to Godley that he issued a statement saying that the "consequences of this committee action go far beyond the injustice done to an outstanding Foreign Service Officer." Godley's defeat, however, was merely a light rebuke to the president. The now accelerating and growing campaign for war powers legislation was a far more serious challenge to his authority and eminence. Consequently, the president informed House Minority Leader Ford that if any such bill reached him, he would veto it.[44]

Fulbright himself had not been very enthusiastic about this proposal, thinking that there was little that Congress could really do to restrain the hand of the president. He believed that public opinion, not legislation, was the best way to keep the president in check.[45] Despite that outlook, he worked hard to improve the legislation which had cleared the Foreign Relations Committee in mid-April. (At that time, he voted only "present," not "aye," because of his belief that the legislation was substantially flawed.)

When the bill reached the floor in mid-July, Fulbright offered several amendments to improve it. One would have simplified the language of the emergency power of the president in order not to give him more latitude for action than he already possessed; another would have required the president "to report to Congress on peacetime deployments of major units by concurrent resolution." Both of these amendments were overwhelmingly defeated, as was an Eagleton amendment which would have placed CIA recruits or civilians under the bill's coverage, a step Fulbright strongly favored. Jacob Javits, who feared that any substantive change to the bill would weaken its general appeal, had thus successfully fought off all such efforts to amend the committee's handiwork. On 20 July the Senate overwhelmingly endorsed war powers legislation, and Fulbright voted with that majority.[46] The bill was then sent to a House-Senate conference committee, where both sides—led by Fulbright from the Senate and Clement Zablocki from the House—sought to reconcile their differences in order to avoid the fate which befell similar legislation in 1972.

Despite Fulbright's doubts about the efficacy of such a bill, he was as responsible as anyone on Capitol Hill for helping to create a new climate in the Congress for such a serious undertaking. Beginning with his opposition to the Vietnam War, he implored his colleagues to challenge the warmaking, aggrandizing imperial presidency of Lyndon Johnson and Richard Nixon. For years, the majority of his colleagues refused to heed his rather dangerous advice, largely because they feared presidential retribution and because they generally agreed with Johnson's and Nixon's policies in the realm of national security and foreign policy.

Watergate appeared to change that situation. It now seemed that each day brought fresh revelations damaging to Nixon's standing in and out of Congress. Alexander Butterfield opened up a huge hole in Nixon's armor when he informed the Ervin committee on 16 July that the president had employed a taping system inside the Oval Office. Later in the month, the Senate Armed Services Committee publicly exposed Nixon's secret bombing of Cambodia during 1969–70, while producing evidence that the Pentagon had employed massive fraud and deception to keep Congress and the American people from learning the truth about that operation.[47]

Nixon later defended that bombing, claiming that it was a necessary tactic to protect American troops in South Vietnam, and he also said that certain key congressmen had been briefed about what was going on. Fulbright and Mansfield replied that the administration had not informed them about those raids. John Sherman Cooper later revealed that knowledge of the bombing was generally known on Capitol Hill. Frank Church went so far as to suggest that the reason the doves remained quiet back in 1969 was their fear that if they spoke out in opposition, it would have been politically dangerous. In Church's view, a condemnation of Nixon's covert attacks would have been equivalent at the time to voting against appropriations for the war.[48] Such a step might have played into the hands of the president, who could be ruthless in defending the well-being and safety of 500,000 American troops from infidels at home.

Because the situation was different in the summer of 1973, Fulbright had no compunction about speaking out. He condemned the fraud practiced by the Pentagon at the time, and he expressed political concern about the current situation in Cambodia, where bombing had been intensified, even after the White House had assured him on 28–29 June that no such escalation would take place prior to 15 August. Consequently, Fulbright invited Secretary Rogers to testify about the situation and to clarify the administration's intentions about the 15 August deadline. Rogers refused to appear, but Fulbright publicly remarked that if Nixon disregarded the injunction to halt the bombing, or continued it without receiving congressional authorization, that action would "precipitate" impeachment by making it "unavoidable."[49]

Nixon, feeling the pressure, sent a letter on 3 August to Mike Mansfield and House Speaker Carl Albert in which he assured these congressional leaders of his intention to comply with the letter of the law. He emphasized that with "the passage of the Congressional Act, the incentive to negotiate a settlement has been undermined. August 15 will accelerate this process." Nixon then went on to warn Hanoi not to mistake "the cessation of bombing in Cambodia for an invitation to fresh aggression or further violations of the Paris agreements. The American people would respond to such aggression with appropriate action."[50] Hanoi, aware of Nixon's domestic plight, would not take this threat seriously.

While Nixon was brooding over his fate, Fulbright was busy taking political soundings in Arkansas. In mid-August, he made known his intentions to run for reelection, and he hoped that Governor Dale Bumpers would find Little Rock a more attractive place to do business than Washington. While traveling through the state, Fulbright focused on the Watergate scandal, saying that it represented an effort to subvert electoral and governmental processes, and he added that the current crisis could have a beneficial impact by allowing Congress to find its proper place in the American political system. Despite his attempts to find something positive about Watergate, he discovered that it had left his constituents "discouraged and frustrated." Upon returning to Washington, he wrote a friend that "I hope my constituents agree with your views about the coming election. I have found that many of my constituents, along with Joseph Alsop and his ilk, are seeking to downgrade the Ervin Committee's work. . . . It is impossible at this time to judge just how this is going to develop."[51]

Watergate soon developed along lines Fulbright had not anticipated. Ironically, it took Nixon himself to spell out, albeit self-servingly, the larger foreign policy implication of Watergate. Speaking to the country on 15 August, he remarked that

> after twelve weeks and two million words of televised testimony, we have reached a point at which a continued, backward-looking obsession with Watergate is causing this Nation to neglect matters of far greater importance to all of the American people. . . . Confidence at home and abroad in our economy, our currency, and foreign policy is being sapped by uncertainty. Critical negotiations are taking place on strategic weapons and on troop levels in Europe that can affect the security of this Nation and the peace of the world long after Watergate is forgotten. Vital events are taking place in South-east Asia which could lead to a tragedy for the cause of peace.
>
> These are matters that cannot wait. They cry out for action now. . . .[52]

Nixon spoke the evening before Secretary Rogers formally resigned his position. Nearly a week later, on 22 August, Nixon announced that he was nominating Henry Kissinger to replace him. This news certainly pleased Fulbright. After all, he and Kissinger had a very friendly relationship in spite of their genuine and strongly held differences over policy in Southeast

Asia. At the core of their friendship was a common, though not necessarily identical, commitment to détente with Moscow and a reconciliation with China. Both favored an accommodation with Moscow along the lines of *Ostpolitik* and arms control, and each supported enlarged trading arrangements and extensive cultural exchanges. Moreover, Fulbright was in agreement with Kissinger's efforts to mediate the conflict in the Middle East along lines he himself favored: their common objective was to have Israel give up land taken from Syria, Jordan, and Egypt in the 1967 war in exchange for security guarantees and diplomatic recognition from those same states.

Fulbright and Kissinger were getting along well for other reasons. Fulbright was already attracted to Kissinger's quick mind and formidible intelligence and found him interesting and stimulating company. In addition, there was the important factor that each man looked at the world in comparable ways. Both deplored the rigid ideological anticommunism that had been so characteristic of American foreign policy. Also, the two men agreed that a given country's internal character was not an issue as long as that country did not threaten vital American security interests because of it. Hence they felt that the human rights issue in the guise of the Jackson amendment should not stand in the way of getting something done with the Russians in the area of trade and arms control. Both understood that détente was both too important and fragile to withstand repeated American poking and prying on a matter of extreme sensitivity to the Soviet leadership. Besides, believed Kissinger, the issue could be better handled in the backroom or under the table in order to give the Russians a chance to make a deal without appearing to have capitulated to the kind of public pressure generated by the implacable Henry Jackson.[53]

Their general rapport notwithstanding, the two men differed profoundly over the extremely important issue of an offensive weapons buildup. Fulbright categorically opposed the construction of the B-1 bomber and the Trident submarine, arguing that if Washington were truly serious about détente it would not seek to increase tensions in that way. He had long believed that the precariousness of the national economy required the diversion of resources from the Pentagon into more productive channels at home.

Kissinger, on the other hand, was committed to a major increase in military spending, believing, like Winston Churchill, that one armed "to parley." Or to put it differently, one acquired "bargaining chips in order to negotiate limits on current or planned weapons systems." Thus Kissinger, like Nixon, was committed to a complex policy which sought to combine a carrot-and-stick approach in the belief that it was the most realistic way of dealing with the Soviets. His modified containment perspective—a blend of George Kennan of the sixties with Dean Acheson of the fifties— placed him somewhere between Fulbright on his left and Jackson on his right. This was an odd alignment for Kissinger, because over the years he had found himself generally in far greater agreement with Jackson than with Fulbright on an entire range of issues and concerns, including the Vietnam War and the size and scope of the military budget.[54]

Kissinger's main objective in late August was to win Senate confirmation. He met with Fulbright and Mansfield on 27 August and probably got from them some sense of what was expected from him. Meanwhile, they learned from him that because of Watergate, the president's authority to conduct foreign policy had been diminished, thereby threatening those initiatives with which the Foreign Relations Committee was in agreement. Weeks before the actual nomination, Kissinger had made it known that he was planning to speak to Fulbright, Mansfield, and Clark Clifford in order to enlist their support in safeguarding those achievements, such as the opening to China and détente. When Kissinger asked Fulbright for his cooperation, Fulbright gave it after realizing that the executive was now so weakened that only Kissinger was left to defend détente from the hard-line challenge to the policy coming from Henry Jackson, a likely presidential candidate in 1976.[55]

Kissinger's confirmation was ensured because the committee shared his perspective and because key members liked and respected him. Yet the Foreign Relations Committee could not easily overlook or simply brush aside allegations that Kissinger had been directly involved with, or had been a major inspiration for, the White House's nefarious wiretapping operation. Consequently, it appointed two members, John Sparkman and Clifford Case, to examine the evidence bearing on his role in this affair. They reported that Kissinger could be taken at his word and that his contact with White House horrors appeared to be peripheral and short-term. Fulbright later confirmed, however, that Kissinger had not told the committee the truth about the nature of his involvement and the extent of his role. And he added that Kissinger failed to reveal the truth about the American role in the toppling of the Allende regime in September 1973, an event which coincided in time with his confirmation hearings.[56]

Kissinger's misrepresentations notwithstanding, committee members knew that if he were turned down, his probable replacement would be a more conservative John Connally. After facing the dilemma of rejecting Kissinger or going along with him in the belief that he would be more careful and cooperative in the future, the Foreign Relations Committee voted sixteen to one to approve his nomination; only McGovern opposed him.[57] Kissinger's pledge to cooperate with the committee in the future and his assurance that the administration would take no further military action in Indochina without first clearing the matter with Congress helped carry the day.

Fulbright issued a statement subsequent to the vote of approval, emphasizing that his endorsement of Kissinger did not mean that he was in sympathy with the administration's wiretap program, its prolongation of the war in Vietnam, or its push for increased military spending. He accepted the inevitability of the Senate's confirmation of Kissinger, and he "trusted" that the secretary of state designate would honor his pledge to work with the Foreign Relations Committee and the Congress on foreign policy matters.[58]

The Senate confirmed Kissinger's appointment on 21 September by a vote of seventy-eight to seven; he was sworn in the next day as secretary of state at a White House ceremony. Shortly after, he went to New York to attend a meeting of the United Nations. Upon his return to Washington, he took possession of his office at the State Department, and, according to the *Baltimore Sun*, his first formal act was to have lunch with Fulbright on 27 September.[59]

Despite his cordial relationship with Kissinger, Fulbright continued to fight against key administration policies. He had long since opposed the construction of the Trident submarine and had spoken out repeatedly against that project. Thus it was not surprising that he strongly supported efforts by Senator Thomas McIntyre to head off its accelerated development. Like others, Fulbright believed that its construction would only intensify the arms race without providing a modicum of additional security for either party. Much to Fulbright's sorrow, the Senate, on 27 September, rejected the McIntyre amendment by a vote of forty-nine to forty-seven. A few days after this exceedingly close vote, Fulbright quoted with approval Charles Yost's telling remark that "when Congress votes funds for a submarine it votes not for one but two, an American and a Soviet."[60]

Meanwhile, there were other issues to tackle, including those of a political-philosophical nature. On 8 October, two days after the start of another war in the Middle East, Fulbright and Kissinger appeared together at a *Pacem in Terris* convocation held in Washington under the auspices of the Center for the Study of Democratic Institutions. Each took this opportunity to defend détente and both rejected the outlook that was associated with the Jackson amendment. In his speech, Fulbright carefully approved of the Nixon-Kissinger balance of power approach to international diplomacy, saying that it marked a tremendous improvement over the ideologically driven foreign policy of earlier administrations. He wondered whether Kissinger—like Bismarck—wasn't an indispensable figure whose framework for diplomacy would atrophy once lesser talents took over. After praising Nixon and Kissinger for their achievements, Fulbright stated that their world view was historically reactionary in perspective and profoundly pessimistic about the possibilities for improving international relations and behavior. And he was also deeply critical of their "bargaining chip" mentality, averring that the Nixon administration "pursues an arms policy which undermines detente and which strains our national economy."[61] He also insisted that the American economy was now in such serious trouble that it was no longer capable of sustaining a global foreign policy without endangering domestic stability. Retrenchment was urgent in order to reestablish a proper domestic economic equilibrium.

Like many of his colleagues, Fulbright had long since recognized the complex interaction between domestic and international events. Unlike most of them, he had believed for a long time that the domestic side of that equation was the most important, a point he made repeatedly during the Vietnam War. For him the objective of a foreign policy was the "securing of democratic values at home. . . . Our national interest," he said, "has to do with the kind of society we have and only incidentally with the kind of society other people live in." Rejecting completely Kissinger's argument that the American experience had a "universal meaning," he pointedly declared that "there is meaning enough in being ourselves, a meaning by no means yet fulfilled, and in letting other people find their own meanings."[62]

Fulbright had spoken about global concerns, but there were also domestic matters needing attention. The most important was war powers legislation, which had been tied up for several months in conference committee. On 4 October, the conference committee issued a report to indicate that the conferees had worked out their differences in a manner that satisfied almost everyone involved. When he discussed the committee's work, Fulbright said that "it came out much better than I could have hoped." He himself had worked hard to find common ground with his House counterparts, whose position on a number of issues was closer to his own than, say, Jacob Javits's, a major architect and key sponsor of the Senate bill. So thanks, then, to the good will and cooperation of the participants, a report was drafted of which the main points were summarized by the committee as follows:

> The essence of the bill is its imposition of restraints and guidelines on the use of the Armed Forces without congressional authorization. Recognizing the necessity of emergency action under conditions of grave threat to the Nation, the bill restricts unauthorized use of the Armed Forces to a period no longer than 60 days.
>
> By the end of that period, the President would be required to terminate military action unless the Congress explicitly authorized its continuation.
>
> Within the 60-day period, the Congress would have authority to require termination of military action by concurrent resolution, a legislative method which is immune from Presidential veto.
>
> In addition, the bill requires the President to consult in advance with the Congress and to report in detail on any military action he may take.[63]

Congress soon passed this legislation, but Nixon vetoed it on 24 October, saying that "the restrictions which this resolution would impose upon the authority of the President are both unconstitutional and dangerous to the best interests of our Nation." He also claimed that if this resolution had been on the books during the Berlin crisis of 1961 or the Jordanian crisis of 1970, the American response might not have been the same. Congress, ignoring Nixon's message, overrode his veto on 7 November marking the first time in 1973 that a Nixon veto was not sustained.[64] Watergate and Vietnam had made it possible to pass such restrictive legislation.

There were also serious problems of an international nature that weighed down everybody in Washington. The resumption of war in the Middle East was troublesome, as Fulbright feared that it could involve the superpowers and thus undermine détente. That conflict, coupled with the resignation of Vice President Spiro Agnew and the firing of special Watergate prosecutor Archibald Cox, further strengthened the bonds already exisiting between himself and Kissinger. Those bonds were such that Fulbright, seeking to protect the secretary from unwanted public exposure, moved committee hearings with him into executive session.[65] This was an ironic development coming when it did. After all, Fulbright had been leading the fight for years for executive openness and restoration of congressional input into the policy-making process. But, because Kissinger was giving Fulbright and the committee what they wanted to hear, everyone seemed to be satisfied with these arrangements.

Fulbright was certainly pleased with his own institutional and personal relationship with the man at the center of the foreign policy network. Now that Kissinger consulted with him almost on a daily basis, he had returned full circle, playing once more the role of a privileged insider whose advice was respected and whose position and eminence were confirmed. That special relationship flourished because both men shared a similar outlook on certain policy matters—such as détente and the need for an American role in securing peace in the Middle East based on the principle of Israeli concessions and guarantees for Israeli security—and because each recognized that the other was indispensable if commonly shared goals were to be reached. Or, to put it differently, Kissinger needed Fulbright and his committee to provide him with support in the face of executive decay and Henry Jackson's challenge to détente, and the committee needed to be reassured that it was properly informed and consulted about the general purpose and direction of American foreign policy.[66]

That rapport notwithstanding, Vietnam still remained a contentious issue, as evidenced by what happened to the proposed nomination of Robert Ingersoll as assistant secretary of state for East Asian affairs. When Ingersoll appeared before the committee on 29 November, he was asked by Fulbright if there was any substance to the rumor that the administration was planning to resume the bombing of North Vietnam. Ingersoll said that if Hanoi attacked South Vietnam, then the administration would have to reassess its position and raise the matter with Congress. Actually, the State Department had been at work trying to determine whether the recently passed War Powers Act had given the White House the authority to retaliate against Hanoi in the face of other legislation forbidding such action.[67]

Like his colleagues, Fulbright was completely opposed to any more bombing. Hence he decided to hold up Ingersoll's nomination until a clarification was received from the administration. On 6 December, Kissinger sent a letter to Fulbright in which he stated that "it is our opinion that the War Powers Resolution does not supersede or otherwise modify . . . legislative restrictions. I understand this is consistent with the weight of Congressional interpretation of this Resolution." He publicly declared that if the administration decided to change its policy, it would first seek approval from Congress before resuming hostilities. Once the committee received this assurance, both in writing and in the form of a public statement, it moved quickly to confirm Ingersoll's nomination.[68]

Always the realist, Kissinger knew that it would be foolish to ignore legislation which had forced Nixon to terminate the bombing on 15 August. Thus he would have to see Le Duc Tho on 20 December 1973 without that bombing card to play, much to Nixon's outrage and Kissinger's disgust. Clearly, everything had changed because of Watergate. As Fulbright later understood, it had gone too far, thereby undermining Nixon's authority precisely at a time when détente had already become a highly politicized domestic issue.

As the year ended, Fulbright was worried about the consequences of Watergate, but at least he could take satisfaction in knowing that an active American military role in Indochina was now over: Kissinger had negotiated a cease-fire in Paris, and Congress had forced Nixon to end the bombing of Cambodia. As concern with the war began to diminish, Fulbright's attention was focused on the Democratic primary in Arkansas. Although he was eager to return to the Senate again, his political future was in the hands of Arkansas Democrats; they would have to decide whether to send him back to Washington for a sixth term.

12 | ARKANSAS RETIRES A REALIST

In early January 1974, William Fulbright officially announced that he was a candidate for reelection. It was a step he took in the mistaken belief that Governor Dale Bumpers would not challenge him for his Senate seat. Fulbright believed that if Bumpers were going to run, he would have conveyed his intention directly to him or through intermediaries who were on friendly terms with both parties.[1] Facing a Bumpers candidacy, the senator would have probably retired rather than risk defeat at the hands of an extremely popular governor.

After filing his papers in Arkansas, Fulbright plunged back into the Washington scene, where he took up the volatile issue of Americans missing in action in Indochina. In a speech to the Senate on 24 January, he castigated Hanoi for its refusal to aid those people involved in the search for missing Americans, arguing that it was in its own interests to do so because an "agreement to co-operate in this unfinished business would indeed be recognized through the world as a mark of humanity and good faith." On 28 January, the Foreign Relations Committee dealt with the issue by taking testimony from individuals who spoke on behalf of the concerned families of those missing in action. It was an emotional occasion, marked by expressions of frustration and despair from senators and witnesses alike.[2]

Several days later, Fulbright and other committee members listened to Secretary Kissinger discuss the Middle East. Afterward, Fulbright publicly praised Kissinger for his efforts to negotiate a settlement to this conflict. Privately, he asked Kissinger to help him in his campaign in Arkansas. Kissinger complied with that request by meeting with him in a well-publicized visit at the Little Rock airport on 15 February.[3] It was a media event designed to show Arkansas voters that Secretary Kissinger, at the height of his power and fame, had a close working relationship with the state's junior senator. With Kissinger's blessing now bestowed, Fulbright hoped that Arkansas Democrats would see the point and vote accordingly.

Much to Fulbright's intense dismay, Bumpers entered the primary race on 11 March, leaving him with the feeling that he had been set up. Fulbright could now either drop out or give the voters a chance to decide the issue for themselves. He made his decision to make a race of it, even though his own poll data showed that Bumpers was unbeatable. It was a decision he would later rue, but once it was made, Fulbright sought to emphasize his seniority, while stressing such issues as Watergate, inflation, and détente. He even floated a proposal to head a mission to Indochina on behalf of the Americans still missing in action, hoping in this way to blunt Bumpers's charge up campaign hill.[4]

On 25 May, the day before the only face-to-face encounter between the two candidates, Kissinger called Fulbright from Jerusalem to apprise him of the current state of negotiations. A well-publicized call, it was another attempt by Kissinger to help his friend who was now in desperate political trouble. On 26 May, Fulbright and Bumpers confronted one another, but because they rarely disagreed about the issues, there was little substantive content to the debate. Fulbright defended his record; Bumpers emphasized his desire to abolish the seniority system, a line Fulbright himself had taken in his first Senate campaign back in 1944.[5]

Faced with an opponent who nicely blended political shrewdness with a shallow populism and personal appeal, Fulbright did not have a chance, and he knew it. Bumpers won a landslide victory, carrying almost every county in the state, including Washington County, Fulbright's home in northwest Arkansas. With his triumph, Bumpers had forced the retirement of the state's most distinguished and best-known political maverick. Ironically, Fulbright lost on the same day that Wayne Morse had won his own primary battle in Oregon. When asked why Morse had won, and he lost, Fulbright answered that Morse "has not been to Washington lately," intimating that his defeat was produced by the adverse voter reaction to Watergate, which indeed was the common denominator of politics during that 1974 midterm election.[6]

After returning to Washington, Fulbright had to deal with current committee business. One such item needing his attention was the nomination of Thomas O. Enders for assistant secretary of state for economic affairs. On 19 June, the committee met in executive session to dispose of the matter. As George McGovern recollects, the discussion was animated as Enders was subjected to a barrage of questions from McGovern and others about his role in Phnom Penh in the spring of 1973. His answers, remembers McGovern, were evasive and poor, which apparently did not bother Hubert Humphrey, who wanted to forget about Cambodia, saying that it was time to put the whole thing on the shelf. McGovern also recollects that although Fulbright was very "sour" about Enders, he voted to confirm him for that new position in the State Department. Looking back at the event, McGovern thinks that only he, Church, and Claiborne Pell voted against Enders, who had so faithfully carried out Kissinger's policy in Cambodia.[7]

When asked years later how he voted, Fulbright said that he could not remember.[8] Assuming that McGovern's memory is reliable, it seems fair to conclude that Fulbright voted for Enders because he did not wish to embarrass Kissinger just after Paul Nitze had resigned as American SALT negotiator or at a time when Kissinger himself was now involved in another running controversy about his role in the Nixon administration's wiretap operation, or just before Kissinger and Nixon were about to leave for Moscow. Fulbright, of course, could not forget that Kissinger had tried to help him in his losing battle with Dale Bumpers.

In late June, there were other, more serious issues to address. As Nixon was preparing to travel to Moscow, Henry Jackson and the military were doing everything in their power to make Nixon's task of negotiating an arms control agreement harder. Without their concerted opposition, Fulbright believed that Nixon could have made greater progress in working out a constructive deal with Moscow. Nixon's problem, argued Fulbright, was not with the Russians but with that hardline Washington establishment which had taken advantage of his weakness to challenge, if not sidetrack, his boldest initiatives on behalf of arms control and the deepening of détente.[9]

The erosion of Nixon's power was such that Fulbright, like many of his colleagues, rallied to Kissinger's side in the context of the renewed controversy over his role in the administration's wiretapping scheme. This issue surfaced after Kissinger declared on 11 June that he would resign if his name were not cleared of any wrongdoing. He requested that the Foreign Relations Committee again investigate those charges which it had examined earlier at the time of his confirmation hearings. So despite the committee's private knowledge that Kissinger was no innocent in the land of bugging, it went to work in July to ascertain the truth as to whether he had lied about his role during his confirmation hearings in September 1973. Predictably, it protected Kissinger by giving him the necessary legitimacy he required just as Nixon himself was facing the clear prospect of a jury trial in the Senate.[10]

While the Foreign Relations Committee examined Kissinger's testimony of September 1973, it was again taking a look at the current situation in Indochina. On 26 June, Fulbright and Secretary of Defense James Schlesinger exchanged remarks on the subject of the foreign military assistance program. Fulbright argued that it had cost the United States vast sums while helping to perpetuate the slaughter in Indochina. Having long since ruled out any economic factor as the reason for long American involvement in the region, he wanted to know why the United States remained so active in the region. Schlesinger answered that the American presence was predicated on a moral commitment tied to a desire to preserve "a free choice" for the peoples of South Vietnam and Cambodia.[11]

Fulbright had heard a similar refrain years earlier from Dean Rusk. He told Schlesinger that

> your idea of a commitment there is a very questionable one. I do not know what the commitment is—a moral commitment because we made a great mistake in intervening and brought destruction on a country?
>
> I think there may be a moral commitment when it is settled to help some of the restoration of the basic infrastructure that we destroyed, but I do not see by any stretch of the imagination that we have a commitment just to maintain Mr. Thieu and this particular type of government. It is obviously not a government of free choice.[12]

On 25 July, Fulbright and Graham Martin, the American ambassador to Saigon, discussed the same program. Again, Fulbright opposed a large funding request for Thieu, and again an administration spokesman defended it on grounds of practical necessity. Fulbright opined that the United States would never leave Vietnam, a view that was seconded by Edmund Muskie, who himself argued that because South Vietnam was a "bleeding sore," he saw no point in giving that regime more aid.[13]

Martin's remarks clearly depressed the old doves on the Foreign Relations Committee, but by this time Vietnam had long since been superseded by other issues, such as détente, the state of the economy, and the question of how and when Nixon would leave office. The last question was answered with his resignation on 9 August 1974. On that same day, Fulbright addressed the Senate, saying that it was vitally important for the country to get over the trauma of Watergate and Vietnam. Hence, he was proposing a pardon for Nixon and an amnesty for the draft resisters. Alluding to Nixon, Fulbright said that he had come to admire his old adversary for his creative and successful attempts to improve relations with Russia and China, and he thought Nixon had moved in the right direction in the Middle East. In a key passage, Fulbright also declared:

> More than any other President since World War II, Mr. Nixon has grasped and acted upon the preeminent necessity of the post war era. As he enunciated it in his fine speech of last June 5 at Annapolis: "In the nuclear age our first responsibility must be the prevention of the war that could destroy all societies. We must never lose sight of this fundamental truth of modern international life." For his grasp of this central truth and for his diligent efforts to implement it—through "shared goals of co-existence" and the "shared practice of accommodation" as he then put it—Mr. Nixon has earned our gratitude and approbation.[14]

A few weeks later, President Gerald Ford pardoned Nixon in what turned out to be the most controversial act of his short presidency, and he also set the stage for a limited amnesty program to come.[15]

Shortly before Ford made these moves, he and Kissinger had offered Fulbright the opportunity to replace Walter Annenberg as the American ambassador to Great Britain, but Fulbright turned it down, probably because of his concern about his wife's health. Meanwhile, he still had work to do. One undertaking which had inspired him back in July and August was a projected public debate on détente. He had planned to hold open hearings that would attract Kissinger, Henry Jackson, James Schlesinger, and others. Nixon's resignation put a crimp in these plans, as Kissinger, the leadoff witness, had to cancel his scheduled 9 August appearance because of Nixon's last and most devastating crisis.[16]

When those hearings finally began on 15 August, without Kissinger, media attention was focused on the Nixon resignation and the drama of the new presidency. Consequently, as Jackson and Schlesinger failed to appear, the great debate, which Fulbright sought to provoke, never took place, and the statements offered by Averell Harriman and George Kennan were not deemed sufficiently newsworthy. By the time Kissinger finally appeared on 19 September, the momentum for that debate had long since been lost; so even his remarks generated little attention.[17]

The fact that the détente hearings began and ended in obscurity deeply troubled Fulbright, and he commented on this point and other matters in a speech to the National Press Club on 18 December. In his prepared remarks, he decried the new journalism of exposé that had shifted the focus of criticism "from policies to personalities, from matters of tangible consequences to the nation as a whole to matters of personal morality of uncertain relevance to the national interest." He reminded his audience that during the Vietnam hearings of the midsixties "our concern was with the events and policies involved rather than the individual officials who chose—or more often were sent—to misrepresent the Administration's position." And he remarked that

it never occurred to me that President Johnson was guilty of anything worse than bad judgment. He deceived the Congress, and he deceived me personally, over the Gulf of Tonkin episode in 1964 and his purposes in the election of '64. I resented that, and I am glad the deceit was exposed, but I never wished to carry the matter beyond exposure. I never had the slightest sympathy with those who called President Johnson and his advisers "war criminals."[18]

After admitting that the object of his committee's concern had been to correct mistakes rather than to punish those who made them, Fulbright noted ruefully that in recent years there had been a "surge of moral extremism in attitude toward politics and political leaders." He deplored this obsession, saying that

the media have acquired an undue preoccupation with the apprehension of wrongdoers, a fascination with the singer to the neglect of the song. The result is not only an excess of emphasis on personalities but short shrift for significant policy questions. I am not convinced, for example, that Watergate was as significant for the national interest as Mr. Nixon's extraordinary innovations in foreign policy. The Nixon detente policy was by no means neglected, but it certainly took second place in the news to Watergate.[19]

Fulbright's words notwithstanding, the singer and his song were not so easy to separate one from the other. Watergate, among other things, was a result of Nixon's paranoia, and détente the product of his political skill and statesmanship. Moreover, the exposure of Nixon's various deeds was very much needed if for no other reason than it helped to educate many Americans about the machinations of a lawless state, thereby sensitizing them to the importance of civil liberties. On another level, though, Fulbright was absolutely right: Watergate and détente did not mix well, with the further development of one affecting the reach of the other. Because of this dialectical configuration, a historic opportunity to move much farther and faster in the area of strategic arms control was apparently lost. That was the greatest and least understood tragedy of the Watergate era, as both Fulbright and Kissinger knew all too well.

The next day—19 December—Fulbright delivered his valedictory address to the Senate. He noted that early in his career his objective had been to work on behalf of an international peacekeeping organization and international education, but not much came from those undertakings. Hence, his efforts were later redirected toward fighting the "excesses of the Cold War," as well as opposing the Vietnam War. He had taken these positions not because he was a pacifist, but because he regarded himself as a rationalist who, in his words, "deplores the vanity and emotionalism which leads a nation to fight unnecessarily, or to arm to the teeth far beyond the necessities of defense or deterrence, at a colossal and debilitating cost with the overkill serving no purpose but prestige."[20]

For years Fulbright had been disseminating such views, but he noted that they "were seldom solicited and, I suspect, even less desired. But I crashed the party and offered them anyway—for better or worse." Looking back on his career, he then wryly observed that "if I am remembered, I suppose it will be as a dissenter. That was not what I had in mind, but when things go contrary to your highest hopes and strongest convictions, there is nothing you can do except dissent or drop out."[21]

CONCLUSION

Years before the coming of the Vietnam War, William Fulbright made something of a reputation for himself in Washington as an opponent of the radical right, whose call for "total victory over communism" he associated with an ideological delusion. Rarely, however, did he challenge the working assumptions of the containment center. Fulbright simply argued from the perspective of a political realist that American security interests required the containment of the leading communist powers.

That commitment notwithstanding, Fulbright began to search in the late fifties for a more constructive American role in world affairs, one which placed greater emphasis on political and diplomatic means and less on military force to uphold world order. Vietnam brought home to him, more clearly than ever before, the fact that local conditions and local histories, not machinations by Moscow or Peking, created revolutionary insurgencies. Hence, he urged policymakers to come to terms with that reality by avoiding fruitless military interventions that did little other than to squander and to waste valuable human and economic resources at home and abroad. The use of the political imagination, not the strict reliance on force, was for him the surest way to enhance American security in a global setting.

Lyndon Johnson paid Fulbright no heed, rejecting categorically his approach, which Johnson equated with surrender to the forces of communism. Knowing Johnson well, Fulbright was aware that his refusal to even consider a compromise in Vietnam had something to do with American politics. That is, LBJ was intent on holding the line in Southeast Asia because he was afraid of what Richard Nixon or Ronald Reagan would say in 1968. Anticipating the argument that Daniel Ellsberg would make years later, Fulbright understood that the long arm of McCarthyism had reached out to grab Johnson, holding him a hostage to the legacy of the 1950s.

The combination of Johnson's intransigence and the magnitude of the disaster in Vietnam led Fulbright to change his mind about some key beliefs. He now saw that the United States was vastly overextended and could no longer afford to pay for Pax Americana. Globalism, as manifested by Vietnam, had produced domestic inflation, social unrest, and widespread cynicism. In Fulbright's view, there was a basic need for the United States to put its own house in order, which is why he repeatedly stressed the point that urgent domestic needs took priority over the interventionist ethic of Dean Rusk. In addition, he realized that the time had arrived for the Senate to challenge and to check the war-making authority of the president. And as a former insider, he began to see that public opinion was something that even a senator could try to educate, in order to restrain a rambunctious, war-minded president. Believing for the first time in the political possibilities of grass-roots democratic protest and dissent, Fulbright went to work, using his position as chairman of a prestigious Senate committee with easy access to the media, to campaign for de-escalation and compromise.

Fulbright took that tack because he did not know what else to do to force the president to change his mind. Like many others, he struggled mostly in vain to overcome the built-in prejudice and tradition operating inside the American political system which favors the president at the expense of critics in Congress or opponents in the country. Given Fulbright's failure to effect much change, one can legitimately argue that his was a futile act of dissent. But what was he supposed to do at that stage, short of taking the road then traveled by Daniel Berrigan or later by Daniel Ellsberg. Simply put, he was not a radical, but a political realist who was appalled by the war's carnage, disturbed by the loss of domestic tranquility and ashamed that the country was behaving so irrationally in Vietnam. And like the "longhairs," he was essentially powerless to do anything about it except either to continue to protest or to drop out.

The situation was not static. The combination of Tet, the political challenge of Eugene McCarthy and Robert Kennedy, the defection of important advisers, and a looming international monetary crisis forced Johnson to alter his position in late March 1968. LBJ's decision to withdraw from the presidential race and to offer Hanoi a partial bombing halt went far to confirm Fulbright's point that the president's reading of the current domestic political situation was a crucial variable in determining just how his Vietnam policy would be made and why.

In 1969, that archrealist Richard Nixon comprehended the situation well; he knew that the country was fed up with the war and wanted out of Vietnam. But by deftly playing the card marked "Vietnamization," he bought time to pursue his search for "peace with honor." As long as Vietnamization appeared to the public as a reasonable way to extricate the country from Vietnam, the policy worked to lower political passions at home. Meanwhile, Nixon was doing everything in his power, including pressuring Moscow and invading Cambodia, to prevent the collapse of the Thieu regime.

Ironically, as the public temperature went down, war criticism mounted in the Senate. Nevertheless, Nixon managed to hold his own in Congress because he had the support of the House and a sizable bloc to work with in the Senate. At the same time, of course, he was making moves which most critics of the war favored, including pushing for a rapprochement with China and détente with the Soviet Union.

It is in that context that one must place Fulbright's gradual public eclipse as a leading Senate dissenter. Although Fulbright worked hard for the Cooper-Church amendment and supported other legislative antiwar measures, he eventually became tired of hitting his head against a wall. Thus Fulbright's fatigue may be one reason why George McGovern, Frank Church, Mike Mansfield, and others moved to the forefront of the legislative struggle against the war. Fulbright's relative inactivity may also have had something to do with the possibility that Henry Kissinger had coopted him at a time when he (Kissinger) was pushing for détente and an opening in the Middle East. Whatever were the precise reasons for Fulbright's loss of zest and zeal, as a major opponent of the war, he should have cosponsored the McGovern-Hatfield amendment both in 1970 and 1971, and he should have given more than the weakest possible endorsement to the Church-Case amendment in 1973.

Détente revived Fulbright's political interest, making him once more an activist in the Senate, where he now battled his old adversary, Henry Jackson. And in 1973, he emerged as a central figure in the struggle to end the bombing of Cambodia and the passage of a war powers resolution. Long before Congress had taken action on such a legislation, Fulbright believed that the war had heightened a constitutional imbalance between the president and the Congress over the increasingly vital question of how and why the United States would employ force in the nuclear age. Although his commitments resolution sought to address that complex problem, it was a minor corrective at best. Nevertheless, Fulbright's work on its behalf helped to create a more receptive environment in the Senate for the later, more significant and far-reaching War Powers Resolution of 1973. Still, he understood that such legislation was really not enough to restrain an interventionist-minded president. As a consequence of the Vietnam War, he had learned that only an aroused public had a chance of preventing such a president from making war, overtly or covertly.

If one sees the token American retrenchment of the seventies, along with that short-lived détente with Moscow, as a benefit for the American people, then Fulbright must receive some of the credit for anticipating and promoting that shift in public policy. Yet Fulbright's effort to publicize the need for limits ran up against the harder realism of Nixon and Kissinger, who looked at retrenchment as a policy of only the last resort. Like Dean Acheson, they preferred to use all forms of power to strengthen American interests in a global setting. Yet their brand of realism, however inadequate it appeared from the Fulbright perspective, was a marked improvement over the universalism of Dean Rusk. They muted ideological disagreements with Moscow and Peking and put relations with them on a firmer footing than ever before.

Fulbright's outlook was more in keeping with the general approach to foreign policy taken by Cyrus Vance, a chastened Vietnam hawk, who became Jimmy Carter's secretary of state. He saw the need to avoid the reckless and indiscriminate use of force in the Third World, and he understood the importance of stabilizing and normalizing relations with Moscow. But once Vance's position was effectively challenged inside the administration by Zbigniew Brzezinski and outside by the Committee on the Present Danger, the realism of the Fulbright perspective no longer had any real standing in Washington.

The election of Ronald Reagan in 1980 confirmed that fact, as a center-right coalition now took power clearly determined to exorcise the last of the limitationists, who in its eyes had helped to make possible the American defeat in Indochina. Peace through strength was the new-old order of the day, and woe to those at home and abroad who rejected that signal call to arms made by a popular president certain in his belief that he spoke for a substantial majority of Americans. Reagan's arms buildup, his Central American policy, and his inflated cold war rhetoric were ample evidence, much to Fulbright's sorrow, that the point of view against which he had struggled for so long had again prevailed.[1]

NOTES

Abbreviations

AD	*Arkansas Democrat*
AG	*Arkansas Gazette*
BS	*Baltimore Sun*
CR	*Congressional Record*
DH	Declassified Hearings of the Senate Committee on Foreign Relations
JWF	J. W. Fulbright Papers, Fayetteville, Arkansas
LBJ	Lyndon Baines Johnson Papers, Austin, Texas
NYT	*New York Times*
PP	Pentagon Papers, Gravel edition.
PPPLBJ	Public Papers of the Presidents: Lyndon Baines Johnson
PPPRN	Public Papers of the Presidents: Richard Nixon
PSCFR	Publication of the Senate Committee on Foreign Relations
UPI	United Press International
WES	*Washington Evening Star*
WPR	U.S. Congress, House, Foreign Affairs Committee, *War Powers Resolution: A Special Report*
WP	*Washington Post*
WS	*Washington Star*

INTRODUCTION

1. Samuel Wells, Jr., and Peter Braestrup, *Some Lessons and Non Lessons of Vietnam: Ten Years after the Paris Peace Accords,* 35; PSCFR, *Causes, Origins and Lessons,* 103; Gabriel Kolko, *Anatomy of War: Vietnam, the United States and the Modern Historical Experience,* 111–14.

2. Norman Graebner, *Ideas and Diplomacy: Readings in the Intellectual Tradition of American Foreign Policy,* vii–x.

3. U.S. Congress, Joint Economic Committee, *The Military Budget,* 88–90.

4. Paul Kattenburg, *The Vietnam Trauma in American Foreign Policy, 1945–75,* 73–75; Ronald Stupak, *American Foreign Policy: Assumptions, Processes and Projections,* 71–89.

1.   HOLDING THE LINE IN ASIA

1. Lee J. Powell, *J. William Fulbright and America's Lost Crusade: Fulbright's Opposition to the Vietnam War,* 25–26.
2. Ibid., 20.
3. Ibid., 241.
4. Eugene Brown, *J. W. Fulbright: Advice and Dissent,* 29–30.
5. Haynes Johnson and Bernard Gwertzman, *Fulbright: The Dissenter,* 468–69.
6. Powell, *Fulbright,* 16, 27; Brown, *Fulbright,* 25–27.
7. Powell, *Fulbright,* 29–30.
8. Lawrence Kaplan, *The United States and NATO: The Formative Years,* 52–57.
9. See Fulbright's speech of 18 January 1951 in Series 72, Box 8, Folder 18, JWF.
10. Powell, *Fulbright,* 39–41.
11. Brown, *Fulbright,* 28; Powell, *Fulbright,* 39–41.
12. Brown, *Fulbright,* 39–41.
13. Powell, *Fulbright,* 28.
14. See Fulbright's speech of 6 March 1952 in Series 72, Box 8, Folder 18, JWF.
15. Powell, *Fulbright,* 41–45.
16. Fulbright, interview with the author; Frank Church, interview with the author.
17. I. F. Stone, *In a Time of Torment,* 331–32.
18. Brown, *Fulbright,* 32–37.
19. CR, 103 (11 February 1957): 1855–69; ibid., 103 (5 March 1957): 3129.
20. CR, 104 (6 August 1958): 16317–20.
21. Brown, *Fulbright,* 37.
22. Fulbright to R. B. McCallum, 14 January 1960, Series 88, File 4, JWF.
23. Ronald Steel, *Walter Lippmann and the American Century,* 523–24; Herbert Parmet, *JFK: The Presidency of John F. Kennedy,* 67–68.
24. Fulbright to McCallum, 7 January 1961, Series 88, File 2, JWF.
25. Fulbright, interview with the author.
26. See television transcript in Series 72, Box 19, Folder 12, JWF.
27. Fulbright, interview with the author.
28. Brown, *Fulbright,* 33.
29. PSCFR, *The U.S. Government, Part I,* 322, 328.
30. J. W. Fulbright, *Old Myths and New Realities and Other Commentaries,* 68–78.
31. CR, 107 (24 July 1961): 12280–81.
32. Ibid.
33. Fulbright to Keith Peterson, 22 July 1961, Series 48, Box 19, Folder 12, JWF.
34. J. W. Fulbright, *Prospects for the West,* 114; J. W. Fulbright, "American Foreign Policy in the 20th Century under an 18th Century Constitution," 1–14.
35. George Ball, *The Past Has Another Pattern: Memoirs,* 370–74; Parmet, *JFK,* 335.
36. Church, interview with the author.
37. See television transcript in Series 72, Box 22, Folder 20, JWF.
38. PSCFR, *U.S. Government, Part II,* 110, 143; George Herring, *America's Longest War,* 105.
39. Fulbright, interview with the author.
40. PP, 2:746; Fulbright, interview with the author.

2. FULBRIGHT GOES ALONG

1. President's Appointment File, LBJ; Anthony Austin, *The President's War*, 120; a perceptive cameo essay on the Fulbright-Johnson relationship is found in David Halberstam, *The Powers That Be*, 697–711.

2. Fulbright to McCallum, 9 December 1963, Series 88, File 2, JWF.

3. Doris Kearns, *Lyndon Johnson and the American Dream*, 205.

4. Lyndon Johnson, *The Vantage Point: Perspectives on the Presidency, 1963–69*, 42–68, 102.

5. President's Appointment File, LBJ; Fulbright, *Old Myths*, V–VIII; CR, 110 (25 March 1964): 6230–32.

6. CR, 110 (25 March 1964): 6230–32; Fulbright to George Kennan, 30 March 1964, Series 73, Box 23, Folder 1, JWF; PPPLBJ, 1963–64: 428.

7. CR, 110 (25 March 1964): 6230–32.

8. Ibid.

9. Ibid., 6238–44.

10. PP, 3:712–15; Fulbright, interview with the author; Seth Tillman, interview with the author.

11. PP, 3:50–51.

12. President's Appointment File, LBJ.

13. Steel, *Lippmann*, 550; see the transcript of this program in Series 72, Box 35, Folder 7, JWF.

14. Fulbright to W. C. Holland, 5 June 1964, Series 48, Box 35, Folder 1, JWF.

15. PP, 3:171–76.

16. PPPLBJ, 1963–64: 734.

17. George Ball, interview with the author; Mike Manatos, interview with the author; Fulbright, interview with the author.

18. Ball, interview with the author; Ball, *The Past*, 360–77.

19. Fred Dutton, interview with the author; Fulbright, interview with the author.

20. Manatos, interview with the author; Fulbright, interview with the author; Ball, interview with the author; Frank Valeo, interview with the author; see also Tristram Coffin, "Washington Watch," in Series 48, Box 45, Folder 1, JWF.

21. Austin, *President's War*, 112; Fulbright, interview with the author; Dutton, interview with the author; Ball, interview with the author.

22. Joseph Goulden, *Truth Is the First Casualty: The Gulf of Tonkin Affair: Illusion and Reality*, 30.

23. Steel, *Lippmann*, 544.

24. Fulbright, interview with the author.

25. PP, 3:78–82.

26. UPI dispatch, 30 July 1964, Series 78, Box 54, Folder 4, JWF.

27. PP, 5:339–41; Fulbright, interview with the author; see also PSCFR, *Hearings on S. 376*, 571.

28. Dutton, interview with the author.

29. Wayne Morse to Norman Thomas, 4 August 1964, Foreign Relations, 1964, Box 50, Wayne Morse Papers; Herring, *America's Longest War*, 121–22.

30. Mark Stoler, "Aiken, Mansfield and the Tonkin Gulf Crisis," PPPLBJ, 1963–64: 927.

31. John Sherman Cooper, interview with the author; I. F. Stone, *Polemics and Prophecies,* 309; Ball, interview with the author.

32. Manatos, interview with the author; Fulbright, interview with the author; CR, 110 (6 August 1964): 19403; Goulden, *Truth Is the First Casualty,* 152.

33. Fulbright, interview with the author.

34. David Halberstam, *The Best and the Brightest,* 150; Fulbright, interview with the author; PPPLBJ, 1963–64: 934; PSCFR, *The U.S. Government, Part II,* 334–35; Warren Cohen, *Dean Rusk,* 218; Kearns, *Johnson,* 328; Fulbright, interview with the author.

35. CR, 110 (6 August 1964): 18399–400.

36. Dutton, interview with the author.

37. Fulbright, interview with the author; CR, 110 (6 August 1964): 18402–10; ibid. (7 August 1964): 18457–60.

38. Ibid. (6 August 1964): 18403; George McGovern, *Grassroots: The Autobiography of George McGovern,* 103.

39. Allen Ellender, Oral History Interview, LBJ; CR, 110 (7 August 1964): 18471; ibid., 116 (10 July 1970): S. 11025.

40. PSCFR, *Causes and Origins,* 54.

41. CR, 116 (9 June 1970): S. 8635–6.

42. Fulbright to John Wallis, 19 August 1964, Series 63, Box 13, Folder 1, JWF.

43. Dutton, interview with the author, Series 72, Box 4, Folder 24, JWF.

44. PP, 3:192–95; DH, Executive Session, 8 January 1965, 165–68.

45. PPPLBJ, 1963–64: 1164; Bundy to Johnson, 1 October 1964, National Security File, Vol. 7, LBJ.

46. Ball, *The Past,* 380–85; Larry Berman, *Planning a Tragedy,* 49–50.

47. Ball, interview with the author.

48. Tillman, interview with the author; Ball, interview with the author; PP, 3:239; Fulbright to McCallum, 27 November 1964, Series 88, File 3, JWF.

49. NYT, 9 December 1964.

50. Bundy to Johnson, 9 December 1964, National Security File, Vol. 8, LBJ.

51. Bundy, interview with the author; Fulbright, interview with the author; Dutton, interview with the author.

3. THE BREAK WITH JOHNSON

1. Mike Mansfield to Lyndon Johnson, 9 December 1964, National Security File, Name File, Container 3, LBJ; Lyndon Johnson to Mike Mansfield, 17 December 1964, National Security File, Name File, Container 3, LBJ.

2. Tristram Coffin, *Senator Fulbright: Portrait of a Public Philosopher,* 225.

3. Cohen, *Rusk,* 244–46; DH, 8 January 1965, 167–68.

4. Douglass Cater to Lyndon Johnson, 26 January 1965, National Security File, Country File, Container 12, LBJ; AG, 15, 21 February 1965; *Christian Science Monitor,* 16 February 1965.

5. PP, 3:321–26, 330.

6. Louis Menashe and Ronald Radosh, eds., *Teach-ins: USA, Reports, Opinions, Docu-*

ments; Fred Halstead, *Out Now: A Participant's Account of the American Movement against the Vietnam War*, 40.

7. John Sherman Cooper, interview with the author; McGeorge Bundy, interview with the author.

8. BS, 2 February 1971.

9. Fulbright to Ernest Deane, 3 March 1965, Series 48, Box 29, Folder 4, JWF; Series 72, Box 24, Folder 21, JWF.

10. Fulbright, interview with the author.

11. Fulbright to McCallum, 31 March 1965, Series 88, File 3, JWF.

12. Fulbright to Johnson, 2 April 1965 (a copy is in the author's possession).

13. Ibid.

14. Kolko, *Anatomy of War*, 163–75; Johnson, *The Vantage Point*, 133–34.

15. PPPLBJ, 1965: 471.

16. Fulbright, interview with the author.

17. Series 72, Box 24, Folder 21, JWF.

18. See Piero Gleyesis, *The Dominican Crisis*, for a superior analysis of this affair.

19. DH, 30 April 1965, 17.

20. Fulbright, interview with the author; Fulbright to Harry Sions, 2 June 1965, Series 48, Box 7, Folder 2, JWF.

21. Fulbright, interview with the author.

22. Ibid.

23. CR, 111 (7 June 1965): 12732–33.

24. Ibid., 12736–40.

25. Fulbright, interview with the author; CR, 111 (15 June 1965): 13656–58.

26. CR, 111 (15 June 1965): 13656–58.

27. See transcript of this interview in Series 72, Box 35, Folder 7, JWF.

28. Ibid.

29. Ibid.

30. *A Record*, Dorothy Territo File, LBJ; PPPLBJ, 1965: 675–76.

31. *Newsweek*, 28 June 1965, 20; Louis Harris, *The Anguish of Change*, 58.

32. Harry McPherson, Oral History Interview, LBJ.

33. Ibid.

34. Berman, *Planning a Tragedy*, 193.

35. Fulbright to McCallum, 19 July 1965, Series 88, File 3, JWF; Fulbright, interview with the author.

36. See Allen Ellender's remarks in CR (1 March 1966): 4349; Fulbright, interview with the author.

37. Carl Marcy to Fulbright, 17 August 1965, Series 48, Box 16, Folder 2, JWF.

38. Halberstam, *The Powers*, 699; Fulbright, interview with the author.

39. Ibid.

40. CR, 111 (15 September 1965): 23855–61.

41. See favorable correspondence in Series 71, Box 31, Folder 7, JWF; AG, 18 September 1965.

42. J. William Fulbright, *The Arrogance of Power*, 59–60; AG, 17, 18 September 1965; George McGovern, interview with the author.

43. This interview is found in Series 71, Box 31, Folder 5, JWF.

44. Ibid.

45. Fulbright, interview with the author; Fulbright to Johnson, 7 October 1965, Series 1, Box 3, Folder 1, JWF.

46. Jack Valenti to Johnson, 19 October 1965, White House Central File, Fulbright, Container 287, LBJ; Fulbright, interview with the author.

47. Fulbright to Ben Cohen, 19 November 1965, Series 48, Box 7, Folder 4, JWF; CR, 111 (22 October 1965): 27465.

48. A transcript of this interview is found in Series 72, Box 27, Folder 24, JWF.

49. Ibid.

50. *Facts on File,* 21–27 October 1965, 381; Fulbright to Cohen, 19 November 1965, Series 48, Box 7, Folder 4, JWF; Halberstam, *The Powers,* 700–701.

51. That speech is found in Series 72, Box 25, Folder 15, JWF.

52. Fulbright to William French, 21 December 1965, Series 48, Box 7, Folder 4, JWF.

4. JOINING THE OPPOSITION

1. Fulbright, interview with the author; Bernard Fall, *Street without Joy: Insurgency in Indochina, 1946–63*; Fall, *The Two Vietnams: A Political and Military Analysis*; Carl Marcy, interview with the author.

2. CR, 112 (24 January 1966): 908.

3. Johnson, *The Vantage Point,* 232–39; Fulbright to William Baggs, 12 January 1966, Series 48, Box 8, Folder 4, JWF.

4. DH, 24 January 1966, 25–45; WP, 25 January 1966; George Kahin and John Lewis, *The United States in Vietnam.*

5. Marcy, interview with the author; Series 72, Box 25, Folder 18–19, JWF.

6. Notes on that meeting are found in the President's Appointment File, Container 28, LBJ.

7. PSCFR, *Supplemental Foreign Assistance, 1966,* 1–98.

8. Church, interview with the author.

9. Manatos, interview with the author.

10. PPPLBJ, 1966: 114; Dutton, interview with the author.

11. H. H. Wilson to Lyndon Johnson, 18 February 1966, FG 431/FR, Container 342, LBJ.

12. CR, 112 (2 February 1966): 1941–43.

13. Ibid.

14. PSCFR, *Supplemental Foreign Assistance, 1966,* 99–200; PPPLBJ, 1966: 144–45; Marcy, interview with the author.

15. A transcript of Fall's testimony is found in Series 72, Box 4, Folder 1, JWF.

16. PSCFR, *Supplemental Foreign Assistance, 1966,* 226–32; CR, 112 (1 March 1966): 4385–86.

17. PSCFR, *Supplemental Foreign Assistance, 1966,* 332–35.

18. PPPLBJ, 1966: 174; PSCFR, *Supplemental Foreign Assistance, 1966,* 439.

19. PSCFR, *Supplemental Foreign Assistance, 1966,* 563–76, 650–51.

20. Fulbright to Fritz Friedman, 10 March 1966, Series 48, Box 48, Folder 1, JWF; Church, interview with the author; a good, brief discussion of this point is found in Cecil

Crabb and Pat Holt, *Invitation to Struggle: Congress, the Presidency and Foreign Policy,* 35–56.

21. This transcript is found in Series 72, Box 24, Folder 8, JWF.

22. Arthur M. Schlesinger, Jr., *Robert Kennedy and His Times,* 736; Joseph Califano to Lyndon Johnson, 19 February 1966, White House Central File, Name File, Container 287, LBJ; PPPLBJ, 1966: 211–15.

23. CR, 112 (1 March 1966): 4381–82.

24. Fulbright to Marriner Eccles, 1 March 1966, Series 48, Box 47, Folder 6, JWF; AG, 6 February 1966.

25. AG, 2 March 1966; CR, 112 (1 March 1966): 4404; Wayne Morse to Fulbright, 3 March 1966, and Fulbright to Wayne Morse, 4 March 1966, Series 48, Box 49, Folder 2, JWF.

26. Fulbright, interview with the author; CR, 112 (1 March 1966): 4383.

27. CR, 112 (7 March 1966): 5145–50.

28. Peter Harkness and Buel Patch, *China and U.S. Far East Policy: 1945–1966,* 279, 287, 292.

29. This transcript is found in Series 72, Box 25, Folder 29, JWF; Fulbright, interview with the author.

30. Harkness and Patch, *China and U.S.,* 282, 292; Fulbright, interview with the author.

31. WP, 14 June 1966.

32. Fulbright to McCallum, 21 March 1966, Series 88, File 3, JWF; Fulbright to Johnson, 19 March 1966, and Johnson to Fulbright, 22 March 1966, National Security File, Country File, Vietnam, Container 212, LBJ.

33. Fulbright to Louis Sohn, 31 March 1966, Series 48, Box 35, Folder 4, JWF; CR, 112 (25 March 1966): 6749–53.

34. CR, 112 (25 March 1966): 6749–53.

35. Ibid. (7 March 1966): 5145–50.

36. Fulbright, interview with the author; Ball, interview with the author; Stuart Symington, interview with the author.

37. CR, 112 (17 May 1966): 10812.

38. Ibid. (25 April 1966): 8869–74.

39. Ibid.

40. Ibid. (28 April 1966): 9325–30.

41. Ibid.

42. This speech is found in Series 72, Box 28, Folder 18, JWF.

43. Ibid.

44. CR, 112 (17 May 1966): 10805–10.

45. Brown, *Fulbright,* 79–87.

46. *Facts on File,* 12–18 May 1966, 173; Harkness and Patch, *China and U.S.,* 187.

47. PPPLBJ, 1966: 496, 502.

48. WP, 28 April 1966; *Life,* 13 May 1966, 4: Harrison Salisbury's *Without Fear or Favor* captures well the position of the *Times* for this period.

49. WS, 18 May 1966.

50. Johnson to Fulbright, 27 May 1966, White House Confidential File, Name File, Container 3, LBJ; William Sullivan, *The Bureau: My Thirty Years in Hoover's FBI,* 64–65, 235.

51. Marcy, interview with the author; Fulbright, interview with the author; Lee Williams, interview with the author.

52. Williams, interview with the author.

53. DH, 30 April 1965, 14–15; Ball, *The Past,* 379; CR, 114 (27 March 1968): 7387.

54. Fulbright, interview with the author; Milward Simpson to Fulbright, 15 June 1966, Series 48, Box 8, Folder 2, JWF.

55. Coffin, *Senator Fulbright,* 313; Fulbright to Chester Bowles, 17 June 1966, Series 48, Box 30, Folder 2, JWF.

56. Fulbright to George Pine, 11 July 1966, Series 72, Box 26, Folder 14, JWF.

57. PPPLBJ, 1966: 718–22.

58. CR, 112 (22 July 1966): 16808–11.

59. A transcript of Moyers's interview is found in the Fred Panzer File, Container 331, LBJ; Dutton, interview with the author.

60. Robert Kinter to Johnson, 28 July 1966, White House Central File, Fulbright, Container 284, LBJ; WP, 25 July 1966.

61. Fulbright to Lewis Douglas, 28 July 1966, Series 48, Box 47, Folder 6, JWF.

62. BS, 23 August 1966; Hubert Humphrey to Fulbright, 17 August 1966, Series 1, Box 11, Folder 5, JWF.

63. WS, 1 September 1966.

64. *Knoxville Journal,* 12 September 1966.

65. See transcript in Series 72, Box 27, Folder 15, JWF.

66. Fulbright to Barbara Tuchman, 20 September 1966, Series 48, Box 27, Folder 6, JWF.

67. AG, 27 October 1966; Fulbright to Lewis Douglas, 22 October 1966, Series 48, Box 47, Folder 6, JWF.

68. Fulbright to Bill Moyers, 1 November 1966, Series 78, Box 20, Folder 1, JWF.

69. Johnson to Fulbright, 3 November 1966, Series 1, Box 3, Folder 5, JWF; WS, 5 November 1966.

70. Harkness and Patch, *China and U.S.,* 203; Herring, *America's Longest War,* 168.

71. Marcy to Fulbright, 28 November 1966, Series 48, Box 16, Folder 3, JWF; WP, 5 December 1966.

72. A copy of that speech is found in Series 72, Box 27, Folder 21, JWF.

5.　　DEADLOCK: I

1. A transcript of this press conference is found in Series 72, Box 27, Folder 3, JWF.

2. Tillman, interview with the author.

3. Fulbright, *Arrogance,* 188–96.

4. *Facts on File,* 12–18 December 1968, 546; Fulbright, interview with the author.

5. See transcripts in Series 72, Box 27, Folder 27, JWF; *I. F. Stone's Weekly,* 30 January 1967, 2; Associated Press dispatch, 24 January 1967.

6. NYT *Book Review,* 19 February 1967.

7. Fulbright to Bennett Cerf, 17 January 1967, Series 70, Box 14, Folder 1, JWF.

8. WP *Book Week,* 19 February 1967.

9. Fulbright's statement is found in Series 72, Box 27, Folder 29, JWF; WP *Book Week,* 19 February 1967.

10. *Facts on File,* 2–8 March 1967; Harkness and Patch, *China and U.S.,* 319; PSCFR, *Salisbury's Trip*; Merle Miller, *Lyndon: An Oral Biography,* 473.

11. Robert Kinter to Lyndon Johnson, 3 February 1967, White House Central File, Fulbright, Container 287, LBJ; Manatos, interview with the author.

12. Fulbright, interview with the author; Marcy, interview with the author; Church, interview with the author.

13. Harry Ashmore, Oral History Interview, LBJ.

14. NYT, 1 March 1967; CR, 113 (28 February 1967): 4715–19; Walter Zelman, *Senate Dissent and the Vietnam War, 1964–68,* 307.

15. Fulbright's statement is found in Series 72, Box 28, Folder 6, JWF.

16. Schlesinger, *Kennedy,* 772–73; PPPLBJ, 1967: 348–54; *Facts on File,* 9–15 April 1967, 115.

17. Fulbright to William Pennix, 31 January 1967, Series 48, Box 53, Folder 4, JWF; *Facts on File,* 9–15 April 1967, 145.

18. CR, 113 (25 April 1967): 10611–12.

19. *Facts on File,* 4–10 May 1967, 145; see transcript in Series 72, Box 28, Folder 14, JWF; Fulbright to Carl Reiner, 1 May 1967, Series 48, Box 53, Folder 2, JWF.

20. *Newsday,* 4 May 1967; Mendel Rivers to Fulbright, 22 May 1967, and Fulbright to Rivers, 23 May 1967, Series 48, Box 53, Folder 32, JWF.

21. Zelman, *Senate Dissent,* 308–9.

22. Fulbright to Irma Jennings, 22 May 1967, Series 48, Box 52, Folder 2, JWF; Fulbright to McCallum, 7 June 1967, Series 88, File 3, JWF.

23. Fulbright to Lyndon Johnson, 19 June 1967, Series 1, Box 3, Folder 7, JWF; Fulbright to Harold Mack, 13 July 1967, Series 48, Box 52, Folder 6, JWF.

24. Godfrey Hodgson, *America in Our Time,* 263–401; Fulbright to Tristram Coffin, 29 July 1967, Series 48, Box 51, Folder 3, JWF.

25. CR, 113 (31 July 1967): 20702.

26. WP, 2 August 1967; W. W. Rostow to Lyndon Johnson, 3 August 1967, National Security File, Country File, Box 56, LBJ.

27. Fulbright, interview with the author.

28. CR, 113 (9 August 1967): 22126–29.

29. Ibid.

30. Ibid.

31. Fulbright to Benjamin Spock, 15 May 1967, Series 48, Box 50, Folder 2, JWF.

32. Fulbright to David Barber, 24 July 1967, Series 48, Box 50, Folder 2, JWF.

33. See speech in Series 72, Box 32, Folder 11, JWF.

34. Fulbright to Perrin Jones, 14 August 1967, Series 48, Box 52, Folder 2, JWF; CR, 113 (9 August 1967): 22126–29.

35. Paul Joseph, *Cracks in the Empire: State Politics in the Vietnam War,* 220–21; Herring, *America's Longest War,* 178; WS, 14 August 1967.

36. Fulbright's statement is found in Series 72, Box 29, Folder 3, JWF.

37. PSCFR, *United States Commitments,* 83–84.

38. PSCFR, *U.S. Government, Part II,* 334–35; Zelman, *Senate Dissent,* 95.

39. PPPLBJ, 1967: 178.

40. *Facts on File,* 7–13 September 1967, 371; Fulbright to Robert Lasch, 23 September 1967, Series 48, Box 52, Folder 4, JWF.

41. This speech is found in Series 72, Box 29, Folder 4, JWF; Fulbright to Erich Fromm, 31 October 1967, Series 48, Box 5, Folder 5, JWF.

42. WPR, 19, 21–22.

43. CR, 113 (30 November 1967): 34363.

44. NYT, 1 December 1967; see transcript of this press conference in Section 72, Box 29, Folder 25, JWF.

45. See transcript in Section 72, Box 29, Folder 25, JWF; *Memphis Commercial Appeal*, 11 November 1967.

46. Mike Manatos to Lyndon Johnson, 28 November 1967, FG 431/FR, Container 342, LBJ.

47. Cohen, *Rusk*, 288; NYT, 13 October 1967.

48. CR, 113 (8 December 1967): 35557–60.

6.   CONTAINING THE CENTER

1. Fulbright to Lewis Douglas, 9 January 1968, Section 48, Box 54, Folder 4, JWF; Fulbright to Lewis Douglas, 20 January 1968, Series 48, Box 54, Folder 4, JWF; Series 72, Box 30, Folder 1, JWF.

2. Fulbright to Lewis Douglas, 20 January 1968, Series 48, Box 54, Folder 4, JWF; Fulbright to Erich Fromm, 1 February 1968, Series 48, Box 54, Folder 4, JWF.

3. See transcript in Series 72, Box 30, Folder 1, JWF; *U.S. News and World Report,* 5 February 1968, 31.

4. Herring, *America's Longest War,* 184–85; Don Oberdorfer, *Tet!,* 172–73, 259; Harris, *Anguish,* 64.

5. Fulbright to Johnson, 7 February 1968, Series 48, Box 16, Folder 5, JWF; Zelman, *Senate Dissent,* 103–4; Marcy, interview with the author.

6. PSCFR, *The Gulf of Tonkin,* 82–83.

7. Ibid., 29–33.

8. Stone, *Polemics,* 326–39; Fulbright, interview with the author.

9. This transcript is found in Series 72, Box 30, Folder 8, JWF; Kolko, *Anatomy of War,* 312–20.

10. Harry McPherson to Lyndon Johnson, 26 February 1968, McPherson File, Box 44, LBJ; President's Appointment File, LBJ.

11. CR, 114 (7 March 1968): 5645, 5653, 5656; Marcy, interview with the author.

12. NYT, 10 March 1968; ibid., 12 March 1968.

13. Fulbright to Barbara Tuchman, 18 March 1968, Series 48, Box 55, Folder 4, JWF.

14. Herbert Schandler, *The Unmasking of a President: Lyndon Johnson and Vietnam,* 308; Cohen, *Rusk*, 307–11.

15. AG, 28 March 1968; Schlesinger, *Kennedy,* 851–53; Series 72, Box 30, Folder 12, JWF.

16. A copy of this speech is found in Series 72, Box 30, Folder 11, JWF.

17. Ibid.

18. Brown, *Fulbright,* 88–102.

19. Hans J. Morgenthau, *A New Foreign Policy for the United States,* 3, 243.

20. BS, 3 April 1968; CR, 114 (2 April 1968): 8569–77.

21. A transcript of this press conference is found in Series 72, Box 30, Folder 12, JWF; Joseph, *Cracks,* 279.

22. Fulbright to Frederick Rebsamen, 22 April 1968, Series 48, Box 55, Folder 3, JWF.

23. Tristram Coffin, *Washington Watch,* Series 48, Box 45, Folder 1, JWF.

24. Harry Ashmore to Fulbright, 17 April 1968, Series 48, Box 54, Folder 1, JWF.

25. *Memphis Commercial Appeal,* 2 August 1968; *Pine Bluff Commercial,* 31 July 1968.

26. Fulbright, interview with the author.

27. A copy of his proposed plank is found in Series 72, Box 30, Folder 18, JWF.

28. Ibid.

29. Fulbright to Ernest Gruening, 2 September 1968, Series 63, Box 15, Folder 4, JWF.

30. Fulbright, interview with the author.

31. WP, 7 February 1970; see also Robert Baker, *Wheeling and Dealing: Confessions of a Capitol Hill Operator,* 270, 273.

32. This speech is found in Series 72, Box 30, Folder 27, JWF.

33. NYT, 26 November 1968.

34. Series 72, Box 30, Folder 30, JWF.

7. AGAINST MILITARISM AND VIETNAMIZATION

1. AD, 16 January 1969.

2. WES, 27 January 1969.

3. UPI dispatch, 4 February 1969, Series 78, Box 65, Folder 1, JWF.

4. Fulbright, interview with the author; Symington, interview with the author.

5. AG, 7 February 1969; Seymour Hersh, *The Price of Power: Kissinger in the Nixon White House,* 25–45; Henry Kissinger, *White House Years,* 39–48.

6. WES, 14 March 1969; BS, 18 March 1969.

7. PSCFR, *Strategic and Foreign Policy Implications,* 184, 185.

8. Ibid., 233–34; Kissinger, *White House Years,* 247; William Shawcross, *Sideshow: Kissinger, Nixon and the Destruction of Cambodia,* 32; Cooper, interview with the author; Church, interview with the author.

9. PSCFR, *Briefing by Secretary of State Rogers,* 4–6.

10. Fulbright, interview with the author; CR, 115 (15 August 1972): S. 13567–69.

11. Erwin Knoll and Judith McFadden, eds., *American Militarism: 1970,* 53–54.

12. David Shoup, "The New American Militarism," 51–56; Jacob Javits to William Fulbright, 26 April 1969, Series 48, Box 6, Folder 24, JWF.

13. CR, 115 (18 April 1969): 9608–10.

14. Ibid.

15. See the transcript of that 18 April 1969 interview in Series 72, Box 31, Folder 10, JWF.

16. See Barry Blechman and Stephen Kaplan, *Force without War: U.S. Armed Forces as a Political Instrument.*

17. Fulbright to McCallum, 26 April 1969, Series 88, File 3, JWF; AD, 30 April 1969.

18. PPPRN, 1969: 365–75.

19. AG, 16 May 1969; Fulbright to John Stevenson, 21 May 1969, Series 48, Box 57, Folder 4, JWF.

20. CR, 115 (18 April 1969): 9607; Fulbright to Harold Willens, 17 May 1969, Series 48, Box 57, Folder 5, JWF; Richard Nixon, *RN: The Memoirs of Richard Nixon,* 514–15.

21. PPPRN, 1969: 432–37.

22. U.S. Congress, Joint Economic Committee, *The Military Budget,* 88–90.

23. Ibid.

24. Powell, *Fulbright,* 240.

25. BS, 5 June 1969; AD, 12 June 1969.

26. Fulbright to Clark Clifford, 21 June 1969, Series 48, Box 17, Folder 1, JWF; PPPRN, 1969: 472.

27. Nixon: *RN,* 484–85.

28. WPR, 19–20.

29. Ibid.; Cooper, interview with the author.

30. UPI dispatch, 2 July 1969, Series 78, Box 63, Folder 3, JWF.

31. PPPRN, 1969: 480; Fulbright to Robert Moore, Jr., 16 July 1969, Series 48, Box 57, Folder 1, JWF; CR, 115 (6 August 1969): 2497–98.

32. Fulbright to Fagan Dickson, 6 September 1969, Series 48, Box 56, Folder 4, JWF.

33. *Washington Daily News,* 10 September 1969; PPPRN, 1969: 731; UPI dispatch, Series 78, Box 63, Folder 3, JWF.

34. NYT, 26 September 1969; PPPRN, 1969: 748–49; Harris, *The Anguish,* 70.

35. CR, 115 (1 October 1969): 27861–64.

36. Ibid.

37. AD, 20 October 1969.

38. Halstead, *Out Now!,* 488–89; Fulbright to John Arthos, 31 October 1969, Series 48, Box 56, Folder 1, JWF.

39. UPI dispatch, 20 October 1969, Series 78, Box 63, Folder 3, JWF.

40. BS, 24 October 1969.

41. PPPRN, 1969: 901–10; Hersh, *The Price,* 131; Harris, *The Anguish,* 70.

42. *Boston Globe,* 5 November 1969; UPI dispatch, 5 November 1969, Series 78, Box 63, Folder 4, JWF; NYT, 11 November 1969; *Boston Globe,* 6 November 1969.

43. Fulbright to George Wald, 8 November 1969, Series 48, Box 56, Folder 3, JWF; AG, 23 November 1969.

44. Fulbright to Coffin, 8 November 1969, Series 48, Box 56, Folder 3, JWF; NYT, 19 November 1969; AG, 20 November 1969.

45. UPI dispatch, 25 November 1969, Series 78, Box 63, Folder 5, JWF; Fulbright to George Kennan, 1 December 1969, Series 48, Box 56, Folder 7, JWF.

46. A copy of this speech is found in Series 72, Box 31, Folder 66, JWF.

47. CR, 115 (15 December 1969): 39146–52; UPI dispatch, 22 January 1970, Series 78, Box 63, Folder 5, JWF. On 22 January 1970, the Senate released a transcript of that closed-door session of 15 December 1969.

8.   CAMBODIA: THE CHALLENGE FROM THE SENATE

1. Fulbright to Fred Harris, 24 January 1970, Series 48, Box 60, Folder 2, JWF. Fulbright to Anthony Austin, 21 January 1970, Series 48, Box 59, Folder 1, JWF.

2. NYT, 2 February 1970.

3. Fulbright's opening statement is found in Series 72, Box 32, Folder 2, JWF.

4. Tad Szulc, *The Illusion of Peace: Foreign Policy in the Nixon Years,* 232–37; WES, 20 February 1970; UPI dispatch, 5 February 1970, Series 78, Box 60, Folder 1, JWF.

5. Fulbright to William Brett, 21 February 1970, Series 48, Box 59, Folder 1, JWF.

6. Fulbright's statement is found in Series 72, Box 34, Folder 4, JWF.

7. PPPRN, 1970: 244–49; CR, 116 (11 March 1970): 6959–60; WP, 13 March 1970.

8. Shawcross, *Sideshow,* 116–22; additional material is found in Hersh, *The Price,* 175–83; AG, 3 April 1970; see also transcript in Series 72, Box 32, Folder 8, JWF.

9. CR, 116 (2 April 1970): 10150–53.

10. Ibid.

11. Kolko, *Anatomy of War,* 408–11; Marcy, interview with the author.

12. PPPRN, 1970: 147; Fulbright, interview with the author.

13. *Indianapolis News,* 4 April 1970; *Richmond Times Dispatch,* 5 April 1970; WP, 5 April 1970.

14. Fulbright to Thomas Watson, 9 April 1970, Series 48, Box 17, Folder 1, JWF; PSCFR, *Impact of the War,* 1–25; Fulbright to Louis Lundbourg, 20 April 1970, Series 48, Box 17, Folder 4, JWF; NYT, 30 May 1970.

15. This statement is found in Series 72, Box 32, Folder 10, JWF; BS, 23 April 1970; Kissinger, *White House Years,* 495.

16. AG, 27 April 1970; this speech is found in Series 72, Box 32, Folder 11, JWF.

17. Series 72, Box 32, Folder 11, JWF.

18. Ibid.

19. Fulbright, interview with the author; BS, 28 April 1970; UPI dispatch, 29 April 1970, Series 78, Box 61, Folder 5, JWF.

20. PPPRN, 1970: 406, 409.

21. Fulbright to Richard Nixon, 1 May 1970, Series 1, Box 4, Folder 5, JWF; WP, 2 May 1970; a copy of Fulbright's speech is found in Series 72, Box 32, Folder 21, JWF.

22. Harris, *The Anguish,* 71; Kissinger, *White House Years,* 512.

23. CR, 116 (12 May 1970): 15080–83; UPI dispatch, 7 May 1970, Series 78, Box 61, Folder 5, JWF; Series 72, Box 32, Folder 11, JWF.

24. Series 72, Box 32, Folder 13, JWF.

25. *Paragould Daily Press,* 9 May 1970.

26. AG, 17 May 1970.

27. WP, 19 May 1970; AG, 22 May 1970.

28. WES, 19 May 1970; PSCFR, *Cambodia: May 1970*; UPI dispatch, 21 May 1970, Series 78, Box 66, Folder 2, JWF.

29. UPI dispatch, 27 May 1970, Series 78, Box 66, Folder 2, JWF.

30. Fulbright to Paul Carroll, 25 May 1970, Series 48, Box 59, Folder 4, JWF; Fulbright to Walter Cronkite, 22 May 1970, Series 78, Box 22, Folder 35, JWF.

31. CR, 116 (28 May 1970): 14709–11.

32. Fulbright to Sam Ervin, 3 June 1970, Series 48, Box 59, Folder 4, JWF.

33. CR, 116 (11 June 1970): 1942; WP, 12 June 1970.

34. WP, 21 June 1970.

35. CR, 116 (22 June 1970): 20745.

36. John Lehman, *The Executive, Congress and Foreign Policy: Studies of the Nixon Administration,* 64; PPPRN, 1970: 546; CR, 116 (24 June 1970): 21674.

37. WP, 26 June 1970; CR, 116 (26 June 1970): 21674; WP, 7 July 1970.

38. CR, 116 (30 June 1970): 22261; WPR, 32.

39. CR, 116 (6 July 1970): 22806–7; AG, 4 July 1970.

40. CR, 116 (10 July 1970): 23746; WPR, 39; CR, 116 (10 July 1970): 23744.

41. See Hersh, *The Price,* 300–301.

42. CR, 116 (14 July 1970): 23838; Fulbright to Olaf Palme, 11 July 1970, Series 48, Box 17, Folder 4, JWF; Kissinger, *White House Years,* 311.

43. NYT, 23 July 1970; ibid., 4 August 1970.

44. Ibid., 5 August 1970.

45. See remarks of Jacob Javits in CR, 116 (10 July 1970): 23718; George McGovern, interview with the author.

46. CR, 116 (1 September 1970): 20683, 30723–24.

47. Ibid.

48. PPPRN, 1970: 825–28; Fulbright to David Bruce, 9 October 1970, Series 48, Box 17, Folder 4, JWF.

49. BS, 20 October 1970; WP, 23 October 1970.

50. Fulbright to Alfred Knopf, 16 November 1970, Series 63, Box 3, Folder 3, JWF; Fulbright to Tristram Coffin, 17 November 1970, Series 63, Box 3, Folder 3, JWF.

51. NYT, 9 November 1970.

52. UPI transcript, 25 November 1970, Series 78, Box 67, Folder 4, JWF.

53. Ibid.

54. NYT, 30 November 1970; WP, 20 November 1970.

55. Kissinger, *White House Years,* 491, 499–500, 1180.

56. J. William Fulbright, *The Pentagon Propaganda Machine.*

57. PSCFR, *Hearings on S.2542,* 1–25.

58. PPPRN, 1970: 1106–9.

59. WP, 12 December 1970.

60. Ibid., 15 December 1970; ibid., 16 December 1970.

61. WP, 16 December 1970; CR, 116 (16 December 1970): 41772–75, 87; Fulbright to Frederick Rabsamen, 16 December 1970, Series 48, Box 61, Folder 2, JWF.

62. Fulbright to Cyrus Eaton, 15 December 1970, Series 48, Box 59, Folder 6, JWF.

63. *Houston Chronicle,* 25 December 1970.

64. Ibid.

9.   DEADLOCK: II

1. WP, 26 January 1971.

2. WP, 29 January 1971; Kissinger, *White House Years,* 990–91; Hersh, *The Price,* 307–10.

3. NYT, 10 February 1971.

4. See Nick Thimmesch's interview with Fulbright in *Newsday,* 14 February 1971; Fulbright to Alfred Knopf, 17 February 1971, Series 49, Box 62, Folder 5, JWF.

5. WP, 18 February 1971; ibid., 26 February 1971.

6. A transcript of this interview is found in Series 72, Box 33, Folder 40, JWF.

7. Fulbright to Dolores Ost, 6 September 1973, Series 73, Box 17, Folder 2, JWF; a transcript of this debate is found in Series 78, Box 70, Folder 2, JWF.

8. Hersh, *The Price,* 309–13; CR, 117 (30 March 1971): 8608–11.

9. PSCFR, *Legislative Proposals;* McGovern, interview with the author.

10. WP, 3 May 1971.

11. PSCFR, *Hearings on S.731,* 483–505.

12. Ibid.

13. See Hersh, *The Price,* 423–24; Kissinger, *White House Years,* 1017–19; WP, 8 June 1971; Fulbright's remarks are found in Series 72, Box 33, Folder 22, JWF.

14. Fulbright's speech is found in Series 72, Box 33, Folder 33, JWF.

15. See Salisbury's *Without Fear or Favor* for an authoritative analysis of this entire affair; Fulbright, interview with the author.

16. Daniel Ellsberg, interview with the author. That letter appeared in the WP, 12 October 1969. See also NYT, 9 October 1971.

17. Ellsberg, interview with the author; Fulbright, interview with the author.

18. UPI dispatch, 18 June 1971, Series 78, Box 68, Folder 3, JWF.

19. NYT, 24 June 1971; ibid., 23 June 1971. Among the publications issued by the committee were *Vietnam Commitments, The United States and Vietnam,* and *U.S. Involvement in the Overthrow of Diem.*

20. CR, 117 (16 June 1971): 20216, 21308.

21. Church confirms that there was "tension" (Church, interview with the author); Fulbright, interview with the author.

22. Fulbright's statement is found in Series 72, Box 33, Folder 27, JWF; Kissinger, *White House Years,* 1025; William Safire, *Before the Fall: An Inside View of the Pre-Watergate White House,* 489.

23. Hersh, *The Price,* 423–25.

24. CR, 117 (30 September 1971): 34236–38.

25. Ibid.

26. PPPRN, 1971: 1030; Fulbright, interview with the author; McGovern, interview with the author; Fulbright to George Ball, 18 February 1972, Series 48, Box 64, Folder 1, JWF.

27. CR, 117 (15 September 1971): 31944–46; Fulbright to Roswald Garst, 1 October 1971, Series 48, Box 42, Folder 2, JWF.

28. PPPRN, 1971: 1114.

29. AD, 29 December 1971.

30. Kissinger, *White House Years,* 1042.

31. Harris, *Anguish,* 73–74; Hersh, *The Price,* 481.

10.   NIXON PREVAILS

1. J. William Fulbright, "Reflections: In Thrall to Fear," 41–62.

2. Ibid.

3. Fulbright to Barnett Petty, 26 January 1972, Series 73, Box 3, Folder 27, JWF; Harry Ashmore to James Gavin, 23 February 1972, Series 48, Box 64, Folder 1, JWF; see Richard Strout in *Christian Science Monitor,* 14 January 1972; *National Review,* 4 February 1972.

4. PPPRN, 1972: 100–106; Hersh, *The Price,* 483–85.

5. NYT, 8 February 1972; Hersh, *The Price,* 485–87; CR, 118 (4 February 1972): 2728; Fulbright to Edmund Muskie, 10 February 1972, Series 63, Box 3, Folder 5, JWF.

6. The transcript of this interview is found in Series 78, Box 11, Folder 3, JWF.

7. WPR, 90, 99–101; CR, 118 (12 April 1972): S. 6048.

8. Kissinger, *White House Years,* 1109, 1198, 1162–63; Hersh, *The Price,* 505–8.

9. NYT, 18 April 1972; Fulbright, interview with the author.

10. NYT, 19 April 1972; Fulbright to Fagan Dickson, 25 April 1972, Series 48, Box 64, Folder 2, JWF.

11. CR, 118 (19 April 1972): S. 6295–96.

12. PPPRN, 1972: 550–54.

13. AD, 27 April 1972.

14. PPPRN, 1972: 583–86; Hersh, *The Price,* 520–23.

15. NYT, 10 May 1972; BS, 10 May 1972.

16. PSCFR, *Causes and Origins,* 2.

17. Ibid., 54, 87, 103.

18. Fulbright, interview with the author.

19. PSCFR, *Causes and Origins,* 24.

20. Fulbright to Clark Clifford, 19 May 1972, Series 48, Box 64, Folder 2, JWF; Fulbright to Jacob Sacks, 25 May 1972, Series 48, Box 64, Folder 7, JWF.

21. Fulbright, interview with the author; NYT, 11 June 1972; ibid., 26 May 1972; WES, 30 May 1972.

22. McGovern, interview with the author; Fulbright to Richard Nixon, 10 June 1972, Series 1, Box 4, Folder 7, JWF.

23. Fulbright to Dante Fascell, 8 June 1972, Series 48, Box 42, Folder 3, JWF.

24. WP, 20 June 1972; NYT, 20 June 1972.

25. UPI dispatch, 21 June 1972, Series 78, Box 71, Folder 2, JWF; ibid., 22 June 1972, Series 78, Box 71, Folder 2, JWF.

26. Fulbright to Charles M. Wilson, 30 June 1972, Series 63, Box 3, Folder 4, JWF.

27. Fulbright to W. R. Stephens, 16 August 1972, Series 63, Box 3, Folder 4, JWF.

28. AG, 12 July 1972.

29. McGovern, interview with the author.

30. CR, 118 (2 August 1964): 26397–98.

31. See the transcript in Series 78, Box 71, Folder 3, JWF.

32. Kissinger, *White House Years,* 1102–3; Harris, *The Anguish,* 74.

33. WP, 4 August 1972; AD, 8 September 1972.

34. Fulbright, interview with the author; Hersh, *The Price,* 558–59; CR, 118 (14 September 1972): 30632.

35. Fulbright to Cyrus Eaton, 22 September 1972, Series 63, Box 35, Folder 4, JWF; AG, 10 September 1972.

36. Fulbright, interview with the author. A hostile review authored by Paul Greenberg, a long-time foe from Arkansas, appeared in the WP, 31 October 1972. A far more favorable critique came from David Calleo, whose review appeared in the *NYT Book Review* on 25 February 1972. Tillman, interview with the author.

37. J. William Fulbright, *The Crippled Giant: American Foreign Policy and Its Domestic Consequences,* 277, 158.

38. AG, 12 October 1972; BS, 12 October 1972.

39. AG, 12 October 1972; CR, 118 (20 October 1972): 33134–36.

40. Kissinger, *White House Years,* 1329–31; Hersh, *The Price,* 577–78, 610.

41. Fulbright, interview with the author; *Ft. Smith Southwest Times Record*, 2 November 1972; WP, 9 November 1972; Hersh, *The Price,* 582, 604–10.

42. Fulbright, *Crippled Giant,* 4–8.

43. Fulbright to Earl Noah, 17 November 1972, Series 48, Box 64, Folder 6, JWF.

44. NYT, 18 December 1972.

45. Fulbright, interview with the author; Fulbright to Reuben Thomas, 30 December 1972, Series 48, Box 64, Folder 7, JWF.

46. Fulbright to Reuben Thomas, 30 December 1972, Series 48, Box 64, Folder 7, JWF.

11. THE TRIUMPH OF THE OPPOSITION

1. Fulbright to Mrs. Lowell Bailey, 5 January 1973, Series 48, Box 65, Folder 1, JWF; Fulbright to Tristram Coffin, 3 January 1973, Series 48, Box 65, Folder 1, JWF.

2. BS, 3 January 1973; NYT, 3 January 1973.

3. Fulbright to Mrs. Amyas Ames, 19 January 1973, Series 48, Box 65, Folder 1, JWF; Fulbright to Mrs. Marriner Eccles, 18 January 1973, Series 48, Box 65, Folder 1, JWF.

4. Fulbright's statement is found in Series 72, Box 34, Folder 18, JWF.

5. PPPRN, 1973: 18–20; Fulbright's statement is found in Series 72, Box 34, Folder 19, JWF; *Ft. Smith Southwest Record,* 27 January 1973; AG, 28 January 1973.

6. AG, 21 March 1973; Fulbright, interview with the author.

7. PPPRN, 1973: 55; NYT, 4 February 1973.

8. Fulbright to Richard Nixon, 5 February 1973, Series 48, Box 31, Folder 4, JWF.

9. Ibid.

10. AG, 4 February 1973.

11. CR, 119 (15 February 1973): 4210–12; AG, 16 February 1973.

12. AG, 11 February 1973.

13. Fulbright to Arthur Schlesinger, Jr., 13 February 1973, Series 48, Box 65, Folder 5, JWF; a transcript of this interview is found in Series 72, Box 34, Folder 24, JWF.

14. PSCFR, *Briefing on Major Foreign Policy Questions,* 1, 5.

15. AD, 11 March 1973; ibid., 21 March 1973.

16. AD, 28 March 1973; CR, 119 (27 March 1973): 9717.

17. WP, 28 March 1973; UPI dispatch, Series 78, Box 64, Folder 2, JWF.

18. An undated memo explaining this point, which either Moose or Lowenstein wrote, is found in Series 48, Box 46, Folder 4, JWF.

19. WP, 31 March 1973; CR, 119 (18 July 1973): 24861–66.

20. AG, 12 April 1973.

21. NYT, 12 April 1973.

22. A transcript of this interview is found in Series 72, Box 34, Folder 27, JWF; AG, 12 April 1973.

23. Henry Kissinger, *Years of Upheaval,* 318–27.

24. PSCFR, *Air Operations,* 2–10; Series 48, Box 46, Folder 4, JWF; Kissinger, *Years of Upheaval,* 347–48; Fulbright, interview with the author.

25. NYT, 1 May 1973; his statement is found in Kissinger's *Years of Upheaval,* 1240–43.

26. Ibid.

27. PPPRN, 1973: 328–33; *Boston Globe,* 2 May 1973; CR, 119 (10 May 1973): H3598.

28. WP, 11 May 1973.

29. CR, 119 (14 May 1973): 15436–37; Church, interview with the author.

30. Church, interview with the author; Tillman, interview with the author; Fulbright, interview with the author; Hersh, *The Price,* 122–23.

31. *Congressional Quarterly,* 16 June 1973, 1556.

32. Church, interview with the author.

33. CR, 119 (12 June 1973): 19159–60.

34. AG, 20 June 1973. In a speech to the American Bankers Association, Fulbright sought to rebut Jackson's argument for his amendment: see CR, 119 (18 July 1973): 24465–68.

35. See transcript of his 24 June interview on "Issues and Answers" in Series 72, Box 34, Folder 33, JWF. His 25 June interview on KATV Little Rock is found in Series 78, Box 73, Folder 5, JWF.

36. PPPRN, 1973: 621–22; Kissinger, *Years of Upheaval,* 358.

37. WPR, 109.

38. AG, 29 June 1973; Fulbright to Lanny Morgan, 10 July 1973, Series 48, Box 65, Folder 4, JWF; Fulbright to George Reynolds, 16 July 1973, Series 48, Box 65, Folder 4, JWF.

39. *Congressional Quarterly,* 7 July 1973, 1854–55.

40. *Congressional Quarterly,* 7 July 1973, 1854–55; CR, 119 (29 June 1973): 22325.

41. Thomas Frank and Edward Weisband, *Foreign Policy by Congress,* 13; Kissinger, *Years of Upheaval,* 355–65.

42. Kissinger, *Years of Upheaval,* 361–65.

43. NYT, 12 July 1973; Fulbright, interview with the author; WP, 12 July 1973.

44. PPPRN, 1973: 644–45; CR, 119 (18 July 1973): H6241.

45. AD, 3 February 1973; Fulbright, interview with the author.

46. WPR, 138–39.

47. NYT, 17 July 1973; Shawcross, *Sideshow,* 287–89.

48. Cooper, interview with the author; Church, interview with the author.

49. AG, 29 July 1973.

50. PPPRN, 1973: 686.

51. AG, 14 August 1973; *Jonesboro Sun,* 21 August 1973; Fulbright to Mrs. Marriner Eccles, 27 August 1973, Series 63, Box 17, Folder 1, JWF.

52. PPPRN, 1973: 697.

53. Tillman, interview with the author; Raymond Gartoff, *Detente and Confrontation: American-Soviet Relations from Nixon to Reagan,* 325–26, 412, 455.

54. Kissinger, *Years of Upheaval,* 261, 235–59, 250.

55. WP, 21 July 1973; Fulbright, interview with the author.

56. Fulbright, interview with the author.

57. WP, 16 September 1973; NYT, 25 September 1973.

58. That statement is found in Series 72, Box 34, Folder 30, JWF.

59. BS, 28 September 1973.

60. CR, 119 (27 September 1973): 31822; ibid., (9 October 1973): 33262.

61. Henry Kissinger, *American Foreign Policy, Expanded Edition,* 255–68; CR, 119 (9 October 1973): 33262–66.

62. CR, 119 (9 October 1973): 33262–66.

63. NYT, 5 October 1973; WPR, 148.

64. PPPRN, 1973: 893–94; WPR, 159.
65. Fulbright, interview with the author.
66. WP, 20 December 1973.
67. NYT, 30 November 1973; WPR, 170.
68. WPR, 170.

12.   ARKANSAS RETIRES A REALIST

1. Fulbright, interview with the author.
2. CR, 120 (24 January 1974): 757; PSCFR, *U.S. POW's.*
3. WP, 30 January 1973; Fulbright, interview with the author; WP, 16 February 1973.
4. Fulbright, interview with the author. Fulbright's approach to that campaign is expressed in an interview he had on 24 April: see transcript in Series 78, Box 73, Folder 5, JWF.
5. AG, 26 May 1974; WP, 27 May 1974; AG, 27 May 1974.
6. AG, 29 May 1974; NYT, 30 May 1974; WP, 30 May 1974.
7. McGovern, interview with the author.
8. Fulbright, interview with the author.
9. CR, 120 (26 June 1974): 21198–99; see also Fulbright's interview on 8 July 1974 edition of "Meet the Press."
10. Kissinger, *Years of Upheaval,* 1119–20. Years later Fulbright confirmed that the committee protected him (Fulbright, interview with the author).
11. PSCFR, *Foreign Assistance Authorization,* 200–201.
12. Ibid., 203.
13. NYT, 26 July 1974.
14. CR, 120 (9 August 1974): 27624–25.
15. Seymour Hersh, "The Pardon: Ford, Haig and the Transfer of Power," 55–78.
16. AG, 24 September 1974; WP, 29 September 1974; Fulbright, interview with the author.
17. WP, 22 September 1974.
18. A copy of this speech is found in Series 72, Box 35, Folder 10, JWF.
19. Ibid.
20. CR, 120 (19 December 1974): 41075–76.
21. Ibid.

CONCLUSION

1. Fulbright, interview with the author.

BIBLIOGRAPHY

MANUSCRIPT SOURCES

Austin, Texas
Lyndon B. Johnson Library. Lyndon B. Johnson Papers.

Burlington, Vermont
University of Vermont Library. George Aiken Papers.

Eugene, Oregon
University of Oregon Library. Wayne Morse Papers.

Fayetteville, Arkansas
University of Arkansas Library. J. W. Fulbright Papers.

New Haven, Connecticut
Sterling Library, Yale University. Walter Lippmann Papers.

Washington, D.C.
National Archives. Record Group 46, Declassified Hearings of the Committee on
   Foreign Relations of the United States Senate: 1961–66.

UNITED STATES GOVERNMENT PUBLICATIONS

U.S. Congress. *Congressional Record,* 1964–74.
———. House. Committee on Foreign Affairs. *The War Powers Resolution.* 1982.
———. Joint Economic Committee. *The Military Budget and National Priorities:
   Hearings.* 91st Cong., 1st sess., 3–24 June 1969, 1970.
———. Senate. Committee on Foreign Relations. *Background Information Relat-
   ing to Southeast Asia and Vietnam.* 91st Cong., 2d sess., 1970.
———. Senate. Committee on Foreign Relations. *Bombing as a Policy Tool in
   Vietnam Effectiveness.* 92d Cong., 2d sess., 12 October 1972.
———. Senate. Committee on Foreign Relations. *Briefing by Secretary of State
   William P. Rogers.* 91st Cong., 1st sess., 27 March 1969.

BIBLIOGRAPHY

———. Senate. Committee on Foreign Relations. *Briefing on Major Foreign Policy Questions by Secretary of State William P. Rogers.* 93d Cong., 1st sess., 21 February 1973.

———. Senate. Committee on Foreign Relations. *Cambodia: May 1970* (Staff Report). 91st Cong., 2d sess., 7 June 1970.

———. Senate. Committee on Foreign Relations. *Causes, Origins and Lessons of Vietnam War.* 92d Cong., 2d sess., 9, 10, 11 May 1972.

———. Senate. Committee on Foreign Relations. *Foreign Assistance Authorization: Hearings on S. 3394.* 93d Cong., 2d sess., 7 June–25 July 1974.

———. Senate. Committee on Foreign Relations. *Harrison E. Salisbury's Trip to North Vietnam: Hearings.* 89th Cong., 1st sess., 2 February 1967.

———. Senate. Committee on Foreign Relations. *Hearings on S. 2542 or S. 2543.* 91st Cong., 1st sess., 10–11 December 1971.

———. Senate. Committee on Foreign Relations. *Impact of the War in Southeast Asia on U.S. Economy: Hearings.* 91st Cong., 2d sess., 15–16 April 1970.

———. Senate. Committee on Foreign Relations. *Impact of the Vietnam War* (Committee Point). 92d Cong., 1st sess., 30 June 1971.

———. Senate. Committee on Foreign Relations. *Laos: April 1971* (Staff Report). 92d Cong., 1st sess., 3 August 1971.

———. Senate. Committee on Foreign Relations. *Legislative History of the Committee on Foreign Relations, 1963–1964.* 93d and 95th Cong., 1972–75.

———. Senate. Committee on Foreign Relations. *Legislative Proposals Relating to the War in Southeast Asia. Hearing on S. 376.* 92d Cong., 1st sess., 20 April–27 May 1971.

———. Senate. Committee on Foreign Relations. *Moral and Military Aspects of the War in Southeast Asia: Hearings.* 91st Cong., 2d sess., 7–12 May 1970.

———. Senate. Committee on Foreign Relations. *Nomination of Henry A. Kissinger: Hearings.* 93d Cong., 1st sess., 10–18 September 1973. Released 4 October 1973.

———. Senate. Committee on Foreign Relations. *Southeast Asian Resolution: Joint Hearings before Committee on Armed Services and Foreign Relations.* 88th Cong., 2d sess., 6 August 1964.

———. Senate. Committee on Foreign Relations. *Strategic and Foreign Policy Implications of ABM Systems: Hearings.* 91st Cong., 1st sess., 6–28 March 1969.

———. Senate. Committee on Foreign Relations. *Supplemental Foreign Assistance Authorization: 1970: Hearings on S. 2542 and S. 2543.* 91st Cong., 1st sess., 10–11 December 1970.

———. Senate. Committee on Foreign Relations. *Supplemental Foreign Assistance Fiscal Year 1966—Vietnam: Hearings on S. 2793.* 89th Cong., 2d sess., 28 January–18 February 1966.

———. Senate. Committee on Foreign Relations. *Thailand, Laos and Cambodia, January 1972* (Staff Report). 8 May 1972.

————. Senate. Committee on Foreign Relations. *The Gulf of Tonkin, 1964 Incidents: Hearings.* 90th Cong., 2d sess., 20 February 1968.

————. Senate. Committee on Foreign Relations. *The United States Government and the Vietnam War: Executive and Legislative Roles and Relationships, Part I, 1945–1961.* April 1984.

————. Senate. Committee on Foreign Relations. *The United States Government and the Vietnam War: Executive and Legislative Relations, Part II, 1961–1964.* December 1984.

————. Senate. Committee on Foreign Relations. *U.S. Air Operations in Cambodia, April 1973* (Staff Report). 93d Cong., 1st sess., 27 April 1973.

————. Senate. Committee on Foreign Relations. *U.S. Involvement in the Overthrow of Diem, 1963.* 92d Cong., 2d sess., 20 July 1972.

————. Senate. Committee on Foreign Relations. *U.S. POW's and MIA's in Southeast Asia: Hearings.* 93d Cong., 2d sess., 28 January 1974.

————. Senate. Committee on Foreign Relations. *U.S. Security Agreements and Commitments Abroad: Hearings.* 91st Cong., 1st sess., 30 September–3 October 1969.

————. Senate. Committee on Foreign Relations. *U.S. and Vietnam: 1944–1947* (Staff Study No. 2). 92d Cong., 2d sess., 1972.

————. Senate. Committee on Foreign Relations. *United States Commitments to Foreign Powers: Hearings.* 90th Cong., 2d sess., 16 August–19 September 1967.

————. Senate. Committee on Foreign Relations. *United States Policy with Respect to Mainland China: Hearings.* 90th Cong., 2d sess., 8–30 March 1966.

————. Senate. Committee on Foreign Relations. *Vietnam Commitments, 1961* (Staff Study). 92d Cong., 2d sess., 1972.

————. Senate. Committee on Foreign Relations. *Vietnam: Policy Proposals and Hearings.* 91st Cong., 2d sess., 3 February–16 March 1970.

————. Senate. Committee on Foreign Relations. *War Powers Legislation: Hearings.* 92d Cong., 1st sess., 8 March–6 October 1971.

U.S. General Services Administration. *Public Papers of the Presidents of the United States: Lyndon Baines Johnson, 1963–1969.* 1965–70; *Richard Nixon, 1969–1974.* 1970–75.

NEWSPAPERS AND JOURNALS

Arkansas Democrat.
Arkansas Gazette, 1964–74.
Baltimore Sun.
Congressional Quarterly Almanac, 1964–74.
Facts on File, 1955–75.
New York Times, 1964–74.

BIBLIOGRAPHY

Washington Evening Star.
Washington Post, 1964–74.
Washington Star.

INTERVIEWS

George Ball, 4 September 1980; 15 October 1982 (by telephone).
McGeorge Bundy, 16 August 1982 (by telephone).
Frank Church, 10 September 1981; 26 October 1982 (by telephone).
John Sherman Cooper, 18 July 1979.
Fred Dutton, 18 July 1979; 31 July 1980.
Daniel Ellsberg, 6 September 1982 (by telephone).
J. W. Fulbright, 17 July 1979; 1 August 1980; 17 February 1982; 9 June 1982; 21
    September 1982; 24 May 1985 (by telephone).
Pat Holt, 16 July 1979.
Haynes Johnson, 11 June 1980.
Norvill Jones, 11 June 1980.
George McGovern, 17 February 1982; 16 August 1982 (by telephone); 26 October
    1982 (by telephone).
Mike Manatos, 20 July 1979; 31 July 1980.
Carl Marcy, 19 July 1979; 10 June 1980.
Stuart Symington, 11 June 1980.
Seth Tillman, 17 July 1979; 12 June 1980.
Frank Valeo, 1 August 1980.
Lee Williams, 12 June 1980.

ORAL HISTORIES

Austin, Texas. Lyndon Baines Johnson Library. George Aiken, Harry Ashmore,
    William P. Bundy, Clifford Case, Frank Church, John Sherman Cooper, Fred
    Dutton, Allen Ellender, Ernest Gruening, Gale McGhee, George McGovern,
    Harry McPherson, Mike Manatos, A. S. Monroney, Thurston Morton,
    Claiborne Pell, George Reedy, Charles Roberts, Leverett Saltonstall, John
    Sparkman, Stuart Symington.

BOOKS AND ARTICLES

Austin, Anthony. *The President's War.* Philadelphia: Lippincott, 1971.
Baker, Robert. *Wheeling and Dealing: Confessions of a Capitol Hill Operator.*
    New York: Norton, 1978.

Ball, George. *The Past Has Another Pattern: Memoirs*. New York: Norton, 1982.
Barnet, Richard. *Roots of War*. Baltimore: Penguin Books, 1973.
Berman, Larry. *Planning a Tragedy*. New York: Norton, 1981.
Blechman, Barry, and Kaplan, Stephen. *Force without War: U.S. Armed Forces as a Political Instrument*. Washington: The Brookings Institution, 1978.
Brown, Eugene. *J. W. Fulbright: Advice and Dissent*. Iowa City: University of Iowa Press, 1985.
Coffin, Tristram. *Senator Fulbright: Portrait of a Public Philosopher*. New York: Dutton, 1966.
———. *Washington Watch*, no. 4, 28 February 1968.
———. *Washington Watch*, no. 11, 18 April 1968.
Cohen, Warren. *Dean Rusk*. Totowa, N.J.: Cooper Square Publishers, 1980.
Crabb, Cecil, and Holt, Pat. *Invitation to Struggle: Congress, the President and Foreign Policy*. Washington: Congressional Quarterly Press, 1980.
Draper, Theodore. *Abuse of Power*. New York: Viking Press, 1967.
Fall, Bernard. *Street without Joy: Insurgency in Indochina, 1946–63*. Harrisburg, Penn.: Stackpole Books Inc., 1963.
———. *The Two Vietnams: A Political and Military Analysis*. New York: Praeger, 1964.
Franck, Thomas, and Weisband, Edward. *Foreign Policy by Congress*. New York: Oxford University Press, 1979.
Fulbright, J. W. "American Foreign Policy in the 20th Century under an 18th Century Constitution." *Cornell Law Quarterly*, 47 (Fall 1961): 1–10.
———. *The Arrogance of Power*. New York: Random House, 1966.
———. *The Crippled Giant: American Foreign Policy and Its Domestic Consequences*. New York: Random House, 1972.
———. "The Legislator." *Vital Speeches*, 15 May 1946, pp. 468–72.
———. *Old Myths and New Realities and Other Commentaries*. New York: Random House, 1964.
———. *The Pentagon Propaganda Machine*. New York: Vintage Books, 1971.
———. *Prospects for the West*. Cambridge: Harvard University Press, 1963.
———. "Reflections: In Thrall to Fear." *The New Yorker* 907 (8 January 1972): 41–62.
Galloway, John. *The Gulf of Tonkin Resolution*. Rutherford, N.J.: Fairleigh Dickinson University Press, 1970.
Garthoff, Raymond. *Detente and Confrontation: American-Soviet Relations from Nixon to Reagan*. Washington: The Brookings Institution, 1985.
Gelb, Leslie, and Betts, Richard. *The Irony of Vietnam: The System Worked*. Washington: The Brookings Institution, 1979.
Geyelin, Philip. *Lyndon B. Johnson and the World*. New York: Praeger, 1966.
Gleyesis, Piero. *The Dominican Crisis*. Baltimore: Johns Hopkins University Press, 1978.

BIBLIOGRAPHY

Goulden, Joseph. *Truth Is the First Casualty: The Gulf of Tonkin Affair: Illusion and Reality.* Chicago: Rand McNally, 1969.

Graebner, Norman. *Ideas and Diplomacy: Readings in the Intellectual Tradition of American Foreign Policy.* New York: Oxford University Press, 1964.

Gravel, Mike. *The Senator Gravel Edition: The Pentagon Papers—The Defense Department History of the United States Decision-Making on Vietnam.* 5 vols. Boston: Beacon Press, 1971-72.

Halberstam, David. *The Best and the Brightest.* New York: Random House, 1972.

———. *The Powers That Be.* New York: Dell, 1980.

Halstead, Fred. *Out Now: A Participant's Account of the American Movement against the Vietnam War.* New York: Monad Press, 1978.

Harris, Louis. *The Anguish of Change.* New York: Norton, 1973.

Harkness, Peter, and Patch, Buel, et al. *China and U.S. Far East Policy: 1945–1966.* Washington: Congressional Quarterly Service, 1967.

Herring, George. *America's Longest War: The United States and Vietnam, 1950–1975.* New York: Wiley, 1979.

Hersh, Seymour. "The Pardon: Nixon, Ford, Haig and the Transfer of Power," *The Atlantic* 252 (August 1983): 55–80.

———. *The Price of Power.* New York: Summit Books, 1983.

Hodgson, Godfrey. *America in Our Time.* Garden City, N.Y.: Doubleday, 1976.

Johnson, Haynes, and Gwertzman, Bernard. *Fulbright: The Dissenter.* Garden City, N.Y.: Doubleday, 1968.

Johnson, Lyndon. *The Vantage Point: Perspectives on the Presidency, 1963–1969.* New York: Holt, 1971.

Joseph, Paul. *Cracks in the Empire: State Politics in the Vietnam War.* Boston: South End Press, 1981.

Kahin, George, and Lewis, John. *The United States in Vietnam.* New York: Dial, 1967.

Kaplan, Lawrence. *The United States and NATO: The Formative Years.* Lexington: University Press of Kentucky, 1984.

Katenburg, Paul. *The Vietnam Trauma in American Foreign Policy, 1945–75.* New Brunswick, N.J.: Transaction Books, 1980.

Kearns, Doris. *Lyndon Johnson and the American Dream.* New York: Harper and Row, 1976.

Kissinger, Henry. *American Foreign Policy.* Expanded edition. New York: Norton, 1974.

———. *The White House Years.* Boston: Little, Brown, 1979.

———. *Years of Upheaval.* Boston: Little, Brown, 1982.

Knoll, Erwin, and McFadden, Judith. *American Militarism: 1970.* New York: Viking Press, 1969.

Kolko, Gabriel. *Anatomy of War: Vietnam, The United States and the Modern Historical Experience.* New York: Pantheon Books, 1985.

LaFeber, Walter. *America, Russia and the World*. 4th ed. New York: Wiley, 1980.

Lehman, John. *The Executive, Congress and Foreign Policy: Studies of the Nixon Administration*. New York: Praeger, 1976.

McGovern, George. *Grassroots: The Autobiography of George McGovern*. New York: Random House, 1977.

Menashe, Louis, and Radosh, Ronald, eds. *Teach-ins: USA, Reports, Opinions, Documents*. New York: Praeger, 1967.

Miller, Merle. *Lyndon: An Oral Biography*. New York: Putnam, 1980.

Morgenthau, Hans. *A New Foreign Policy for the U.S.* New York: Praeger, 1969.

Morris, Roger. *Uncertain Greatness: Henry Kissinger and American Foreign Policy*. New York: Harper and Row, 1977.

Nixon, Richard. *RN: The Memoirs of Richard Nixon*. New York: Grosset and Dunlap, 1978.

Oberdofer, Don. *Tet!* Garden City, N.Y.: Doubleday, 1971.

Parmet, Herbert. *JFK: The Presidency of John F. Kennedy*. New York: Dial Press, 1983.

Powell, Lee. *J. William Fulbright and America's Lost Crusade: Fulbright's Opposition to the Vietnam War*. Little Rock, Ark.: Rose Publishing Company, 1984.

Safire, William. *Before the Fall: An Inside View of the Pre-Watergate White House*. New York: Ballantine Books, 1977.

Salisbury, Harrison. *Without Fear or Favor*. New York: Ballantine Books, 1981.

Schandler, Herbert. *The Unmaking of a President: Lyndon Johnson and Vietnam*. Princeton: Princeton University Press, 1977.

Schemmer, Benjamin. *The Raid*. New York: Harper and Row, 1976.

Schlesinger, Arthur, Jr. *The Imperial Presidency*. Boston: Houghton Mifflin, 1973.

———. *Robert Kennedy and His Times*. Boston: Houghton Mifflin, 1978.

Schurmann, Franz. *The Logic of World Power: An Inquiry into the Origin, Currents, and Contradictions of World Politics*. New York: Pantheon Books, 1974.

Shawcross, William. *Sideshow: Kissinger, Nixon and the Destruction of Cambodia*. New York: Simon and Schuster, 1979.

Shoup, David. "The New American Militarism." *The Atlantic Monthly* 223 (April 1969): 51–56.

Steel, Ronald. *Walter Lippmann and the American Century*. Boston: Atlantic and Little, Brown, 1980.

Stoler, Mark. "Aiken, Mansfield and the Gulf of Tonkin Crisis: Notes from the Congressional Leadership Meeting at the White House, August 4, 1964." *The Proceedings of the Vermont Historical Society* 50 (Spring 1982): 80–94.

Stone, I. F. *In a Time of Torment*. New York: Random House, 1967.

———. *Polemics and Prophecies*. New York: Random House, 1970.

———. *I. F. Stone's Weekly*. 30 January 1967.

Stupak, Ronald. *American Foreign Policy: Assumptions, Processes and Projections*. New York: Harper and Row, 1976.

BIBLIOGRAPHY

Sullivan, William. *The Bureau: My Thirty Years in Hoover's FBI*. New York: Norton, 1979.

Szulc, Tad. *The Illusion of Peace: Foreign Policy in the Nixon Years*. New York: Viking Press, 1978.

Wells, Samuel, and Braestrup, Peter, eds. *Some Lessons and Non Lessons of Vietnam: Ten Years after the Paris Peace Accords*. Washington: Woodrow Wilson International Center for Scholars, 1983.

UNPUBLISHED SECONDARY WORKS

Brown, Donald E. "Fulbright and the Premises of American Foreign Policy." Ph.D. diss., State University of New York at Binghamton, 1982.

Riddell, Thomas. "A Political Economy of the American War in Indochina: Its Costs and Consequences." Ph.D. diss., The American University, 1975.

Zelman, Walter. "Senate Dissent and the Vietnam War, 1964–1968." Ph.D. diss., University of California at Los Angeles, 1971.

INDEX

INDEX

LBJ's Vietnam policy, 32, 33, 34, 37, 53–54; and Nixon's Vietnam policy, 110, 118, 141, 168, 177–78, 181; and resolution on Vietnam, 12–13

Church-Case amendment: (1972), 153, 154, 156; (1973), 171, 172, 174, 175, 199

Church resolution, 12–13

CIA (Central Intelligence Agency), 9, 18, 19, 116, 180

Clark, Joseph, 43, 46, 53, 80, 102

Clifford, Clark, 44, 68, 112, 113, 116–17, 184; criticized by Nixon administration, 130, 168; and Fulbright, 29, 156; as secretary of defense, 93, 95, 97, 99, 100

Coffin, Tristram, 73, 118, 135

Colby, William, 121

Colegrove, Albert, 10

Colson, Charles, 168

Connally, John, 185

Cooper, John Sherman, 40, 99, 113, 121, 181; and Cooper-Church amendment, 128, 137; and Tonkin Gulf Resolution, 24, 26

Cooper-Church amendment: (1969), 19; (1970), 128, 129, 130, 131, 132, 133; modified, 137, 138, 140, 179, 199

Cox, Archibald, 187

Crippled Giant, The (Fulbright), 161–62, 164

Cronkite, Walter, 79, 102, 129

Cuban Missile Crisis, 10, 13, 16

Dean, John, 173, 174, 176, 177

Demilitarized Zone (DMZ), 99, 107, 137

Democratic National Committee, 26, 101

DE SOTO, 18, 23, 24, 29, 95

Diem. *See* Ngo Dinh Diem

Dirksen, Everett, 20, 24, 46, 115

Dodd, Thomas, 46, 53

Dole, Robert, 130–31

Dole amendment, 130–31, 132

Dominican Republic crisis, 38, 39, 43, 44, 45, 46, 47–48, 54

Dougherty, Bp. John, 127

Douglas, Lewis, 71, 73, 93

Draft resisters, amnesty, 194

Drew, Elizabeth, 168, 174

Dulles, John Foster, 60

Dutton, Fred, 23, 26, 54

Eagleton, Thomas, 152, 159, 177, 178

Eaton, Cyrus, 132, 161

Eisenhower, Dwight D., 7, 8, 9, 46, 103; and Vietnam, 10, 13

Ellender, Allen, 24, 26, 27, 34

Ellsberg, Daniel, 144–45, 197, 198

Enders, Thomas O., 173, 191–92

Erlichman, John, 173, 174

Ervin, Sam, 129, 169, 176

Ervin Committee (Watergate), 169, 176, 181, 182

"Face the Nation," 13, 110, 135, 141, 172

Fairbank, John K., 60

Fall, Bernard, 51, 56, 81

Fascell, Dante, 157

Faubus, Orval, 58, 83, 100

FBI (Federal Bureau of Investigation), 68

Federal Communications Commission (FCC), 133–34

Finney, John, 172

Flanders, Ralph, 6

Ford, Gerald, 161, 177, 180, 194

Formosa Resolution of 1955, 146

Frankel, Charles, 44

Frankel, Max, 77–78

Fromm, Erich, 93

Fulbright, J. William: advocates negotiations with North Vietnam, 52–53, 58, 83, 118, 138; and Agnew, 127, 130, 131, 134, 135; approves certain Nixon policies, 194, 195; as author of *The Arrogance of Power,* 75, 76–78, 85, 161; as author of *The Crippled Giant,* 161–62, 164; as author of *Old Myths and New Realities,* 22; as author of *The Pentagon Propaganda Machine,* 136, 142; and bombing policy, 52, 99, 135–36, 144, 153–54, 159–60, 165, 174, 177–78, 181, 188; and break with LBJ, 1, 8, 31–32, 36, 42–45, 46–47, 49, 103; and Cambodia, 122, 124–27, 128, 138, 170–71; as chairman of Foreign Relations Committee, 5, 8, 31, 53–54, 72, 88, 95, 102, 136,

INDEX

Herrick, John, 25
Hersh, Seymour, 147, 175
Herter, Christian A., Lectures (Fulbright), 63–64, 66–67, 75, 77, 85; "The Arrogance of Power," 66–68; "The Higher Patriotism," 63; "Revolutions Abroad," 64
Hickenlooper, Bourke, 53, 91
Hilsman, Roger, 12
Ho Chi Minh, 45, 79, 80, 83, 91, 101, 114
Hollings, Ernest, 68
Holt, Pat, 20, 45, 54
Hughes, Harold, 130
Humphrey, Hubert, 10, 20, 24, 40, 72, 101, 102, 192

ICBMs (intercontinental ballistic missiles), 160
Ingersoll, Robert, 188
"Issues and Answers," 95

Jackson, Henry, 83, 130, 136, 160–61, 162, 184, 194; challenges détente, 175–76, 183, 192, 199
Jackson amendment: (1972), 160–61; (1973), 175–76, 183, 186, 188
Javits, Jacob, 26, 67, 130, 141; and war powers bill, 132, 142, 152, 180, 186
Johnson, Alexis, 105
Johnson, Jim, 100, 127
Johson, Lyndon B., 6, 51, 113, 114, 123, 146, 154; and bombing halt, 97, 99, 100, 135, 198; and containment, 18, 19–20, 37, 62, 164; and determination to win, 70, 81, 92, 93, 97; and Dominican Republic, 38, 43, 44, 45; and Foreign Relations Committee, 53, 54–57, 58, 63, 76, 79–80, 95–96; and Fulbright's break with, 1, 8, 31–32, 36, 42–45, 46–47, 49, 103; and Fulbright's opposition on Vietnam policy, 50, 52, 55–56, 66, 67, 68, 70–71, 72, 82, 85; and good relations with Fulbright, 14–19, 22, 24–28, 35, 36, 39–40, 55; and Great Society, 43, 61; as incumbent candidate (1968), 96–97, 99, 119, 198; and Nixon's war policies compared to, 106, 110, 112, 117, 118, 120; opposition to his policies, 34, 37–38, 44, 53, 57, 86, 90; and presiden-

tial campaign (1964), 8, 21–22, 29, 33, 55; and public opinion, 61, 84, 94; rejects compromise on Vietnam, 52, 77, 80, 168, 197; retirement and death, 97, 102, 167; and Southeast Asian Resolution, 20, 24–29, 43, 59, 80–81, 87–89, 94–95, 132; and Soviet Union, 23, 83–84; and support for policies, 19–21, 72, 73, 74, 82, 93, 180; and Tonkin Gulf affair, 23–26, 69–70, 89, 195; and war escalation, 16, 29–30, 31, 34–35, 37, 44, 45, 74, 87
Joint Economic Committee, 111, 112, 132
Jones, Norvill, 54, 145
Judiciary Subcommittee on the Separation of Powers, 169

Kalb, Marvin, 135
Katzenbach, Nicholas, 87–89, 143
Kennan, George, 11–12, 56, 57, 58, 79, 118, 184, 194
Kennedy, Edward, 106, 130, 166, 168, 177–78
Kennedy, John F., 6, 11, 23, 45, 46; and assassination, 13; and executive power, 12; and foreign affairs, 9–10, 12–13, 14; as presidential candidate, 8
Kennedy, Robert, 58, 81, 96, 97, 100, 101, 103, 198
Kent State University, student protest, 126–27
Khanh. *See* Nguyen Khanh
Khmer Rouge, 170, 178–79
Khrushchev, Nikita, 9, 31, 148
Kinter, Robert, 71, 79
Kissinger, Henry, 136, 145, 152, 160, 161, 200; becomes secretary of state, 182–86; and China, 146, 149; and détente, 149, 150, 174, 186, 194; and Foreign Relations Committee, 166–67, 184–85, 192–93; and Fulbright, 174–75, 182–83, 185, 186, 187–88, 190–91, 194, 199; and Middle East conflict, 188, 190, 199; as National Security Adviser, 106, 107–8, 124, 154; outlook on foreign policy, 132, 140, 149, 178–79, 183–84, 186, 188; and Paris talks, 123, 146–47, 151, 163–64, 165, 168, 171, 175; supports bombing, 173, 178–79, 188–89; and Watergate, 178, 189, 196

INDEX

Mitchell, John, 135
Mitchell, Martha (Mrs. John), 135
Mondale, Walter, 141
Monroney, Mike, 96
Moose, Richard, 120, 128, 138, 171, 173
Moose-Lowenstein reports: (1970), 120, 128, 138; (1973), 173
Morgenthau, Hans, 2, 98
Morse, Wayne, 61, 62, 69, 83, 99; and elections, 102, 191; and Fulbright, 17, 25, 46; and funding the war, 40, 58, 87; opposes Vietnam commitment, 10, 15, 37, 53; and Tonkin Gulf Resolution, 24, 25, 26, 59, 94–95
Moscow summit meetings: (1972), 147, 152, 154, 156–57, 158; (1974), 192
Moyers, Bill, 49, 52, 71, 73, 82
Mudd, Roger, 142
Mundt, Karl, 53, 96
Muskie, Edmund, 151, 158, 174, 177–78, 193
My Lai Massacre, 118–19

Nasser, Gamal, 7, 8
National Commitments Resolution, 84–85, 87, 101, 113
National Liberation Front (NLF), 57, 76, 148
National Press Club, 67, 194
National Security Council, 155
NATO (North Atlantic Treaty Organization), 5, 7
Neibur, Reinhold, 74
Nelson, Gaylord, 26, 27, 134
New Mobilization, 117–18
Ngo Dinh Diem, 10, 12–13
Nguyen Cao Ky, Marshal, 126, 129
Nguyen Chanh Thieu: and election of 1971, 147; and Hanoi's opposition to, 119, 123, 132, 144; invades Laos, 140; Nixon prevents overthrow of, 178, 199; and Nixon support for, 110, 112, 113, 115, 117, 119, 123, 126, 132, 144; and opposition to in U.S., 152, 163, 193; rejects Kissinger initiatives, 164; and veto over U.S. policy, 134
Nguyen Khanh, 22
Nitze, Paul, 192
Nixon, Richard M., 18–19, 62, 84, 96, 197;

and Cambodia, 122, 124–27, 128, 129–30, 136–38, 173–74, 176–79, 181–82, 189; and China, 146–47, 149, 151, 157, 199; confronts critics, 117, 130, 168–69; and executive power, 106, 125, 131, 132, 167, 169, 170–72; and Foreign Relations Committee, 126, 132–33, 177, 179; and Fulbright's approval, 194, 195; and Fulbright's early expectations of, 105, 106–8, 110; and Fulbright's opposition to policies, 115, 117, 119, 121, 122–23, 125, 138–39, 186; and Paris talks, 123, 143–44, 151, 167, 168, 189; and presidential campaign (1972), 158, 160, 161, 163, 164; and public opinion, 117, 120, 125, 129, 133, 135, 141, 143, 155–56, 160; rejects conciliation, 114, 123, 134, 148; resigns, 193–94; and USSR, 111, 147–48, 149, 152, 156–57, 161, 175–76, 192, 199; and Thieu regime, 110, 112, 113, 115, 117, 119, 123, 126, 132, 144; and Vietnam commitment, 108, 110, 111, 166, 200; and Vietnamization, 112–13, 116, 117, 126, 137, 140, 198–99; and war escalation, 135, 138, 140–41, 148, 152–54, 165; and war in Laos, 116, 119, 122, 141, 142; war policies compared to LBJ's, 110, 112, 117, 118; and war powers bill, 179–80, 187; and Watergate, 172–73, 174, 178, 180–81, 184, 187, 189; and Watergate investigation, 169, 176, 182

Oberdorfer, Don, 54
Old Myths and New Realities (Fulbright), 22
Operation Rolling Thunder, 34
OPLAN 34-A, 18, 23, 25, 29, 95

Paris agreement (1973), 167, 171, 173, 182, 189; and Article 20, 171, 173
Pastore, John, 130
Paul, Roland, 116
Pell, Claiborne, 53, 192
Pentagon Papers, 144–45, 150, 154
Pentagon Propaganda Machine, The (Fulbright), 136, 142
Pfaff, William, 98
Phoenix program, 121
Pincus, Walter, 116

INDEX

Truman, Harry S, 4, 5, 6, 98, 162, 164
Truman Doctrine, 5, 150, 162
Tuchman, Barbara, 73

United Nations, 4, 21, 83, 109, 146, 185; as agency for economic aid, 34, 167; as agency to end Vietnam War, 17, 89, 90, 91
United States Information Agency, 156
USS *Maddox,* 24, 25, 89

Valenti, Jack, 47
Valeo, Frank, 20
Vance, Cyrus, 116, 200
Vanocur, Sandor, 41
Vietnamization, 153; and Cambodia, 128, 137, 138, 140, 179; and Fulbright, 115, 119, 120–21, 122–23, 134, 160; and Moose-Lowenstein report, 120, 128, 138; and Nixon, 112–13, 116, 126, 137, 140, 198–99; and public opinion, 117, 125, 135, 143, 198–99
Vietnam Moratorium, 115–16

Wald, George, 117–18

Wallace, George, 102, 127, 148
Wallace, Henry, 4
War Powers Act, 132, 142, 143, 152, 179–80, 186–87, 188, 199
Washington summit meeting (1973), 175–76
Watergate, 86, 182, 191, 193–94, 195–96; effect on Nixon's presidency, 172–73, 174, 178, 180–81, 184, 187, 189; investigation of, 169, 176, 182
Westmoreland, William, 44, 81–82, 91, 95, 96
Wheeler, Earle, 23, 107
White, William Allen, 3
Williams, Lee, 68–69
Wilson, H. H., 54–55
World Bank, 34, 37

Yost, Charles, 185
Young, Steve, 46

Zablocki, Clement, 180
Zagoria, Donald, 60
Ziegler, Ron, 171